A CONCISE HISTORY OF SWITZERLAND

Despite its position at the heart of Europe and its quintessentially European nature, Switzerland's history is often overlooked within the English-speaking world. This comprehensive and engaging history of Switzerland traces the historical and cultural development of this fascinating but neglected European country from the end of the Dark Ages up to the present. The authors focus on the initial Confederacy of the Middle Ages; the religious divisions which threatened it after 1500 and its surprising survival amongst Europe's monarchies; the turmoil following the French Revolution and conquest, which continued until the Federal Constitution of 1848; the testing of the Swiss nation through the late nineteenth century and then two World Wars and the Depression of the 1930s; and the unparalleled economic and social growth and political success of the post-war era. The book concludes with a discussion of the contemporary challenges, often shared with neighbours, that shape the country today.

CLIVE H. CHURCH is Emeritus Professor of European Studies at the University of Kent, Canterbury. He has also been a Fellow of the French CNRS, a Visiting Professor at the University of Sussex and a National Research Fund Fellow at the Universität Freiburg in Switzerland. His recent publications include *Swiss Politics and Government* (2004) and, as editor, *Switzerland and the EU* (2006).

RANDOLPH C. HEAD is Professor of European History at the University of California Riverside. He has held fellowships from the Institute for Advanced Study, the American Philosophical Society and the Newberry Library. His publications on early modern Switzerland include numerous articles and essays along with two books, *Early Modern Democracy in the Grisons* (1995) and *Jenatsch's Axe* (2008).

CAMBRIDGE CONCISE HISTORIES

This is a series of illustrated 'concise histories' of selected individual countries, intended both as university and college textbooks and as general historical introductions for general readers, travellers and members of the business community.

A full list of titles in the series can be found at:
www.cambridge.org/concisehistories

A Concise History of Switzerland

CLIVE H. CHURCH

RANDOLPH C. HEAD

CAMBRIDGE
UNIVERSITY PRESS

CAMBRIDGE
UNIVERSITY PRESS

University Printing House, Cambridge CB2 8BS, United Kingdom

Cambridge University Press is part of the University of Cambridge.

It furthers the University s mission by disseminating knowledge in the pursuit of education, learning and research at the highest international levels of excellence.

www.cambridge.org
Information on this title: www.cambridge.org/9780521143820

© Clive H. Church and Randolph C. Head 2013

First published 2013
7th printing 2018

Printed in the United Kingdom by Clays, St Ives plc

A catalogue record for this publication is available from the British Library

Library of Congress Cataloguing in Publication data
Church, Clive H., author.
A concise history of Switzerland / Clive H. Church, Randolph C. Head.
pages   cm. – (Cambridge concise histories)
ISBN 978-0-521-14382-0 (pbk.)
1. Switzerland – History.   I. Head, Randolph Conrad, author.   II. Title.
DQ54.C47   2013
949.4–dc23
2012031494

ISBN 978-0-521-19444-0 Hardback
ISBN 978-0-521-14382-0 Paperback

*In memory of Margaret Ann Church, wife, friend
and facilitator of studies of Switzerland*

CONTENTS

ILLUSTRATIONS

FIGURES

MAPS

ACKNOWLEDGEMENTS

We would like to acknowledge the generous help of the Swiss National Fonds in providing us with the opportunity of spending time in Switzerland working on the book, Head in Berne and Zurich and Church in Fribourg. Equally, we must thank the host departments concerned, the Institut für Schweizergeschichte and André Holenstein in Berne, the Historisches Seminar and Simon Teuscher in Zurich, and Institut für schweizerische Zeitgeschichte in Fribourg for providing such welcoming and supportive environments. We also owe a great deal to the Swiss libraries and institutions who have helped us, including the National Library in Berne, the Schweizerisches Landesmuseum in Zurich and the Swiss Historical Dictionary, and notably Lucienne Hubler and Stephanie Summermatter.

On a more personal level, we have both contracted many debts of gratitude to Swiss colleagues. In the initial gestation of the project, the support of Thomas Cottier and Thomas Maissen was critical. They set it on its way. Later Urs Altermatt, Catherine and Louis Bosshart, Paolo Dardanelli, François Jequier, David Luginbühl, Thomas Metzger, Carlo Moos, Damir Skenderovic, Siegfried Werklein and Michel Walter all discussed, provided suggestions and, especially, read drafts for Church. He is also grateful for the inspiration of the late Christopher Hughes and for the help of Pro Helvetia in earlier times. Regula Schmid read drafts of two chapters for Head, who also extends thanks to Thomas Maier, Rainer Hugener and the historians at the Arbeitsstelle Culmanstrasse for their support. Their friendship and support were greatly appreciated. However, none of the above is responsible for any of the work's errors. Finally, we are also grateful to anonymous readers, to Liz Friend Smith, Elizabeth Spicer and Jo Breeze of CUP and their colleagues, and to the many Swiss individuals and institutions who helped us with images, maps and charts.

ABBREVIATIONS

AIDS	Acquired immune deficiency syndrome
AHV/AVS	Old Age and Survivors' pension system
ASUAG	General Swiss Watch Industry Company Limited (Allgemeine Schweizer Uhrenindustrie AG)
AUNS/ASIN	Action for an Independent and Neutral Switzerland
BGB/PAB	Burghers, Artisans and Peasants Party
COCOM	[US] Coordinating Committee for Multilateral Export Controls
COMCO	Swiss Federal Competition Commission
EFTA	European Free Trade Association
EC	European Community, later EU (European Union)
ECHR	European Convention (or Court) on Human Rights
EEA	European Economic Area
FDP	Free Democratic Party (Radicals)
FINMA	Swiss Financial Market Supervisory Authority
GATT	General Agreement on Tariffs and Trade
GDP	Gross Domestic Product
HSBC	Hong-Kong and Shanghai Bank Corporation
MP	Member of Parliament
NA	Nationale Aktion gegen die Überfremdung von Volk und Heimat
NATO	North Atlantic Treaty Organization
NSDAP	German National Socialist Workers party (Nazi Party)
OECD	Organization for Economic Cooperation and Development
OEEC	Organization of European Economic Cooperation
PBD	Conservative Democratic Party
SMH	Swiss Corporation for Microelectronics and Watch-making Industries Ltd (Société de Microélectronique et d'Horlogerie)
SPS	Swiss Social Democratic Party

SVP/UDC	Swiss People's Party
UBS	formerly Union Bank of Switzerland; known simply as UBS after its 1998 merger with Schweizerische Bankgesellschaft
UN	United Nations
UNESCO	United Nations' Educational, Social and Cultural Organization
UNICEF	United Nations' International Children's Emergency Fund.
UNRRA	United Nations' Refugee Relief Agency
USSR	Union of Soviet Socialist Republics
VAT	Value Added Tax

Making the Swiss

Time, myth and history

Modern nations are layered entities embracing geographical regions, their specific political systems, local populations and cultures, and the various communities within and beyond them. When the nation in question, like modern Switzerland, has clearly traceable roots that go back 500 years and more, the layers become complex, woven into a historical fabric that tenaciously influences how both insiders and outsiders view it. Such a fabric is a critical feature of Switzerland's history. We can say with confidence that people calling themselves 'Swiss' have lived north of, and to some extent in and even south of, the central Alps since the late 1400s. They took this name from Schwyz, which was just one of the *Orte* (places) that made up the Grosser Oberdeutscher Bund Stetten und Lender (Great Upper German League of Cities and Territories) – the political alliance that formed the core of what eventually became modern Switzerland.

This book traces a path that began among this loose network of relatively autonomous communities north of the Alps – among them Schwyz – that began joining into alliances by about 1300. These developed into a ramshackle but surprisingly durable Confederacy by the 1450s, and survived Europe's tumults to become the multi-lingual and multi-religious federal republic of 2013. Switzerland's relative political stability since its constitutional foundation in 1848, in a Europe otherwise much troubled by political crisis, led many observers to emphasize the continuity from those earliest associations to the present, and to pay much less attention to the many bitter conflicts that divided the Swiss, and to the ties that linked them to other regions no longer part of Switzerland. Modern historians have recovered the conflict as well as the continuity that characterized this region – not least the four significant internal wars between 1444 and 1715 – leading to a more nuanced picture.

For all of its durability, the Swiss political system throughout its evolution has also always been something of an outlier. In 1300, no one expected the various leagues that were forming among modest towns and thinly settled mountain valleys to replace the God-given order of aristocracy and Holy Roman Emperor, even locally. In 1600, an oath-bound Confederacy including both Catholics and Protestants seemed out of place among the divinely appointed kings ruling their (theoretically) orthodox subjects. And after 1800, the rising nation-states of Europe, shaped by supposedly natural borders and idealized ethnic unity, looked askance at the polyglot Confederation sprawled messily, but sometimes threateningly, across the Alps. Never has there been anything particularly natural about Switzerland. Neither dynasty, nor religion, nor language ever united Switzerland's denizens, leaving history – the human capacity to adopt shared stories and to imagine a community – as the primary foundation of modern Swiss identity as it emerged and thrived. Indeed, the emergence of Swiss identity around 1500 was specifically founded on the region's history as contemporaries understood it (but which, as modern historical research shows, contained a good deal of myth). That identity, once established, had important consequences for later developments, because it could be adapted and revived as a foundation for political and economic survival and success in the turbulent nineteenth and especially twentieth centuries. Though Switzerland was conquered and reconstituted during the Napoleonic Wars, and twice surrounded and isolated during the wars from 1914 to 1945, its history (both as a shared set of stories and as a long and legitimate political past) ensured that a recognizable Switzerland re-emerged from each European catastrophe, changed but not dissolved.

Understanding the modern nation-state of Switzerland therefore requires considering *both* the empirical history of events and institutions *and* the culturally embedded stories and myths that the Swiss themselves accepted, and which thus shaped their options and choices through the centuries. William Tell never existed, yet his actions repeatedly affected the course of Swiss politics, as shown in the chapters that follow. Each chapter addresses not only the dynamic events that characterized each period in the region that became Switzerland, but also investigates the changing ways in which the political actors understood their political world. That world changed enormously from the 1300s to the twenty-first century: not surprisingly, the Swiss people's understanding of who they were, politically, and what (if anything) held them together, changed as well. Myth shaped history for the Swiss, just as history (re)wrote their myths.

Before laying out the nine chapters through which this book traverses Switzerland's complex history, a double-edged question raised by Jonathan Steinberg deserves our attention: 'Why Switzerland?' We can ask, first, how and why it was that a separate modern nation-state – one characterized both by a lasting dedication to direct-democratic decision-making and by tenacious hesitation to follow the political norms of their neighbours – emerged in this region, equally distinct from the Italian city-states to the south, the French monarchy to the west, and the princely Empire that became Germany and Austria to the north and east. Neither dynasty, nor language, nor religion brought about a Swiss national identity that could bolster a Swiss political nation. Instead, modern Switzerland seems in an important sense the result of its inhabitants' own decisions – a *Willensnation*, a nation resting on its inhabitants' will – and of its own and its neighbours' willingness to accept its various forms through the centuries as a single and continuous political unit. In other words, although people often overlook this today, Switzerland was – and is – a real polity with real politics, and not an untroubled island set amidst spectacular mountain scenery.

Second, we can ask why modern readers might be interested in the many complex details of Switzerland's past. One reason might be that for thinkers from Jean-Jacques Rousseau in the eighteenth century to various political theorists in the twentieth, Switzerland seemed to provide a useful model for the political organization of an often violent Europe – although attempts to apply a Swiss model, from California to Yugoslavia, have met with mixed success. More modestly, we can say that in addition to appealing to those interested in understanding the – often ignored and misconstrued – Swiss of today through their past, Switzerland's history also helps us to broaden our understanding of the full range of political possibilities available to Europeans through the centuries.

The chapters that follow provide a history of Switzerland as a political entity and not just as a region. In consequence, the pre-historical, Roman and early medieval events in and around the Central Alps receive only the briefest mention in Chapter 1, along with a sketch of modern Switzerland's geography, since, as already suggested, no such entity can be discerned before the 1300s. Most of Chapter 1 thus concentrates on the period from about 1200 to the late 1300s, when a series of developments shared across Western Europe, but inflected by this region's location on a series of dynastic, linguistic and cultural boundaries, opened up new political possibilities. The decline of several major aristocratic lineages, most importantly the Hohenstaufen, allowed lesser political forces north of the Alps to flourish, including both regional families such as the Habsburgs (whose subsequent career forms an essential part of European history) and various urban and rural corporate associations. All of these, and further players too, participated in a bewilderingly complex landscape of feuds, alliances and ruptures that slowly consolidated into a new configuration. Although all communities in the Confederacy that began taking shape in the fourteenth century were Germanophone, many of them maintained comparable ties to Italian, French and Romansh-speaking neighbours, some of whom later became Swiss themselves. The various corporate and communal associations, including cities like Berne, Lucerne and Zurich, and rural valleys like Glarus, Uri and the Haslital, increasingly joined together to contain aristocratic violence and secure the peace. When the great demo-graphic and economic crisis of the Black Death hit in 1348, the region's aristocracy suffered further losses, leaving alliances of com-munes as the primary political force for a critical half-century, during which they consolidated and worked out their first common laws.

In Chapter 2, we trace the series of internal and external struggles that transformed the loose alliance networks of the later 1300s into a more firmly constituted and militarily potent political actor, the Swiss Confederacy (known in German as the *Alte Eidgenossenschaft*) that came to dominate the Swiss region. First called 'Swiss' after military victories against Habsburg forces in 1386, the members of the emerg-ing Confederacy expanded their territorial and political scope by purchasing or seizing territory from the regional nobility, but also faced bitter internal divides that reached a peak in the 'Old Zurich War' of 1436–50 that pitted Zurich and its Habsburg backers against most other members of the Confederacy, headed by Schwyz. Zurich's defeat demonstrated that individual members of the Confederacy were no longer fully free political actors. In the second half of the fifteenth century, Swiss infantrymen briefly dominated the European military stage, defeating and destroying the Dukes of Burgundy in the 1470s, repelling the Habsburgs and the southern German nobility in the 1490s and becoming arbiters of northern Italy in the 1510s. Victory allowed the Confederacy to grow both through adding new members – including bilingual Fribourg – and by buying or seizing control over neighbouring territories, many of which were French- or Italian-speaking. The Confederacy's success also encouraged the emergence of a shared set of stories about who they were, and why their alliances were favoured by God. These stories centred on the dramatic figure of William Tell and the 'three Confederates' who were thought to have sworn the first Confederate oaths in the unstable period around 1300.

The end of Swiss military predominance, dramatically demonstrated at Marignano in 1515 and Bicocca in 1522, coincided with a new wave of internal division triggered by Europe's religious schism, setting the stage for Chapter 3. The Reformation movement to reject the Roman church and its theology that began with Martin Luther in Wittenberg found a series of key protagonists in Switzerland, where first Ulrich Zwingli and then the French immigrant Jean Calvin contributed to the creation of a second magisterial church, the Reformed or Calvinist, in opposition to Rome. Some of Zwingli's earliest followers also helped found the movements we now call Anabaptist or Mennonite. Even as the Confederacy was reaching its modern borders through Berne's seizure of the Vaud in 1536, it was also becoming divided by religion, since only a minority of its thirteen full members accepted the teachings coming from Zurich and Geneva. In 1531, a first civil war over religion erupted in Switzerland: although Zwingli lost his life in one of its battles, the result was an unwilling stalemate between the religious parties. Since these were often bitterly divided, and attached to outside confessional allies as much as to one another, Switzerland's survival in this period owed more to its neighbours' corresponding weaknesses than to anything else. The religious status quo was tested in two further civil wars, and modestly revised in the Protestants' favour in 1715, but remained a lasting obstacle to further development French of the Confederacy's shared institutions. Ever-narrower oligarchies monopolized influence and public revenue in the cantons, even as economic growth – accelerated by Switzerland's ability to remain outside the Thirty Years War and later European conflagrations – slowly transformed the countryside.

The uneasy balance that characterized Switzerland after the formal recognition of its political autonomy in 1648 persisted into the eighteenth century, as traced in Chapter 4. On the one hand, the political ossification of the Swiss Ancien Régime continued: the cantons became increasingly both oligarchical and liable to internecine struggles over power, precedence and profit. Nevertheless, neither absolutism nor princely rule ever emerged. Regular popular challenges to oligarchy, fuelled in part by the mythical history of liberation, represented one constraint: Francophone subjects of Berne in the Vaud found the story of William Tell just as inspiring as did anti-oligarchical rebels in German Switzerland. Equally, the patricians' occasional willingness to set long-standing conventions aside and to yield to some demands in order to preserve their positions, as in Geneva, was another. On the other hand, despite apparent stasis, change continued in the intellectual, patriotic and economic spheres, the last led by domestic textile production. Notably, Enlightment thinking flourished, including contributions from local patricians as well as both émigrés and Swiss who emigrated abroad. At the end of the century, change began to accelerate, encouraged by the spillover from the French Revolution. In the end, despite or because of its growing conservatism, the Ancien Régime could not cope with these challenges and abdicated in face of French arms and local agitation for political reform.

Chapter 5 opens with the French invasion of 1798, which led to an immediate revolution that replaced the old Confederacy with a French-inspired and French-dominated Helvetic Republic. The Republic's failure to win general acceptance opened a half-century of fluidity characterized by incessant constitutional experiments and contention over the validity of any new order. Lacking internal legitimacy and unable to fulfil French demands, the Helvetic Republic was replaced by fiat in 1803 by Napoleon's Mediation regime, which brought stability on sufferance, along with economic growth. Napoleon's military decline allowed supporters of the Ancien Régime to make a new bid for power, but full restoration of the Ancien Régime was blocked by the victorious Allies, leaving the country with an unstable compromise order in which all parties sought to legitimate their proposals, at times through appeals to the tradition of William Tell and the virtuous old Confederates – seen alternatively as patrons of restoration or forerunners of more democracy. Strengthening liberal demands for reform in the press and in public institutions led in 1829–31 to a series of quasi-revolutionary upheavals in the cantons, which wrote finis to hopes for a restoration of the Ancien Régime. This Regeneration did not end contention, however, because, on the one hand, pressures continued for reform at the national level and, on the other, demands for more radical social and political change came into conflict, sometimes violently, with emerging Catholic conservatism. In the end, the conflict led to civil war in 1847–8, triggered by religious and economic tension as well as by political disagreements. The victory of radical liberals allowed them to draft the first Swiss national constitution, creating for the first time a single sovereign federal republic out of the many quasi-sovereign cantonal states.

Chapter 6 traces the implementation of the new order and the creation of a functioning new state, with surprising lack of resistance from either the defeated conservatives or the continental powers. This success rested on the moderation of the new government and on the willingness of the defeated to use the new system to their own advantage. Switzerland's new order won international acceptance, while the country also developed a leading-edge industrial economy based on railways and factory production. The new federal politics faced a powerful challenge from a new cantonal democratic movement in the 1860s, which ultimately produced both a new federal constitution in 1874, making Switzerland a tighter federation, and also a new clash with the Catholic Church. Switzerland's uncertain place in an increasingly nationalist Europe also spurred renewed interest in the Swiss past: the pact of 1291 between Uri, Schwyz and Unterwalden (lost until the eighteenth century and published only in the 1830s) became a new cornerstone of national pride and led to the creation of a national holiday on 1 August. This was part of an institutional development of Swiss identity, and helped to make the Swiss an increasingly nationally minded people. The economic depression of the 1870s stimulated the emergence of a socialist movement that helped to crystallize party structures across the political spectrum. By the turn of the century, Catholic conservatives had been brought first into the political process, and then also into government, thanks to the expansion of direct democracy in 1891 to allow partial constitutional revision by popular initiative. Broader inclusion helped develop a new overarching sense of national identity, and encouraged a new bourgeois alliance directed against socialists and foreigners.

Chapter 7 covers Switzerland's part in the European crisis from 1914 to 1945 and beyond. The newly self-confident and democratic Swiss nation found itself under an unprecedented triple pressure during the First World War, involving neutrality, linguistic unity and social harmony. The mishandling of the 1914 mobilization and its economic consequences led to a social outburst in the form of a General Strike in 1918, which in turn brought forward the introduction of proportional representation for national elections. The new voting system triggered a virtual revolution in the domestic political system in the 1920s, just as entry into the League of Nations revolutionized the country's diplomatic situation. New stresses emerged in the inter-war period, thanks to the post-1929 economic slump and the spillover of Europe's ideological conflicts, which all found resonance within Switzerland. Well into the 1930s, proto-fascist as well as liberal and socialist-communist groups remained active, though each had to adapt their programmes to the distinctive historical context and deep-seated democratic political culture of the Swiss system.

Late in the 1930s, the government also began to batten down the hatches because of the threatening European situation. Nonetheless, when the war came, the country still found itself encircled. Real fears of a German invasion provoked a radical new defensive strategy based on an Alpine fortress, the 'Reduit', and a newly self-conscious defence of Swiss traditions under the heading of 'spiritual national defence'. Nevertheless, the government also engaged in what many thought were dubious relations with the Axis powers. Hence, Switzerland found itself at odds with the Allies both during the war and immediately afterwards, leading to a renewal of its stand-alone neutrality in an increasingly interconnected global scene. This, and the country's ability to survive the war, boosted its self-confidence, encouraging the conviction that Switzerland represented a 'special case' of stability and democracy in a divided world.

The course of this 'Sonderfall' (as ideal and reality) occupies Chapter 8. The belief in Swiss exceptionalism expanded with the surge of prosperity that followed the war, further supported by the nation's increasing political and social harmony and by its successful new international role, facilitated by the Cold War. Only in the 1960s – as in other Western nations – was Switzerland's post-war satisfaction (and self-satisfaction) challenged by dissident intellectuals, the 1968 movement, women, youth unrest and (from the right) by opponents of migration and economic cosmopolitanism. The Swiss consensus overcame all these challenges, along with the two economic depressions, in the 1970s. Political and cultural polarization increased in the 1980s, however: even as the political centre moved somewhat to the right, more fissures opened up in the Sonderfall as the country was gripped by new movements against migration and UN entry on the one hand, and environmentalist and anti-army coalitions on the other. The Swiss state itself lost credibility on all fronts after high-profile cases of corruption and insider dealing, and by revelations that it had been spying on many of its own citizens.

Finally, Chapter 9 traces how, from the 1990s down to the present, these fissures became increasingly large cracks. The end of the Cold War and the acceleration of globalization forced the Swiss to rethink their neutrality, to deal with growing numbers of third-world asylum seekers, and to cobble together a new policy for relations with the EU, once Swiss voters had rejected membership in the European Economic Area. Pressure for new approaches grew when, for the first time since the war, the country suffered a significant economic slowing in the 1990s and the first decade of the 2000s. Anxiety about Switzerland's place in the world helped foster the growth of a new populist movement, the Swiss People's Party, similar to, but more effective than, those found elsewhere in Europe. Such populist supporters of the old Sonderfall view of Switzerland seemed to gain the upper hand for a while after 2003, but from 2007 onward the forces of consensus and pragmatism began to reassert themselves. Even so the country remained divided between inward- and outward-looking communities, so that politics became increasingly polarized, as was the case elsewhere in Europe. In fact, in the last twenty years or so, the country has become much more of a normal European state.

Indeed, the tension between the sense of distinctiveness and the reality of Switzerland's deep and abiding connections to its European neighbours represents a striking element of continuity in the nation's history. Champions of Swissness have always been able to point to features that set the region apart, from its confederal structure and the dominance of communal institutions in the late Middle Ages – justified by the mythical bravery of William Tell and the idealized prudent and pious leaders who formed the first Swiss alliances – down to the current populist leaders who continue to point to events in the thirteenth and fourteenth centuries as the grounds for Switzerland's special nature. Claims to distinctiveness and claims to continuity have thus themselves been a conservative constant, and one that has deeply influenced historians' descriptions of Switzerland through the centuries. Yet historical events, from the bitter divisions of the Old Zurich War of the 1440s through the Reformation and the era of Revolution to the civil conflict of 1847–8 that finally produced a single Swiss nation-state, show that Switzerland was never separated from European events, and that conflict often broke the bounds of comity and stability emphasized by the conservative vision. The many ways in which William Tell has been mobilized, from conservative icon to revolutionary agitator, show that neither conflict nor continuity alone capture the Swiss trajectory: it is their intertwining, captured in history and myth, in institutions and in culture, that make modern Switzerland both a distinctive and a profoundly European construct, and one deserving of being better known.

I

Before Switzerland

Lordship, communities and crises,
c. 1000–1386

Modern historians concur that 'the Swiss' and 'Switzerland' are concepts that emerged only in the 1400s, and that a modern state of Switzerland emerged only in the early nineteenth century, taking its final shape in 1848. Geographical and historical conditions of the region in and north of the central Alps after the year 1000, however, did provide the conditions in which a Swiss people and a Swiss political system could emerge, and shaped those people and that system in important ways. A pivotal feature of the physical and human geography described in this chapter is complexity and diversity. Neither the landscape, nor the societies, nor the institutions found in this region around the year 1000 provided any notable unity for its inhabitants. Rather, a Swiss identity emerged only through historical evolution, and remains to the present characterized by an internal variety in language, religion and culture that distinguishes Switzerland from most other European nation-states. Broad historical trends stretching back to the central Middle Ages allowed for political innovation and flexibility within the framework of noble rule in the region by 1250; this flexibility opened opportunities for various actors between 1250 and 1386 to produce a loose but stable network of alliances among cities, towns and mountain valleys – the early Swiss *Eidgenossenschaft*, or Confederacy. The loose Confederacy of around 1386 was the immediate precursor of the Old Confederacy (*Alte Eidgenossenschaft*) that took shape between 1386 and 1513, and thereafter remained largely stable until 1798.

GEOGRAPHIES AND STRUCTURES IN A FRAGMENTED REGION TO 1250

Modern Switzerland occupies 41,285 square kilometres, which makes it one of the smaller European states. More than half of this space is occupied by the Alps and their northern outliers, the pre-Alps; another 1,740 square kilometres are occupied by water, including two major lakes located on current national boundaries, Lake Geneva and Lake Constance. The Swiss Alps include most of the highest mountains in Europe, although the highest peak, Mont Blanc, lies in France near the Swiss border. The Alps have long been settled, and Alpine passes have since Roman times connected the Italian peninsula to France and Germany. Deep valleys reach between the pre-Alps and far into the Alps themselves from both north and south, providing arable land and access to passes; agrarian settlements also spread higher up the slopes – as high as 2000 m during the High Middle Ages (~1000–~1300). The pre-Alpine spurs extending north from the major ranges consist of steep hill country and lower peaks, as does the Jura range which runs in an arc along Switzerland's north-western border. Between the Alps and Jura lie the Swiss midlands, with relatively level although by no means flat terrain, which have formed the centre of both agriculture and population throughout the last millennium. All of Switzerland's major cities, from Geneva to St Gallen, are located in the midlands, though several, notably Lucerne, are nestled among pre-Alpine ranges. Modern Switzerland does not extend beyond the southern edge of the Alps, which subside abruptly into the North Italian plain. At the peak of the pre-modern Confederacy's power, efforts to incorporate the south slope of the Alps and even the city of Milan on the north Italian plain took place, but ultimately the Swiss were pushed back to the mouths of the deep valleys that cut into the mountains.

Two major European rivers, the Rhône and the Rhine, have their springs in modern Switzerland, along with the Inn, tributary to the Danube, and several northern tributaries to the Po. The upper river valleys provided pathways towards a series of mountain passes, control over which always represented an economic and political prize. The lowest Alpine pass, the Brenner (1370 m), lies in modern Austria, too far east for travellers between Italy and the northern Continent, whereas the Swiss passes offer shorter routes, though at altitudes over 2000 m. The Alpine routes across Switzerland fall into three major groups. To the west, the upper Rhône leads to the Great St Bernard and the Simplon passes, and south to Turin and Milan. In the east, various routes – the Julier, the Septimer, the Splügen, the San Bernardino – connect the upper Rhine to Como and Milan. The third route through central Switzerland, the St Gotthard, only opened for international trade around 1200, and connects Basle to Milan via major Swiss tributaries to the Rhine. In addition to its directness, the St Gotthard offered the advantage of lake transport from Lucerne far into the Alps at Fluelen in Uri and then from the Maggadino plain far south toward Milan. Its opening triggered economic growth and broader horizons in the formerly isolated valleys, as became evident in their precocious emergence as privileged corporate communities headed by local noble clans in the 1200s. Along each mountain route, local communities maintained paths, provided draft animals and in the winter sleds, and charged travellers and merchants to pass by, as well as using the passes to connect with their own immediate neighbours. Since the times of Hannibal, armies have also crossed the Alps. In the Middle Ages, it was above all German Emperors who brought troops south through the mountains on the way to their coronations in Rome, or to assert their imperial rights in Italy as successors to the Emperors of classical Rome.

Switzerland's striking landscape shaped patterns of human settlement and of economic exploitation of the environment. The midlands have always been the core zone for population and agriculture, providing the staple grains essential for all pre-modern economies. Since their hilly terrain is well watered and generally well drained, the midlands are fertile, though not suitable for the high-intensity cultivation that developed on Europe's wider plains. Subsistence agriculture extended far – and high – into the Alpine massif as well, but commercial growth during the High Middle Ages encouraged more and more Alpine dwellers to adopt herding as a primary occupation. With suitable investment in paths and irrigation ditches, the summer riches of the high meadows – the actual 'alps' – allowed the production of meat, fats and cheese, high-value products for export that could pay for imported grains. The region's fractured landscape ensured that both midlands and pre-Alps remained modestly

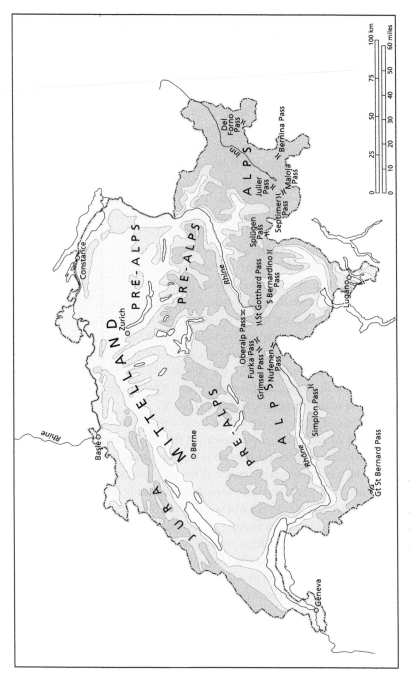

Map 1.1 Switzerland: physical

populated; the cities and towns that sprung up along the Swiss lakes and rivers were correspondingly small in European comparison, though numerous. Several of the oldest and most significant lay at key points on the region's most important lakes and rivers, including Basle, Chur, Geneva, Lucerne and Zurich.

In the Middle Ages, trade was the second major occupation of the region's people, after agriculture. In addition to local trade that expanded with population growth and economic expansion, the confluence of several major trans-European routes ensured a steady stream of long-distance trade. In addition to the crucial north–south routes across the Alps to Italy, east–west trade on an axis that reached as far as Nuremberg and Poland to the north-east and Genoa and Barcelona to the south-west crossed the Swiss midlands north of the Alpine massif. Local producers of silk, wool and linen textiles became contributors to and beneficiaries of this route, which in the Middle Ages centred on entrepôts at Geneva and later Lyons; later, such routes also took Swiss emigrant craftsmen far into north-central Europe as well. Cities including Fribourg, Berne and St Gallen thrived at various times owing to this trade. Mining, in contrast, never flourished, because the central Alps are unusually bereft of significant mineral deposits.

In the pre-modern period, human and animal muscles provided energy for almost all undertakings, along with water power that turned mills and drove fish into weirs. During the early Industrial Revolution, water power provided Swiss factories with an enviable advantage, and it remains important to the present in the form of hydroelectric generation. Wood, another universal energy source in pre-modern Europe, was abundant in most of Switzerland, being used to heat forges as well as houses and baths. Even before the modern period, deforestation became a major problem far into the mountains, since the rivers made rafting logs downstream to Swabia and Austria relatively easy.

As all of Europe thrived in the High Middle Ages, the Swiss region saw steady expansion of population and of cultivated land. By the end of the thirteenth century, the population may have reached 800,000 (although records are too sparse for accurate measurements). A notable feature of this period was the expansion of existing cities and the founding of many more. In medieval society, cities enjoyed a particular legal status that included a group of citizens who were personally free, rather than serfs, along with the privilege to hold markets and conduct business under favourable terms. The older Swiss cities had bishops (Basle, Chur, Geneva, Lausanne, Sion), or cloisters (Lucerne, Zurich) as their nominal lords, while most of the newer cities (e.g. Berne, Fribourg, Schaffhausen) resulted from lordly foundations intended to demonstrate prestige, secure roads, encourage trade and increase population. In periods of political fragmentation, even minor lords founded cities, often minuscule; this explains the region's unusual density of cities, which also resulted in a surprisingly urbanized population by 1200.

The attractive environment of the Swiss midlands drew diverse settlers from pre-history onwards including Celts, Romans and Germanic migrants such as the Franks, Burgundians and Alemanni. During the central Middle Ages, Germanic languages even spread south of the Alps with the Goths and Lombards, but by the year 1000, the rough distribution of German as well as three post-Roman languages (French, Italian and Rhaeto-Romance) in the region was well established. Never in the pre-modern period did political boundaries follow linguistic divides, however, and shifts in the boundaries between languages continued well into the fifteenth century. The Alps generally separated Italian from French, with Rhaeto-Romance increasingly restricted to higher valleys in the eastern Alps. Of the various Germanic invaders, the Alemanni had the most influence on the German spoken in modern Switzerland, which shares many features with that of south-west Germany. In the history of the Swiss Confederacy after 1300, German was the primary language, although the Confederacy gained Romance-speaking allies and subjects; only in Fribourg did French and German coexist in politics and administration from the fourteenth century onwards.

Christianity spread into the Swiss region during the Roman period, with evidence for bishoprics at centres from Geneva to Chur by the mid-400s. The Germanic invaders arriving in the fifth and sixth centuries were initially pagan, but by 700, the christianization of the region was largely complete. Multiple ethnic communities and political fragmentation ensured a complex ecclesiastical terrain as well. Seven separate bishoprics held authority in the region (Basle, Chur, Como, Constance, Geneva, Lausanne and Sion/Sitten), mostly with considerable territory outside the future Switzerland.

These sees in turn belonged to no fewer than five archbishoprics (Besançon, Mainz, Milan, Tarentaise and the patriarchate of Aquileia), and were punctuated by numerous autonomous abbeys and cloisters. Most of the German-speaking areas adhered to the newly founded Bishopric of Constance after 600. Founded to evangelize the Alemanni, this enormous diocese spread far to the north, which led to growing disjunctions when the Swiss began to separate from their Swabian neighbours. None of this prevented a lively spiritual life and visible support for local churches from emerging, but it did enable divergent responses to conflicts involving the church, such as the Investiture Controversy, the schisms of the fourteenth century and the Reformation.

Politically, all of modern Switzerland once belonged to the Roman Empire, unlike regions further north and east. The territory was divided among several Roman provinces, but these left few traces; after the collapse of Rome, various Germanic kingdoms claimed shifting slices of the region with equally ephemeral results. The brief reunification of Western Europe under the Franks around 800 brought all of Switzerland under a single ruler again, but beginning with the Treaty of Verdun in 843, successor kingdoms again claimed various parts of the central Alps and the midlands. By the 1030s, both major regional powers, the Kingdom of Burgundy in the west and the Duchy of Swabia in the north, belonged to the German Empire – and both were beginning to fragment, leaving local aristocrats as the main political forces. In the south, German claims to Lombardy steadily lost significance as first feudal dynasties, and then the Italian cities – especially Milan – became autonomous.

Along with the decaying kingdoms and duchies and the regional noble dynasties, the High Middle Ages brought new political actors onto the scene: these included urban communities, ecclesiastical foundations and eventually rural communities as well. The key legal and cultural change that enabled this development was the emergence of the political corporation as a legitimate political actor. Starting with monasteries and cathedral chapters, 'bodies' of members (Latin: *corpora*) gained the ability to possess property and privileges, and to exercise lordship. This development allowed all sorts of corporate entities to operate within the lordship-based political culture of medieval Europe. Initially, many towns and cities enjoyed support and sponsorship of expanded privileges from their lords (feudal or ecclesiastical), since a thriving town enhanced its lord's resources and prestige. After 1100, however, urban interests increasingly diverged from those of the nobility: urban elites valued peaceful trade and manufactures, whereas the fragmentation of political authority across Europe generated growing feudal violence amongst the aristocracy. The privileges and personal freedom to be found in cities, moreover, provided an environment in which organized resistance to lords' authority was not only possible, but often successful. Especially in the band of territory from central Italy to the Netherlands, including the future Swiss regions and the western parts of Germany, cities succeeded in becoming autonomous political actors, often bolstered by royal or imperial privileges that could be gained through political support – or bought for hard cash – from often beleaguered rulers. Similar privileges could be obtained from bishops, abbeys, and other lords as well.

Within the Empire, the status of 'imperial liberty' (*Reichsfreiheit*) represented the greatest autonomy: imperial free cities (and other imperially privileged entities, including abbeys and rural communes) were 'subject to the Emperor alone', and often possessed imperial privileges to appoint their own imperial bailiff and to operate courts with no right of appeal. Within the imperial cities, political authority lay in the hands of a limited number of full citizens, usually local knights and merchants, who formed the corporation that embodied the city's privileges. As internal autonomy increased, other social groups sought to join the politically active citizenship. The most important were craftsmen organized into guilds, which regulated and limited production and trade in specific goods. Guilds usually pursued both charitable and political goals as well as regulating their crafts, and led other social groups in seeking the formation of larger political councils on which they could be represented, or outright guild regimes in which only guild members played a part. By the fourteenth century, a wide range of internal arrangements characterized the cities that joined the Swiss Confederacy. While by no means democratic by modern standards, they offered more inhabitants a chance to participate in political life than under aristocratic dominion, and encouraged a culture that rejected aristocratic values and celebrated the 'common man' (if not the common woman).

1.1 Urban Guilds. In this sixteenth-century representation from Basle, a guild's leadership enjoys a sumptuous banquet while ostentatiously displaying their (notably plebeian) coats-of-arms and matching outfits. Guilds in the High Middle Ages led opposition to merchant oligarchies in the towns, but, like other Swiss institutions, became bastions of family privilege and solidarity after about 1500.

Urban autonomy was common across medieval Europe, and many rural communities adopted corporate forms of organization in the High Middle Ages, but rural communities with imperial liberty emerged in only a few areas, notably in the central Alps. Valley communities in the mountains from the Valais to the Grisons organized as political corporations bearing seals and administering justice, and once they had gained sufficient legal privileges and autonomy, joined as equal members the networks of alliances among communes that characterized the entire region. Several factors enabled this development: location on the passes critical to imperial policy in Italy, the relative weakness of the major feudal dynasties and the high degree of cooperation demanded by pastoralism in the Alps, which encouraged strong collective institutions. Living in a diverse landscape of nobles, towns and cities also provided models and sometimes the impetus to organize on corporate lines. Historians have pointed to the emergence of alliances that included both urban and rural communes as a distinctive feature that enabled the Swiss leagues to thrive and survive after 1500, even as primarily urban alliances elsewhere foundered.

As the importance of imperial privileges illustrates, the ideal of universal Christian monarchy in the form of a 'Roman' Empire remained powerful in medieval Europe. By 1000, this Empire was a largely Germanic institution, including all of modern Switzerland and with claims in Italy, though the name Roman Empire or later Holy Roman Empire remained. As it took shape, the Swiss Confederacy never challenged the principle of its subjection to imperial authority, and Switzerland remained formally part of the Empire until its dissolution in 1806, even though its jurisdictional autonomy was recognized by the Treaty of Basle in 1499, and its total exemption from imperial authority by the Peace of Westphalia in 1648. Indeed, from the thirteenth to sixteenth century, the members of the Confederacy eagerly sought and proudly proclaimed their imperial liberties and loyalties, because imperial authority bolstered their hard-won political autonomy against local lords. The situation in these lands was rendered more complex, however, when one powerful regional family, the Habsburgs, joined the small number of dynasties contesting the imperial throne after 1273. When they united their local power with imperial authority, the Habsburg Emperors were well placed to consolidate their power over their family's territories, including those in Switzerland. At the same time, however, imperial politics and the Habsburgs' new realms to the east in Austria repeatedly distracted them from their south-west German homeland, allowing political rivals, including the early Swiss Confederacy, to thrive. Crucially, the Habsburgs never gained undisputed imperial authority in the years between 1308 and 1438, despite repeated efforts. By the time Habsburg Emperors sat unchallenged on the throne after 1438, the Swiss Confederacy had not only consolidated, but had also appropriated most Habsburg lordships south of the Rhine.

1.2 Habsburg castle. The Swiss lands are dotted with medieval castles, such as the Habichtsburg, an early seat of the Counts of Habsburg who took their name from the 'falcon's castle' strategically located on the Aar in central Switzerland. Many castles were abandoned as the regional nobility declined after 1300, or were destroyed by communal militias during the region's political conflicts. This image of the Habsburg from the early seventeenth century shows that the castle avoided this fate, serving instead as the seat of Habsburg servants, then of Bernese administrators after 1415.

At the peak of the High Middle Ages around 1250, diverse social forms and political organizations flourished in and north of the central Alps. The region shared in trends that characterized all of Western Europe, including growing population and economy, increased commercialization, the rise of autonomous and corporately organized communities and a thriving if heterogeneous

Christian religious life organized by a single church. Inhabitants of
the region spoke Lombard Italian, Franco-Provençal or Alemannic
German, although church affairs still took place in Latin. By the mid-
1050s, the region had been incorporated into the German Empire,
even as that Empire began to fragment as a system of political
dominion; as a result, no single dynasty prevailed. Divided economically, culturally and politically, the region that was to become the
Swiss Confederacy had a relatively open political system and
society that allowed multiple responses to the crises that lay on the
horizon: overpopulation, agrarian breakdown, the Black Death and
the continued fragmentation of public order across central Europe.
How the important actors in the region responded helps explain the
foundations of the political system that emerged fully by the beginning
of the sixteenth century: the pre-modern Confederacy of XIII sovereign cantons, along with its diverse subjects, dependants and allies.

PEACEKEEPING NETWORKS AND POLITICAL ALLIANCES: FORERUNNERS OF THE OLD CONFEDERACY

The extinction around 1200 of several major regional dynasties in
the region north of the Alps set the stage for later developments. The
Kings of Burgundy vanished after 1032, and the southern parts of the
Duchy of Swabia fell into the hands of the Dukes of Zähringen in
1098. Their family in turn expired in 1218, while the Hohenstaufen
dynasty of Emperors and Dukes of Swabia effectively ended in 1250
with the death of Frederick II. The collapse of major dynasties
created opportunities for lesser families – in this region, the House
of Savoy and the Counts of Habsburg eventually emerged as the new
dynasts – but also weakened public order and led to increased local
violence and feuding. The imperial interregnum from 1250 to 1273
exacerbated such problems. Papally sponsored anti-Emperors challenged the Hohenstaufen Emperors' authority until 1257, when the
disputed election of two candidates without substantial followings in
the German lands accelerated the decay of imperial authority. The
failure of existing authorities to maintain order encouraged a solution that appeared across medieval Europe in times of political chaos:
the regional peace alliance.

When Emperors and nobility failed to maintain the peace and protect the roads, other political actors – cities, abbeys and even rural communities – stepped into the breach out of vital self-interest. Such leagues were akin to the Peace of God movement that had earlier emerged in France: the members swore collective oaths to obey the laws, to resist violence and to submit their disputes to arbitration rather than reaching for their weapons, as the feudal nobility was prone to do. Some such alliances included local nobles – particularly weaker families or branches threatened by more powerful rivals – while others were directed against them. Peace alliances reflected the interests of local elites, whether these were petty nobles, urban faction leaders or powerful family heads in rural communities, and frequently shifted as local political constellations changed. To take one example, the city of Berne began seeking allies in the 1240s, reaching out to other cities such as Fribourg (1243) and Solothurn (1295), but also nobles (Savoy, 1256), ecclesiastics (Bishop of Sion, 1252) and rural communes (the Land Valais together with its bishop, 1250). The terms of each alliance reflected the circumstances of the contracting parties, and often described a fixed territory within which the allies agreed to help defend each other against all aggressors, along with provisions for peacefully arbitrating disputes. Since central authority continued to decline through the mid-1200s, multiple overlapping peace alliances (either for a set number of years, or without expiration) became a regular feature of political and legal life in much of Germany. Just north of the Alps, one network of alliances centred on Berne in the west, while further east, Zurich and the other towns participated in ever-changing groupings oriented to the upper Rhine and the Grisons passes, often including cities far into modern Germany.

One particular peace alliance between the rural mountain valleys of Uri, Schwyz and Nidwalden has come to symbolize the founding of the Swiss Confederacy. Purportedly drafted and sealed in early August 1291, the actual document displays numerous peculiarities, and may well have been written down in 1309 or even later; it nevertheless highlights some unusual features of peace alliances in the central Alps. The document included typical promises of support and adjudication, and the parties vowed to accept no judges from outside the region. The distinguishing element in this alliance is the parties involved: the *homines, universitas* or *communitas* of Uri,

1.3 The Bundesbrief between Uri, Schwyz and Unterwalden. Rediscovered only in the eighteenth century, this charter – dated to 'early August' of 1291 but most likely drafted in the early 1300s – recorded an alliance among the communities of Uri, Schwyz and Unterwalden to preserve the peace, administer justice 'without foreign bailiffs', and resolve their conflicts through arbitration. Similar in content to many contemporary alliances, this particular document was unusual in recording only rural communities as members. In the nineteenth century, it became an icon that identified the three cantons as founding the Confederacy in 1291.

Schwyz and Nidwalden respectively, that is, the political corporations of three rural valleys, who noted they were renewing an earlier alliance. Each of these entities did have a legal and corporate existence by 1291, as shown by the seals each attached to the document and the claims to imperial liberty that each made. Uri, astride the St Gotthard Pass, gained a formal charter of imperial liberty in 1231, although the other two parties' claims were less secure. Local aristocrats led the valleys and probably organized the alliance, yet their choice to do so as valley corporations rather than as individuals demonstrates that rural communities in the Alps played an important role in the peace alliance movement by *c.* 1300.

Several reasons explain the numerous new alliances established in this region right after 1291. First, the imperial interregnum had ended in 1273 with the election of a local noble, Rudolf of Habsburg, to the imperial throne. Local communities, who generally preferred imperial law to the depredations of the regional nobility, on the whole welcomed this development. Rudolf set to work restoring imperial power across Germany, and gained a great victory over Ottokar II Premysl, King of Bohemia, in 1278 that brought his family extensive territories in Austria. This made the Habsburgs one of the most powerful (and longest-lasting) dynasties in European history. In the family's older territories north of the Alps and in Alsace, Rudolf supported regional peace alliances to pacify his new Empire. On his death in 1291, however, a rival dynast, Adolf of Nassau, was elected Emperor, renewing fears of civil war and disorder. The year 1291 was thus a reasonable time to restore or expand local peace alliances: along with their pact with Unterwalden, Uri and Schwyz also signed a three-year peace alliance with Zurich later in the year. On Adolf's death in 1298, the electors chose Rudolf's son Albrecht as Emperor. Albrecht's reign was characterized by constant rebellions across the Empire as he sought to re-establish imperial authority, and ended with Albrecht's murder by his own nephew in 1308.

Albrecht's murder and the subsequent instability highlight the political forces active in the region. On the one hand stood networks of peace alliances comprising cities, rural communities, ecclesiastics, and the lesser nobility. These networks were mutable and often evanescent, but their ongoing formation created a set of expectations about maintaining the public peace – by force of arms if needed – that all participants accepted. On the other hand stood an equally complex network of greater and lesser noble families united by marriages and divided by inheritance disputes. Members of each network constantly negotiated with others to create coalitions and to manage crises. Although feuding and wrangling were constant, major wars were rare in this environment. As in Italy, disputes often resulted from the death of dynasts (setting off competition over inheritances)

1.4 Emperor Rudolf I Habsburg: funerary sculpture. After the violent imperial interregnum of 1251–73, many in the Alpine foothills welcomed the election of Rudolf, leader of the ambitious regional Habsburg dynasty, as Emperor. Rudolf's award of Austria to his family elevated the Counts of Habsburg to dynastic players of European stature, but subsequently distracted the family from their roots in the German south-west. Fears of renewed strife upon Rudolf's death in 1291 set off a wave of new local and regional peace alliances, perhaps including the one depicted in illustration 1.3, which is dated to that year.

or factional disputes within a powerful city (producing angry exiles seeking to overthrow new regimes). The constant negotiations this environment demanded also spurred the rise of politically astute communal leadership capable of seizing opportunities or resisting outside control, thus enabling the emergence of a territorial political system based on alliances rather than on lordship.

Albrecht's death removed the most powerful force for unity in the Swiss region, while subsequent purges of his noble murderers and their kin further destabilized local power networks. The subsequent elections of non-Habsburg Emperors also gave the Habsburgs' local rivals in the region powerful outside allies who could offer imperial privileges to weaken their Habsburg competitors. Existing struggles over resources and authority were thus exacerbated, leading to even greater incentives to expand the existing network of peace alliances. It was in this context that a long-standing struggle over grazing rights between the valley of Schwyz and the abbey of Einsiedeln triggered what is traditionally seen as the first major battle of Swiss history at Morgarten on 15 November 1315. A column of troops headed by Duke Leopold of Habsburg, brother of the current Habsburg claimant to the imperial throne, and including contingents from Zurich and other midlands towns, marched towards Schwyz in retaliation for several bold attacks on the abbey, of which the Habsburgs claimed to be protectors. Leopold's force was surprised and driven off in headlong flight by companies from Schwyz and its local allies. The local leadership celebrated their victory with a new, more ambitious peace alliance joining Uri, Schwyz and Unterwalden, while Emperor Louis the Bavarian responded to the defeat of his Habsburg rival by confirming the imperial liberty of the three valleys.

The pattern of local fragmentation entangled in imperial politics continued to encourage the construction of interlocking peace alliances all across southern Germany. Wherever lordship was weak – and the period's economic crises and the Black Death weakened the nobility disproportionately – local peace alliances expanded in membership and in scope. Zurich, Berne, Lucerne, the three Inner Swiss valleys and various other entities established multiple, overlapping leagues, some of which were perpetual, rather than made for a fixed term. Communal entities with dubious claims to autonomy were particularly eager to bolster their position through such alliances.

Lucerne, legally subject to Habsburg rule, was among the most aggressive in seeking allies both urban and rural, including a 1332 formal alliance with the three valley cantons, who were not only its local trading partners but also shared in the lucrative trade through the St Gotthard. Like most peace alliances, the 1332 treaty contained a clause nominally respecting Habsburg rights. However, Lucerne's citizen elite had formed urban conspiracies that swore oaths of unity directed against their Habsburg bailiff in 1328 and 1332, making it evident that the alliance with Uri, Schwyz and Unterwalden was intended to undermine the Habsburg position.

Political turmoil in the towns also shaped the network of local alliances. Most notably, an urban revolution in Zurich that installed a guild regime in 1336 became an important driver of events well into the 1350s. The city had gained imperial liberty under the nominal control of the abbess of the Fraumünster after the Duchy of Swabia dissolved. A council consisting at first of petty nobles, but increasingly dominated by a few merchant families, controlled the city. Craftsmen and poor denizens did not count as 'burghers' and had little influence, while the urban noble families felt excluded as well. As Zurich's crafts thrived, the craftsmen's guilds became more powerful and their exclusion from political influence began to exacerbate other tensions. Conflict reached a breaking point in 1336 when the urban craftsmen rose up under the leadership of an impoverished noble, Rudolf Brun, and established a new guild-based regime that exiled Brun's chief rivals. Similar revolutions took place in many German cities in this period, and Zurich's new constitution in fact closely followed the one established in Strasbourg in 1334.

Under the new constitution, Rudolf Brun became mayor for life, backed by a council of guildsmen and urban aristocrats, and spent most of the following decades seeking recognition of the city's regime and his position in it. Since his merchant rivals had generally supported Habsburg authority in the region, Brun turned primarily to anti-Habsburg parties, including Constance, Schaffhausen and Basle, and gained imperial support from the Wittelsbach Emperor Louis IV and then from the Luxembourg Emperor Charles IV. Continuing struggles with the exiles, who had settled in nearby Rapperswil and attempted a coup in 1350, eventually produced a crisis. After efforts to reach an accommodation with local Habsburg agents failed and Archduke Albrecht II appeared near the city with troops, Brun established a permanent alliance with Lucerne, Uri and Schwyz in 1351. This treaty later became a model for further intra-Swiss leagues, though all parties retained the right to make future treaties, as was typical at the time. Although the situation for Zurich seemed dire, Austrian affairs once again distracted the Archduke, allowing Zurich and its allies to seize Glarus and Zug and impose similar alliance treaties on them. In 1353, Berne – part of an existing network of alliances further west – expanded its ties to the eastern network built around Zurich, Lucerne and the three valleys. The network of partners, though still unstable, was growing denser.

By the 1350s, two alternatives for organizing regional political life had emerged across Europe, which faced each other directly in the Swiss region: administration by lords who used new bureaucratic methods to build up effective peace-keeping, judicial and tax systems; or networks of semi-autonomous corporate communities linked by alliances that regulated regional policy, while each ally managed its own internal affairs. Both systems had roots reaching far back before 1350, but the economic and demographic crises that grew after the 1320s and culminated in the Black Death after 1347 weakened the lordly alternative even in well-administered kingdoms such as France and England, where the period after 1350 was characterized by disruption. The much less effective administration of central European dynasts like the Habsburgs suffered even more. Particularly in the band of territories from Italy to the Netherlands – characterized by stronger corporate organization than further east, but weaker noble administration than further west – the second alternative, government by corporate communities, thrived.

A key feature of both alternatives was the organization of government into territories that included all inhabitants, replacing geographically diffuse personal linkages of authority based on lordship and privilege. Lords and communal magistrates alike sought to bring everyone living in their domains, regardless of feudal status, under a uniform territorial law and its courts, paying taxes to a single territorial authority, and universally liable for military service to the territory's ruler. The Habsburgs put great effort into consolidating a closed territory in the region by acquiring lordships, cloisters, and imperial territories through purchases or pledged loans

(*Verpfändungen*), and created a systematic register in 1307, the *Habsburg Urbar*, that listed their possessions and privileges. The costs of this strategy often strained the dynasty's financial resources to their limits, and beyond.

The members of the Swiss alliances pursued similar goals, especially after the 1350s. Wealthy citizens and the city governments began purchasing vacant or indebted lordships, and also extended their jurisdiction by offering urban citizenship to individuals and whole communities outside the city walls. Berne was the most aggressive and most successful in these tactics, building up an urban territory that eventually made it the largest city-state north of the Alps. The rural cantons, too, sought to expand their lordship over new areas: Uri reached over the St Gotthard into the upper valley of the Ticino with a combination of alliances, military campaigns and purchases of territory, while Schwyz looked north to Lake Zurich and beyond.

Communes were intent on ruling over their acquisitions and their new subjects, just as lords were, though their distinctive political culture allowed for more consultation and inclusion of local elites in political affairs. Urban purchases of lordships, and especially the habit of making lords and communities outside the city walls citizens, clashed directly with the efforts of the Habsburgs and other regional dynasts to build their own closed territories. The intensification of governance, whether lordly or communal, ensured a rising level of clashes from 1352 to 1386. Rival claims, disputed jurisdictions, bribes, pressure and outright violence characterized the tactics on both sides of this struggle for territorial dominance. Although the legal and political framework continued to rest on lordship and privilege – which could be exercised by communes as well as by aristocrats – more and more participants recognized that rival systems with incompatible visions of political order were in conflict, thus adding ideological hostility to local power struggles taking place domain by domain.

Tensions rose throughout the 1360s and 1370s. In 1365, during a moment of Habsburg vulnerability, Schwyz simply seized Zug and forced the by no means reluctant population to ally with the Confederates. The Habsburgs, meanwhile, concentrated on controlling the strategic city of Basle, with considerable success in the late 1370s. In the early 1380s, Berne took advantage of a conflict within the divided noble family of Kyburg to absorb the strategic towns of Burgdorf and Thun. The papal schism after 1378 created additional fractures and pressures, since the pro-Avignonese Habsburgs faced mostly pro-Roman antagonists in southern Germany and Switzerland. War dragged on between France and England too, while civil strife inside the Italian city-states flared throughout this period (notably in the 1378 Ciompi revolt in Florence).

Significantly, six Confederate towns and communities passed a first common statute, the so-called *Pfaffenbrief* (Treaty on Clerics, also known as the Priests' Charter), in 1370. This agreement added two critical innovations (absent in peace alliances) that demonstrate the growing control over their territories that the Swiss communities sought: a clause demanding that all inhabitants of communal territories (including nobles) swear fealty to the territory's government, and a clause forbidding clerics from appealing to church courts except for internal and spiritual matters. The treaty, in which the six signatories (Zurich, Lucerne, Zug, Uri, Schwyz and Unterwalden) described themselves for the first time as an *Eidgenossenschaft* (oath-comradeship), established a common law, thus turning what had begun as a network of peace alliances into a nascent territorial power.

The pivotal crisis for the future Switzerland came in 1386. On the Habsburg side, Duke Leopold III had become sole lord over the family's western territories, including Switzerland, in a division of the dynasty's patrimony in 1379. The division weakened both branches, and Leopold's problems were exacerbated by his conflicts with Emperor Wenceslas as well as by financial pressure. On the Swiss side, Zurich feared the revival of its old foe Rapperswil, a Habsburg stronghold, while Lucerne resented the intrusive administration of the Habsburg bailiff over the city. Recognizing Leopold's weakness, the cantons struck during the winter of 1385–6: Zurich seized Rapperswil and Lucernese bands raided Habsburg territories and awarded the inhabitants of several surrounding lordships urban citizenship (subverting their status as Habsburg subjects). After negotiations failed, Leopold raised an army and led it towards Lucerne in July 1386. At Sempach on 9 July, a smaller force from Lucerne, Uri, Schwyz and Unterwalden inflicted a serious defeat on Leopold's forces in which Leopold lost his life – killed, as later Habsburg propaganda put it, 'by his own [subjects], on his own

1.5 Battle of Sempach. The Battle of Sempach helped
consolidate the early Swiss alliances, and eventually became a
focal point for the Confederacy's emerging identity. A chapel
erected in the 1470s, about a century after Sempach,
commemorated the battle as part of the Confederacy's
founding. The mural depicted here was painted and repainted in
the sixteenth and seventeenth centuries, and highlights the
'heroic deed' of Arnold Winkelried – also first recorded in the
1470s – in seizing the enemy's spears to open a breach in their
defences.

[territory], for the sake of his own [authority]'. Two years later, the
German urban leagues faced their lords in a similar battle at
Döffingen, where they lost as decisively as the Swiss had won.

The Battle of Sempach had both immediate and long-lasting consequences. In the short term, the death of Leopold and much of the
local nobility who had accompanied him gave the cities and valleys a
further advantage in building up their territories. Moreover, membership in the *Eidgenossenschaft* became more attractive in light of
the deep crisis of Habsburg power in the region. Basle's council was
able to turn back Habsburg influence and regain its freedom of
movement, while the valley of Glarus gained membership in the
Swiss alliance after a battle at Näfels in 1388. When Rudolf
Schöno, mayor of Zurich, sought to swing the city back towards

the Habsburg camp in 1393, pressure from its allies joined with internal dissent to force his removal and the city's repudiation of the alliance. Instead, nine future cantons signed an agreement, the *Sempacherbrief* (Sempach treaty) that regulated their joint conduct of war. Meanwhile, rather than reaching a permanent peace, the Swiss and the Habsburgs – now leading territorial rivals – signed a series of extended truces that held until 1415.

Contemporaries fully recognized the significance of the battle: a legitimate lord had led an army of nobles to punish commoners who had seized his people and territory – and had been defeated. The two most dynamic political formations of the period, dynastic rulers and urban leagues, had faced off, and the leagues had won. Chroniclers all over Europe noted this strange event with concern, while the perfidy of the 'rude peasants' of Switzerland entered Habsburg family history as a lasting theme. For the *Eidgenossen* themselves, the battle became a moment to commemorate God's protection of their alliance from tyranny. A chapel to celebrate the victory was consecrated in 1387 and became the site of annual memorials. Only at the end of the fifteenth century did the story appear that one soldier, Arnold Winkelried, had swung the Battle of Sempach by throwing his body onto the wall of noble spears, thus opening a breach for his fellows; Winkelried's supposed deed quickly became a core myth for the Swiss, illustrating the brave self-sacrifice that justified their autonomy.

With this victory, and with the *Pfaffenbrief* and *Sempacherbrief* to regulate territorial jurisdiction and military affairs, the network of alliances in the region transcended its origins as a peacekeeping mechanism. Against external powers, most importantly the Habsburg dynasts with their many claims in the region, the Swiss had reached a stalemate of equals sustained in battle and in negotiations. Against local aristocrats, they had taken advantage of weakness to acquire many of their domains. Against villages, churches and other local institutions, they had proved capable of incorporating them, whether as citizens or subjects, into increasingly coherent territories. Backed by their alliances, the cantons were emboldened to reach out for more territory, accelerating the decline of the region's remaining noble families. Contemporaries and the Swiss themselves recognized that a new political force, the *Eidgenossenschaft*, now existed.

Nevertheless, the Confederacy of the 1390s was not in any sense a state, much less a nation. Importantly, no single document united all of the later cantons (usually considered to be eight, although Solothurn also signed the *Sempacherbrief*.) All of the cantons also remained part of the Empire, and continued to accept the legal framework of lordship and privilege by which the Empire operated. Each member retained the right to make further alliances and to follow its own interests, as long as new pacts did not directly contradict the existing ones. Political pressure to put the Swiss network above others did limit how far each canton could go, but Zurich and Berne in particular strenuously resisted any limits on their diplomatic freedom. Although all of the original eight cantons spoke German, and shared a certain contempt for Romance, especially Italian, mores and attitudes, their shared language did not in itself increase their cohesion or limit their alliances with neighbouring Romance-speaking communities or lords. As in the polyglot kingdoms around them, language played only a minimal role in Swiss nation-formation before the seventeenth century.

The members of the *Eidgenossenschaft* of 1393 had very different political interests, social structures and perspectives. Berne's politics lay primarily in the hands of a small group of families with noble estates outside the city, who looked mostly south and west in their ambitions, playing a complex game of alliance and rivalry with the Houses of Savoy and Burgundy. Zurich remained a manufacturing and trading city with interests south-east to the eastern Swiss passes and north-east to the textile and trading cities of St Gallen, Constance, Schaffhausen, and Ulm, none of which were then part of the Confederacy. The Inner Swiss (Lucerne, Uri, Schwyz and Unterwalden) followed territorial interests south across the St Gotthard pass into Italy. The search for territorial opportunity brought some cantons up against others: Obwalden and Lucerne faced Berne to their west, while Schwyz and Zurich competed to their east. Finally, urban cantons had different horizons and different internal structures from the rural valley members of the Confederacy. Among the VIII cantons making up the alliance, Zurich, Berne and Lucerne contrasted with Uri, Schwyz, Unterwalden and Glarus (with Zug halfway in between, structurally and socially). The citizens of the rural cantons often sympathized with rural communities under urban rule, whereas the cities were drawn towards their peers in southern Germany and down the Rhine.

The relatively open and heterogeneous political and social constellation that had given rise first to peace alliances, then to political leagues in the formation of the Swiss Confederacy, remained in place after 1386. What had changed was that the *Eidgenossenschaft* of the Swiss was poised to take advantage of that openness as a group with shared interests. The course of events after 1386 belongs to the next segment of Switzerland's history. Here, we will conclude with some highlights of the social and cultural developments that helped shape events into the 1400s.

EUROPEAN CULTURE AND SOCIETY IN THE SWISS LANDS

The most important feature of Swiss society and culture in the High Middle Ages was its continued participation in the major trends that transformed Western Europe as a whole. Switzerland experienced depredations from the Magyars and Islamic raiders before 1000, like its neighbours, and recovered socially, economically and politically after 1000. Cities began to grow after 1050, and in the twelfth and thirteenth centuries, houses of Dominican and Franciscan friars were popular, as they were elsewhere. The thorough penetration of Christian practices far into the mountains is demonstrated by the decorated church ceiling of Zillis in the Grisons Alps, dating to 1109–14. In 153 metre-square murals, themes from the Bible and the life of St Martin were vividly illustrated for the congregation. Local lords, and increasingly local communities, also found themselves forced to take sides in the great European ecclesio-political struggles of the Middle Ages, from the Investiture Conflict to the Great Schism. And not least, as in any agrarian society, the steady pulse of demography and rural production lay behind all other Swiss events in the period.

The most cataclysmic development affecting Switzerland before 1386 was the crisis of overpopulation beginning *c.* 1300 that reversed with the Black Death of 1347–9 – dates that correspond closely with the emergence of the Confederacy. Some evidence suggests that *c.* 1300 Swiss regions were less overpopulated than other parts of Europe, though the spread of Walser migrants into the

1.6 Annunciation to the Shepherds, Zillis, *c.* 1110. The
elaborate mosaic of images painted on the ceiling of the church
of St Martin in Zillis, on a major pass route through the
Grisons, provides an unparalleled representation of popular
religious culture in the region around 1100. Since the region's
population relied heavily on shepherding at the time, the
Annunciation to the Shepherds was a natural topic for one of
the images.

highest valleys in the Alps during the 1200s demonstrates that the
pressure to find new land was strong. The Black Death that ended
this pressure affected the Swiss midlands severely, though the Alpine
regions seem to have been less afflicted. The best estimates suggest
that the territory comprising modern Switzerland went from some
800,000 inhabitants after 1300 to fewer than 600,000 by 1400,
owing to repeated waves of plague. It is difficult to connect either
overpopulation before 1347 or rapid population decline afterwards

to specific political events, however. The guild revolution in Zurich in 1336 probably reflected economic pressure from high grain prices, but we lack direct evidence. Similarly, a major political crisis broke out in 1350, but no documents connect it directly to the Black Death. In general, we can say that the lesser aristocracy in particular faced economic as well as demographic headwinds in the late 1300s that made the growth and consolidation of communal polities easier, as seen in England, France and Italy as well as the German lands. It is also possible that the mountain valleys took on unusual significance in the Confederacy because they suffered less disruption from the plague than the midland cities, though intense (but poorly documented) social conflict took place in Uri in the late 1350s.

Nineteenth- and twentieth-century Swiss historians of this period often highlighted the 'peasant and herder' societies of the Alpine valleys, arguing that strong local solidarity and wild, elemental courage made mountain warriors the backbone of Swiss autonomy. Several early battles in Swiss history were fought primarily by men from the mountains, and because of their prowess, mercenaries from Inner Switzerland found an eager welcome in Italy and beyond by 1400. The combination of poverty and inaccessible terrain, commercial pastoralism, connections to the outside world through the passes and the local strength of corporate organization did set these regions apart. In the romantic version of nineteenth-century writers, the democratic Inner Swiss fought bravely for freedom against tyrannical aristocrats because of the natural liberty of the mountain meadows, abetted by the physical toughness that the herder's life demanded. Modern research has revealed how little democracy existed at the time, although the society of these valleys was characterized by a less vertical social hierarchy, more dependence of local elites on popular support and broader political participation than in most areas of Europe. The society of the Alpine valleys thus played a role in the Confederacy's emergence, but most historians now agree that it is not the primary explanation.

The midlands cities were more tightly bound to European developments and to the complex hierarchies of feudal Europe. Many historians have remarked that the Swiss cities combined features of Italian city-states and German imperial cities: they developed substantial territories like the Italians, but remained organized corporately like the Germans. All of the Swiss cities remained modest in size, and their cultural contributions were correspondingly modest. One illustrative achievement from the period is the Codex Manesse, a manuscript volume containing the richest surviving collection of late *Minnesang* – the German version of feudal love poetry – along with spiritual and didactic texts. Compiled in Zurich after 1300, it was a product not of the nobility, but of an urban family, the Manesse, who had aristocratic ambitions. Illustrated with 137 miniatures of knights at their adventures, and carefully ordered according to the noble status of each poem's supposed author, the text illustrates how aristocratic values thrived in the heart of the urban commune. Many similar products reflecting aristocratic and Christian ideas

1.7 Courtly culture in the towns. Among the whimsical images of lords and ladies in the Codex Manesse, produced for a successful burgher family in Zurich shortly after 1300, the scribe included one with his own name, Hadlaub. The book contains songs and poems from Europe's aristocratic culture, which set the tone for the increasingly wealthy urban elites as well.

and culture are found among the art, architecture and physical objects from the period.

During a recent renovation undertaken on a house in Zurich, traces of the Jewish population of the medieval city came to light as well. Evidence about the small number of Jews present in Switzerland before 1347 is scant, although we know they experienced persecution ranging from accusations of ritual murder in Berne in 1294 to outright pogroms during the Black Death, as occurred all over Europe. In Zurich, a well-off Jewish family commissioned lively decorations on the walls of a stately townhouse on the Brunnenhof before 1349; a second community thrived in the late 1300s, leaving signs of what was probably a school and small synagogue on the Froschaugasse. Some twenty Jewish families lived in the city at the time, involved in money-lending and urban trade, before rising anti-Semitism in the fifteenth century once again led to their expulsion in 1436. Here too, Swiss patterns matched broader European trends in both timing and consequences.

In the High Middle Ages, the region that produced the late medieval Swiss Confederacy and eventually the modern nation-state of Switzerland was an engaged participant in the culture of the medieval West as a whole. The region's inhabitants took advantage of the openness of feudal society and politics to carve out their own set of political institutions, even as they continued to share in broader European cultural and social developments. After the Battle of Sempach, in which one of Europe's leading aristocratic dynasts fell to a nameless commoner, Europeans recognized that this region and its emerging power system had characteristics that set it apart from others. As national states began to consolidate across Europe during the fifteenth century, the key issue was whether the loose *Eidgenossenschaft* of 1400 would be reabsorbed by the emerging dynastic-administrative states around it, or whether the larger region's structures were still sufficiently open for a different kind of state to emerge.

2

Creating the Swiss Confederacy, 1386–1520

Around 1400, the loosely organized *Eidgenossenschaft* or Confederacy of rural and urban communes, bolstered by mutual support at moments of crisis and by a few agreements on jurisdiction and military affairs, had become significant political players in the region stretching from Lake Geneva to Lake Constance. A century later *c.* 1500, a widely recognized Swiss Confederacy negotiated treaties with the Habsburg Emperors, the kings of France and other major European powers about military cooperation and dominion over northern Italy. Repeated wars as well as profound changes in the European political milieu and in relations among the Swiss themselves made this unexpected transformation possible.

Across Europe, leagues that began as desperate efforts to control violence in the High Middle Ages showed themselves capable – especially in Italy, the western German lands and the Netherlands – of evolving into stable political alliances with offensive and defensive capacities. The thriving Italian city-states in the fourteenth century proved that communal polities could become politically dominant; as they demonstrated in the fifteenth century, they could also produce new nobilities and revert to aristocratic government. The *Eidgenossenschaft* of the Swiss followed a different path. The small size of the units involved – Zurich and Berne were tiny compared to Florence and Milan – and the combination of rural and urban communes made the Swiss Confederacy distinctive. Moreover, aristocratic dynasties remained vital in the north beyond 1400, including the Habsburgs and Savoy along with

40

2.1 Swearing to the alliances. Mutual oaths among communal members provided a potent alternative to lordly dominion in the late 1300s and early 1400s. In this image, citizens of Lucerne swear to uphold the Confederate alliance of 1351, documented in the charter held by the figure upper right. Swiss consciousness of how their alliances, and the oaths they took to protect them, constituted their Confederacy appears in this depiction of oath-swearing from an illustrated chronicle produced in early sixteenth-century Lucerne.

regional houses like the Toggenburg and Württemberg, meaning that the Confederacy's members could survive only through cooperation and mutual support. By 1500, however, despite the persistently diverse interests among its members, it was the Confederacy as a whole, rather than Berne or Zurich or Schwyz, that had become significant on a European scale.

Growing polarization between the emerging Confederacy and the region's dynasts – above all, the Habsburg family, who permanently regained the imperial throne in 1438 – added an ideological dimension to political contestation. Most contemporaries equated the Confederacy's usurpation of Habsburg and other noble territories with the peasant rebellions that all European nobles feared; from the Swiss perspective, aristocratic efforts to suppress communal privileges demonstrated that the region's dynasts had become tyrants worthy of deposition by the pious common man. A nearly unbroken sequence of Swiss military and political successes from 1386 to 1499 heightened such tensions, and led defenders of the Confederacy to produce songs, myths and histories intended to legitimate the new political entity that was taking shape. Composed mostly after 1450, this material reflected the circumstances of the 1400s, even though most of the events it reported, including the increasingly iconic story of William Tell, were set around 1300.

This body of literary and historical material – what Swiss call the 'saga of liberation' (*Befreiungssage*) – is significant in understanding both Swiss history and modern Swiss political culture, since it became the accepted foundation for political discussions among the Swiss for the next five centuries. Urban patricians in the 1500s, rebellious rural communes in 1653, Enlightenment intellectuals in the early 1700s and political activists in the era of the French Revolution all referred to William Tell's fight against Habsburg tyranny. Modern historical research has established that the saga included many events that either never took place, such as the rebellion of William Tell, or which were described anachronistically. Nevertheless, its emergence must be included among the transformations of the long fifteenth century that produced a coherent Confederacy.

THE EUROPEAN CONTEXT

The events that produced a lasting Swiss Confederacy in the 1400s can only be understood in their larger European context. Across Europe, central authorities of all kind faced enormous challenges around 1400, since political fragmentation and local lawlessness were widespread. Major wars affected most European states, while repeated popular rebellions created great anxiety among feudal aristocrats. The demographic and economic consequences of the Black Death, which kept populations down and labour scarce well into the 1400s, exacerbated conflict. After about 1470, however, the balance tilted across Europe. This can be seen most vividly in the consolidation of powerful 'new monarchies' in France, England and Spain. Characterized by bureaucratic administration, standing armies and significant representative institutions, these new monarchies created the foundations for early modern and modern European states. In Italy, the city-states mostly became hereditary principalities – the major exception being Venice; in the Empire, territorial principalities played a growing role in politics and society, while the Empire's own institutions expanded in the imperial reform of 1495. Political consolidation was accompanied by increasingly rigid social hierarchies and a new wave of repression directed against those who diverged from Christian ideals. At the same time, intellectual innovation beginning in Italy transformed education, religion and eventually elite culture as a whole, as Renaissance ideas spread across Europe.

Swiss developments closely followed European trends, although Switzerland's location near several hotspots of European contention, including the nascent Burgundian realm and northern Italy, put particular pressure on the Confederacy's members while lending the entire Confederacy greater European salience. Six major episodes of conflict transformed the Confederacy between 1386 and 1500 and illustrate its development. The first two, which continued the trends of the late 1300s, fit the European pattern of weakened traditional authorities and aggressive new political actors. The Appenzell wars of 1403–9 belong among the most significant and successful peasant rebellions in a rebellious era, while the Swiss seizure of the Aargau from the Habsburgs in 1415–19 demonstrated the strength of the *Eidgenossenschaft*'s network of alliances. The third conflict, the Old Zurich War of 1436–50, was a complex affair involving dynastic politics, Swiss–Habsburg relations and rivalries within the Confederacy itself. These first three conflicts also deeply influenced the narratives of Swiss liberation that were emerging around 1450.

The last three conflicts – the Burgundian War of 1474–7, the Swabian War of 1499 and finally Swiss involvement in the Italian Wars after 1494 – show that the Confederacy had become a significant player in European politics (more significant, indeed, than it would be in later periods). In each of these conflicts, however, the internally conflicted nature of the Confederacy also became evident. Shared institutions and shared agreements helped manage these circumstances, and also reveal how the Confederacy was evolving. In particular, the emergence of a Swiss Diet, the *Tagsatzung*, after 1420; the treaties that ended the Old Zurich war in the early 1450s; and the *Stanser Verkommnis* of 1481, together with the acceptance of Fribourg and Solothurn as members of the Confederacy, document the emerging outlines of the Swiss polity as it existed from the early 1500s until 1798.

CONSOLIDATION AND REVOLUTION, 1386–1415

The loose Swiss Confederacy that existed in 1386 could grow because of weakness among both the local and higher nobility in the region. This weakness allowed the urban cantons, especially Berne, to expand their territories through purchase, mortgage and other tactics, thus bringing more and more subjects under their governance. The rural cantons sought expansion as well: notably, Uri signed a protection agreement with the Leventina valley south of the St Gotthard pass, and in cooperation with the other Inner Swiss pressed its influence further south, initiating the century-long process of appropriating the valley of the Ticino.

The emergence of an aggressive peasant movement in the hills of Appenzell provides a vivid demonstration of how limited noble power was around 1400. Like other rural areas, the inhabitants of Appenzell had established corporately organized economic and legal communes in the 1300s. In 1377, these communes became members of the Swabian league of cities, along with the city of St Gallen, which shared in the region's thriving linen manufactures and subjection to the Abbot of St Gallen. When a new abbot, Kuno von Stoffel, sought to restore the abbey's control over – and its income from – its subjects after 1379, the peasants insisted the abbot was violating 'old traditions'. They therefore systematically withheld death dues, married non-subjects and otherwise ignored his commands. Resistance from Appenzell and St Gallen led Kuno to put his abbey under Habsburg protection. The Appenzellers responded by destroying their bailiff's castle and allying with Schwyz, which took charge of military affairs. The peasant militia inflicted a series of humiliating defeats on the abbatial and Habsburg forces at Voglinsegg in 1403 and at the Stoss in 1405, inspiring a wave of excitement among the Habsburg-ruled peasantry of the region around Lake Constance. As one contemporary report put it, 'All the peasants would gladly be Appenzellers.' A struggle over feudal dues and administration had provoked a social revolution.

From 1404 to 1408, a Bund ob dem See (Alliance above the Lake) centred on Appenzell and its Schwyzer allies destroyed castles and drove out noble administrators around the region. The new alliance aimed at creating a peasant confederacy of remarkable size, and resembles the contemporary Hussite rebellion in Bohemia. However, though the Appenzellers ignored episcopal and papal condemnations, their movement lacked the religious dimension that welded the Bohemian rebels into a lasting movement. A minor defeat at Bregenz, inflicted by the Swabian noble-communal league of St Jörgenschild, ended the seeming invincibility of the Appenzell militia, after which truces and legal judgments terminated open hostilities. On paper, Appenzell returned to obedience to the abbot, but in reality, the commune remained autonomous. The members of the Swiss Confederacy took a limited part in these events. Schwyz, whose territorial interests lay towards Appenzell, provided support and military leadership at crucial moments; Zurich counselled peace, mediated and sought to stabilize its own hinterland to prevent the movement from spreading.

Appenzell was not the only region where mountain communities expelled regional lords in this period. In the upper Rhone valley, seven valley communities collaborated to limit Savoyard influence by expelling the lords of Raron and gaining oversight over the Bishops of Sion. In the Grisons, ministerial noble families like the Planta and commoner elites built a network of communal alliances between 1367 and 1446. The League of the House of God limited the Bishop of Chur, while the Grey League extended a regional peace alliance at the headwaters of the Rhine by establishing a common court and regular assemblies. Joined by the League of the Ten Jurisdictions after 1436, these leagues formed a separate confederacy in the Grisons that became a lasting ally of the Swiss.

Each of these rural movements rested on the leadership of elites who were neither poor nor unsophisticated, and who often had ties to the existing aristocratic system and to nearby urban communes. Earlier Swiss historians often ascribed democratic practices and legitimacy to these movements, and to the emerging Confederacy as a whole, in ways that the evidence does not support. Only a limited number of citizens had political rights in Swiss political corporations, and even where most arms-bearing males could attend public assemblies, a few clans typically monopolized offices and controlled most decisions. Still, communal leaders – even those carrying noble titles – gained legitimacy from their communes, rather than from aristocratic status. Communal support for leadership, especially in the rural cantons, and the very real rejection of noble prerogatives that drove many of these movements also encouraged the increasing ideological divide between nobles and commoners – whom the nobles derogated as 'coarse peasants' regardless of their status or authority. This divide shaped both events and the historical mythology of the Confederacy.

IMPERIAL POLITICS, THE AARGAU AND THE SWISS DIET, 1415–1436

The seizure of the Aargau in 1415 brought a key strategic territory under Swiss control and simultaneously spurred the creation of the Confederacy's first formal institutions. The Aargau lies at the very centre of the Swiss midlands where the Aar, Reuss and Limmat rivers meet – flowing from Berne, Lucerne and Zurich – and there lay the Habichtsburg, the castle that gave the Habsburg family its name. The Habsburgs had comital rights in the Aargau after 1173, and by 1415, much of the Aargau was under direct administration of a Habsburg bailiff in the town of Baden.

In 1415, Emperor Sigismund called a church council in Constance to end the papal schism, in which three rival popes each claimed to be the sole head of the church in Rome. The schism divided western Christendom from the 1370s, since everyone faced the choice of which Pope to support. The council summoned the claimants in the intention of deposing them all; when the Habsburg duke Frederick IV helped one claimant escape, Sigismund seized this welcome opportunity to weaken his Habsburg rival by invoking the imperial ban and inviting Frederick's enemies to seize his territories. The leaders of Berne had long had their eyes on the strategic and prosperous region down the Aar from the city, and swiftly seized the western Aargau. The other Confederates hesitated, but when promised further privileges from Sigismund, seized the eastern and southern Aargau. Resistance was modest, and soon the Confederates were the (slightly dubious) lords over the Aargau. The validity of the Confederates' title was subject to the vicissitudes of Habsburg–imperial relations, but payment to Sigismund of 10,000 gulden to mortgage several crucial lordships provided a legal foundation sufficient to make the Aargau permanently Swiss.

Possession of this strategic territory was of great importance; the challenge of administering the Aargau, which became not a member but a *subject* of the Confederacy, had equally lasting consequences. The Bernese quickly absorbed the territory they had seized, but the areas that had been taken jointly formed a condominium. After some poorly documented experimentation, the seven participating cantons began jointly appointing a chief magistrate for their shared territories, with the power of appointment rotating biennially. This officer, the *Landvogt*, collected taxes, administered high justice and called out the local militia in the name of the seven cantons. Although the Confederates confirmed the liberties and privileges of the Aargau's inhabitants, governance was founded entirely on the basis of lordship.

Significantly, the cantons decided to make policy for their new subjects by majority vote among the conquerors. Although the Aargau produced only modest revenues, the necessity of inspecting each *Landvogt*'s accounts and of swearing in the new incumbent also meant that representatives of the cantons had to meet regularly, which they began doing in the town of Baden. From these beginnings, the

Swiss Diet (the *Tagsatzung*) emerged. In contrast to other parliaments appearing at the time, the Diet rested not on the three estates of the clergy, nobility and commoners, but rather on corporate states that sent delegates bound by instructions from home. The meetings provided the occasion to discuss other shared concerns, although unanimity was required for any decisions not related to the condominiums. Regular Diets ensured that the leading politicians in the cantons knew each other and became familiar with their allies' situations, and provided a valuable forum both for mediation of conflicts and for military planning later in the century.

Acquisition of lordship over the Aargau was thus a decisive step for the loosely organized Confederacy of the fourteenth century. It closed a strategic territorial gap between Berne and the eastern Confederates, drawing Berne and its existing network of alliances closer to the rest of the Confederacy – especially since Berne now possessed a substantial slice of usurped Habsburg territory, thus aligning its political interests more closely with the anti-Habsburg central and eastern cantons. Increasing coherence in the Confederacy also generated conflict, however. The territorial interests of the individual cantons – still fully autonomous beyond the pacts that connected them – began impinging not only on neighbouring lordships, but also on other Confederates. Major disputes in the Valais and in Zug in the 1420s threatened the Confederacy when various ties put members on opposite sides. Greater territorial integrity also raised the question of how far the Confederacy as a whole could bind the actions of its individual members. The actual pacts connecting the members dated back to the fourteenth century, and addressed such questions only vaguely if at all. *Ad hoc* solutions overcame some potential internal conflicts, but these issues nearly destroyed the Confederacy during the struggle from 1436 into the 1450s known as the Old Zurich War (*Alter Zürichkrieg*).

CONTESTING THE NATURE OF THE CONFEDERACY, 1436–1460

Instability characterized most of Europe from the 1420s to the 1450s. Particularly in south-west Germany, where authority was deeply fragmented, public order was tenuous and armed feuding ubiquitous.

2.2 Deathbed of Frederick VII of Toggenburg. Although the Habsburgs lost ground in the Confederacy after 1400, major dynasts such as Frederick controlled wide swathes of territory in the region. When Frederick died in 1436 without a will or direct heir, his conflicting promises and alliances, and the strategic placement of his domains in eastern Switzerland, provoked the Old Zurich War of 1436–50, which nearly destroyed the Confederacy.

Compared to Germany, the peace alliances of the *Eidgenossenschaft* succeeded in limiting public violence, but a serious economic slowdown in the 1430s and 1440s hit them as well. It was a dangerous time for small political entities, but also offered opportunities. Indeed, Zurich and Berne used their financial resources to expand their territorial holdings during these years at the expense of the remaining petty nobility. Schwyz, too, sought control over the pass trade through the

Grisons by reaching out to the southern end of Lake Zurich, fuelling a rivalry with Zurich that would last several centuries. Zurich and Schwyz both courted the Count of Toggenburg, the last major feudal dynast in eastern Switzerland. Well into the early 1400s, the counts kept accumulating strategic inheritances, but it became clear by the 1420s that the last count would have no direct heir. The rivalry for Count Frederick VII's favour, and thus for his lands, became more and more virulent until his death in 1436 unleashed open war inside and outside the Confederacy.

The struggle over the Toggenburg legacy was bitter, but a second dynastic event made it an existential threat to the Confederacy: in 1438, Albrecht II Habsburg, son-in-law of Sigismund, became Emperor, initiating 300 years of Habsburg sovereigns. Not since 1308 had the Swiss faced a Habsburg Emperor who combined in one person both imperial authority and his family's claims in the region. The truce between the Confederacy and the Habsburgs after 1386 had resolved nothing, nor had the Habsburgs ever accepted their loss of the Aargau in 1415. Although Albrecht soon died, he was succeeded by his cousin Frederick III, who was intent on restoring his family's possessions, and thus refused to confirm the imperial privileges of the Swiss. Frederick's desire to regain the Aargau and other lost domains turned a local feud into a war that eventually involved France and the south German princes as well as the Swiss.

The war, largely consisting of raids, skirmishes and attacks on peasants, fell into two phases. From 1436 to 1442, Zurich's high hopes of obtaining substantial territories from the Toggenburg inheritance were dashed by the bold actions that Ital Reding, long-term *Landamman* (chief magistrate) of Schwyz, took to seize several critical territories. Reding's hostility to Zurich gained support from Berne during a series of arbitrations undertaken by the Confederates: the Bernese leaders apparently felt that Zurich was a greater rival than rural Schwyz, and tilted the arbitrations toward the latter. Meanwhile, Habsburg administrators moved aggressively to re-establish control over critical parts of the upper Rhine valley, whose lordship they claimed after the extinction of the Toggenburger. Zurich's troops were defeated in a few skirmishes, its limited gains of 1436 were reversed and increasingly onerous penalties weighed on the city.

Hedged in, Zurich turned to the new Emperor, Frederick III, who boldly proposed a grand bargain: with imperial support, Zurich would obtain large parts of the Toggenburg inheritance; in exchange, Zurich would cede its recent acquisitions from the Counts of Kyburg to the Habsburgs, and support full Habsburg restitution in the Aargau. The deal would be enforced by a new eastern confederation including Zurich, St Gallen, Appenzell and the Habsburgs, which would neutralize the dangerous Swiss and bring the region into the Habsburg sphere of influence. Challenged by its allies for making an alliance with the 'hereditary enemy', Zurich's negotiators pointed to

2.3 Battle of St Jakob an der Sihl. Although they defeated Zurich and Habsburg troops outside the city at the chapel of St Jakob in July 1443, the coalition headed by Schwyz and supported by Berne was unable to take Zurich itself. A bloody stalemate with incessant raiding of the peasantry and numerous atrocities ensued. The bitterness of the struggles, which spread across eastern Switzerland, delayed a final peace and reconsolidation of the Confederacy until 1450.

the diplomatic freedom that the city retained in its old alliances with
the Confederates, and insisted that the pact with Austria reflected its
rights as a free imperial city.

The possibility that the Habsburgs might regain hegemony
over their south-western lordships became a matter of European concern. In the Empire, the electoral princes (*Kurfürsten*) supported the
Confederacy as a way to limit Habsburg power, while Frederick
formed an alliance with the King of France, who was eager to find
distraction outside France for the mercenaries, known as *Armagnacs*,
released by the waning of the Hundred Years War. Zurich experienced
a major defeat in July 1443 at St Jakob an der Sihl. A Confederate
army overran a force consisting of city militia, Swabian nobles and
Habsburg cavalry, Mayor Stüssi was killed and a long siege ensued.
In the summer of 1444, an Armagnac force marched towards Alsace
and Switzerland to subdue Basle and support Zurich. It was met
outside Basle by a hastily assembled force of about 1,500 troops
from Berne and Solothurn: nearly all the Swiss were killed, but the
French pulled back and played no further part in the struggle.
Widespread skirmishing and devastation continued, along with several minor battles in which Confederate forces defeated various combinations of Habsburg and local troops, but failed to capture many
towns or fortified places.

The war was accompanied by a wave of propaganda from all sides.
For the Confederates, Zurich's plan for a new anti-Confederacy
under Habsburg hegemony constituted betrayal. Frederick appealed
for French assistance by evoking 'the dangerous example of servants
rising up against their masters, and peasants against the nobles', while
the Zurich cleric Felix Hemmerli circulated a polemic against Swiss
rebels, whom he described as 'coarse, gluttonous, wrinkled, rough
and with strangely shaped bodies'. Such increasingly clear polarization
between the 'Swiss' – seen as peasants, for better or for worse – and the
lords found a reflection in the Swiss liberation narrative when it was
first written down in the 1470s by men who had experienced the Old
Zurich War.

Although fighting petered out after 1446, the intense animosity
that had developed between the parties delayed a final settlement for
years. Finally, after a series of complicated arbitrations, in which
Berne played a decisive role, a peace was reached. Zurich received

back almost all of the territory it had lost, but the Toggenburg inheritance went to other claimants, including Glarus and Schwyz. The most important clause subjected Zurich (and all the Confederates) to mediation if their actions impinged on the shared alliance: henceforth, the *Eidgenossenschaft* would have priority over each canton's right to make alliances. In the wake of the peace, several original alliances from the fourteenth century were reissued under the original dates, but missing crucial clauses protecting Habsburg authority; the originals were destroyed. A loose network of alliances had become a binding confederacy of partners.

The Old Zurich War represented a key turning point in the fate of this region. Had Zurich built up its own rival confederation in partnership with the Habsburgs, it is hard to imagine that the Swiss network would have survived the coming centuries of turmoil. Three other important features of the Swiss situation also became visible during the conflict. First, under the conditions of fifteenth-century warfare, no noble or urban military force was capable of defeating the Swiss. The events of the following half-century would repeatedly confirm this fact, until the emergence of artillery and modern fortifications. Second, the Confederacy had become the key territorial power in the region north of the Central Alps, just as principalities were becoming the key territorial powers further north and further south. The Confederacy would deal with Visconti and Sforza Milan, with the Dukes of Württemberg and with the Habsburgs as territorial peers. Finally, while future conflicts within the Confederacy often began with events in Zurich or in the mountains, their resolution would remain impossible until Berne took sides. As the largest and eventually richest canton, with a close-knit aristocratic urban elite in charge, Berne had become the arbiter of the Confederacy.

THE CONFEDERACY AND ITS NEIGHBOURS, 1460–1499

The Old Zurich War produced a more integrated Confederacy, changing both political balances within the cantons as well as their relationship with neighbouring powers. In consequence, the political issues during the half-century after 1450 had a different flavour. In place of territorial consolidation of individual cantons through piecemeal acquisition, outright conquest and the accession of new members characterized the period to 1536, when Swiss western expansion reached its modern limits with Berne's seizure of the Vaud and Geneva's entry as an associate. The new members included Fribourg and Solothurn (1481), followed by Schaffhausen, Basle (both 1501) and finally Appenzell, which became a full member in 1513. Ambitious efforts to expand south of the Alps remained confined to the Alpine foothills: the III Grisons Leagues seized the Valtellina in 1512 and held it until the Napoleonic period, the Ticino valley came under Swiss sovereignty in the form of several condominiums, while the Val d'Ossola slipped back out of Swiss hands before 1500. Territorial expansion and the consolidation of the great powers around Switzerland led to regional wars that included two spectacular Swiss victories, first against Burgundy in 1476–7, then against the Habsburgs and Empire in 1499. Expansion and victory altered the balance of power inside the Confederacy, along with the social and political balance between each canton's elite (which gained in influence and wealth) and the body of the citizenry. These issues reached a crisis in 1481, and were resolved in the *Stanser Verkommnis*, which accelerated the consolidation of the cantons as sovereign and territorially defined polities.

The events between 1458 and 1460 that brought the Thurgau under Swiss jurisdiction illustrate how the issues described above were intertwined. In particular, the role of autonomous bands of militarily trained men from various cantons – often only tenuously controlled by the magistrates – was critical, and reveals how mercenary experience was shifting the political forces within the Confederacy. The first phase of the Swiss takeover was the so-called Plappart War of 1458. As described in later sources, the rejection of a Bernese coin sporting the image of a bear (a *Plappart*) during a festival in Constance as a mere 'cow-plappart' triggered outrage among the Swiss attendees. The accusation showed the growing divide in identity between the Swiss and their neighbours in Swabia, perhaps accentuated by the insinuation of bestiality in the term of abuse 'cow-Swiss'. The insult provoked an impromptu band of troops to savage the Thurgau (under the jurisdiction of Constance at the time) and to demand reparations for their honour. The band had official support from Lucerne, although

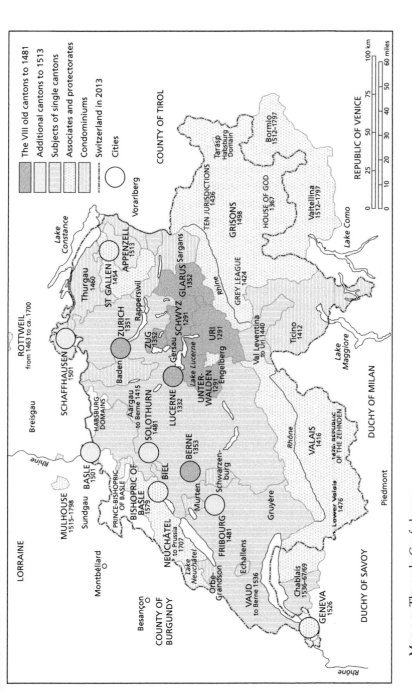

The VIII old cantons to 1481
Additional cantons to 1513
Subjects of single cantons
Associates and protectorates
Condominiums
Switzerland in 2013
Cities

LORRAINE

ROTTWEIL
from 1463 to ca. 1700

Lake
Constance

Breisgau

Vorarlberg

COUNTY OF TIROL

MULHOUSE
1515–1798

Sundgau

SCHAFFHAUSEN
1501

Thurgau
1460

ST GALLEN
1454

APPENZELL
1513

Rhine

BASLE
1501

PRINCE-BISHOPRIC
OF BASLE

HABSBURG
DOMAINS

ZURICH
1351

Baden

Rappperswil

Sargans

TEN
JURISDICTIONS
1436

Tarasp
Habsburg
Domain

BISHOPRIC OF
BASLE

Aargau
to Berne 1415

ZUG
1352

Gersau

SCHWYZ
1291

GLARUS
1352

Rhine

GREY LEAGUE
1424

Bormio
1512–1797

BIEL
1579

SOLOTHURN
1481

LUCERNE
1332

Lake Lucerne

URI
1291

GRISONS
1498

HOUSE OF GOD
1367

Montbéliard

NEUCHÂTEL
to Prussia
1707

BERNE
1353

Murten

UNTER-
WALDEN
1291

Engelberg

Val Leventina
to Uri 1440

Valtellina
1512–1797

Lake Como

Besançon

Lake
Neuchâtel

Schwarzen-
burg

Ticino
1412

COUNTY OF
BURGUNDY

Orbe-
Grandson

FRIBOURG
1481

Gruyère

Rhone

VALAIS
1416

Lake
Maggiore

DUCHY OF MILAN

Echallens

1476 REPUBLIC
OF THE ZEHNDEN

VAUD
to Berne 1536

Lower Valais
1476

Chablais
1536–67/69

GENEVA
1526

Rhone

DUCHY OF SAVOY

Piedmont

REPUBLIC OF VENICE

0   10   20   30   40   50 miles
0   25   50   75   100 km

60 miles

Map 2.1 The early Confederacy

men from a number of cantons participated; on their way home, they triggered a pro-Swiss coup in the Habsburg town of Rapperswil, divided between a loyalist faction known as 'Christians' and a pro-Swiss faction known as 'Turks'. In September 1460, irregular troops from Unterwalden and Lucerne again marched into the Thurgau after declaring a feud against the Habsburgs. To curb the movement, the remaining cantons sent their own contingents, and the territory quickly fell into Swiss hands. The Thurgau quickly re-emerged as a condominium under the same arrangements as the Aargau. Sigismund of Habsburg sold the now isolated city of Winterthur to Zurich in 1467, closing the remaining gap in Swiss control in this region. Direct action by militarily experienced citizens brought territorial additions to the Swiss, but their lawlessness and disrespect for existing hierarchies caused both urban and rural elites considerable anxiety.

Such matters were overshadowed in the 1470s by larger shifts in Western Europe. One legacy of the Hundred Years War between France and England was the uncertain status of Burgundy, which by the mid-1400s included territories stretching from the northern Netherlands down to the County of Burgundy around Besançon. The Valois Dukes who assembled these lands had their eyes on a crown for their 'middle realm', and energetically expanded their holdings to this end, funded by the prosperous Low Countries. Their ambitions were alternatively useful and alarming to the Kings of France and the German Emperors, but they were a direct threat to many small domains in their path, among which Berne, immediately to the south-east of the County of Burgundy, was significant.

Charles the Bold's accession as Duke triggered a complex series of diplomatic realignments that led, ultimately, to major Swiss participation in the struggles that destroyed Charles and his hopes. Both Sigismund of Habsburg, regent of his family's western holdings and King Louis XI of France, alarmed at Charles's ambitions, played critical roles. Sigismund initially sought Burgundian assistance against the Swiss, paid for by mortgaging his territories in Alsace to Charles. As his doubts about Charles's intentions grew, however, Sigismund changed sides and reached a long-term accommodation with the Swiss in 1474 that accepted Habsburg's territorial losses to the Confederacy – an astonishing concession – in exchange for support against the Burgundian possession of Alsace. Not coincidentally, Louis helped negotiate this treaty's terms, which made conflict between Charles and the Bernese, reluctantly supported by the rest of the Confederacy, inevitable. After a series of skirmishes and Berne's seizure of the Vaud from Charles' ally Savoy in 1475, the three major battles at Grandson, Murten and Nancy went from bad to worse for the Burgundians. At Grandson on 2 March 1476, a Burgundian army under Charles's personal command was driven back and his luxurious baggage train captured (major pieces remain in the Bernese Historical Museum and other Swiss museums). At Murten, a few months later, Charles lost half of his army, some 9,000, against a few hundred Swiss losses. Finally, at Nancy on 5 January 1477, a unified Lotharingian–Swiss–Alsatian army destroyed Charles's forces and killed the Duke himself. One of the most dynamic and ambitious potentates in Europe had fallen to the Confederacy, dramatically raising its stature as a potential ally.

Military and political success put the nature and extent of the Confederacy into question in new ways. During the war, the Confederacy gave little support to Berne's expansionist agenda, and afterwards, the eastern cantons refused to back Berne, ensuring that neither the Vaud nor the County of Burgundy remained in Swiss hands, though Fribourg did move closer to the Confederacy. Moreover, as the French negotiators quickly learned, cash directed to individual leaders or to a canton's common treasury was usually sufficient to bring about policies they desired. Greater Swiss power, it turned out, meant greater opportunities for corruption and internal disputes. Meanwhile, a growing divide between urban and rural areas enhanced the centripetal forces in the Confederacy. City magistrates already feared the undisciplined 'free companies' of young men, like those who had ravaged the Thurgau. Similar spontaneous cavalcades culminated in the 'Sow-banner campaign' (*Saubannerzug*) of 1477, when some 1,700 ex-soldiers, mostly from Inner Switzerland, marched to Geneva to demand the pay they had been promised for service during the Burgundian war. Behind their banner – whose symbols of the boar and the club symbolized popular unrest – lay not only anger at being cheated out of loot at Nancy, but also a growing rural population that faced harsh landlords backed by the authority of the cantons themselves. Urban landholders and powerful family heads in the rural cantons used their wealth and connections to pressure the poorer peasantry as land became scarce. The resulting social tensions were exacerbated by the flow of pensions and bribes from powers outside Switzerland, which mostly ended up in the pockets of political insiders. Swiss success on the European stage thus accelerated the emergence of sharp social differences inside the cantons.

The men in charge of politics, who increasingly adopted an aristocratic way of life, seemed a far cry from the 'noble peasants' of the liberation narrative that was beginning to circulate. In 1469–71, for example, the city of Berne was torn by social tensions between the urban guilds and the aristocratic council members who wanted to keep their feudal jurisdictions free from the city's control. The struggle broke out after a commoner was elected mayor, and was triggered by a decree that forbade citizens to wear aristocratic clothing. The authorities in the rural cantons often lacked the means to quell outbreaks of popular dissatisfaction, while Berne, Zurich and Lucerne seemed more interested in expanding their ties to additional cities, rather than remaining within the bounds of the Confederacy that had been affirmed at such a high cost during the Old Zurich War. When the three towns sealed a new permanent pact with Solothurn and Fribourg – cities in Berne's orbit that had been drawing closer to the Confederacy – the rural cantons objected. New members were being slipped into the Confederacy, they claimed, tilting the balance towards the cities. That Fribourg lay on the language border and had a bilingual patriciate was inconsequential in the debates over its admission to the Confederacy; indeed the rural cantons objected to more cities, not to more French-speakers, in the Confederacy. Tensions rose further in 1478 after the council in Obwalden instigated resistance to Lucerne's administration of the Entlebuch, a rural area lying between the two cantons.

Assisted by the mediation of the hermit Niklaus von Flüe of Obwalden, a compromise, the *Stanser Verkommnis*, emerged in 1481 to resolve both urban and rural cantons' complaints. On the one hand, Solothurn and Fribourg joined the Confederacy through treaties with the existing VIII cantons, while a new statute forbade unauthorized assemblies, and bound all the cantons to help suppress unrest. This measure strengthened the territorial integrity of all the cantons and the authority of each canton's existing regime. On the other hand, the primacy of the first VIII cantons was acknowledged, and Solothurn and Fribourg had to accept a second-tier membership that substantially

2.4 St Niklaus von Flüe. Military success in the Burgundian
Wars (1474–7) only increased social and political tensions
within the Confederacy. A stalemate over admitting new urban
members and controlling the free-lance militias from rural
regions threatened the Confederacy's survival in 1480. The
intervention of the hermit (and former high magistrate) Niklaus
von Flüe of Obwalden brought about the *Stanser Verkommnis*,
which reaffirmed the magistrates' authority in both cities and
rural cantons. Niklaus was canonized in 1947 as the patron
saint of Switzerland.

restricted their freedom of action. The settlement of 1481 thus represented another modest step toward political and territorial coherence
for the Confederacy, and away from the freewheeling flexibility of the
earlier alliances. It also reinforced the authority of cantonal magistrates
over their citizens and subjects, and contributed another element to
Swiss mythology, the selfless hermit Niklaus (who was beatified in 1648
and declared a saint in 1947).

That this agreement had not resolved rising social tensions between
peasants, burghers and rising magnates became clear in 1489, when

the powerful mayor of Zurich, Hans Waldmann, ran afoul of Zurich's citizens and rural subjects. By this time, the city had consolidated its hold over a broad territory whose inhabitants enjoyed limited local self-government while answering to city-appointed bailiffs for taxes, justice and military service. City administration imposed substantial burdens on its subjects. When Zurich purchased Winterthur in 1467, for example, the costs were covered by a head-tax and property tax on all inhabitants of city and country, with every taxpayer carefully recorded and assessed. Waldmann came from a relatively modest background but rose quickly to prominence in Zurich during the 1460s and 1470s. Like many strongmen in this period, military experience and marriage to a rich widow enabled his rise. He served as a captain of Zurich's troops at Murten in 1476 and as a mercenary in Germany, bringing him wealth and prestige that he deployed to gain further influence inside Zurich. His stature as leader of one of the two most influential cantons, in turn, made him vital to Swiss negotiations with outside powers, which brought him direct pensions from the King of France and Maximilian of Habsburg, heir to the imperial throne. By 1485, his dominance of Zurich politics seemed complete. He advanced Zurich's interests in peace with the Habsburgs and mercenary service for Milan, while also intensifying the city's administration over its own rural subjects.

The emergence of strongmen with near-dictatorial powers was common in the urban states of fifteenth-century Europe. Just as regularly, such rulers faced factional rivals eager to replace them and popular unrest from citizens who resented the hollowing out of republican constitutions. Waldmann, however, faced an additional source of unrest that sealed his fate: well-organized rural communities. When the city began cracking down on rural textile manufacturing and ordered all rural families to kill their dogs (the better to allow aspiring urban elites to enjoy hunting, the peasants believed), rural unrest combined with citizen dissatisfaction to trigger a rebellion. Several factors made such uprisings particularly common across Switzerland. First, Swiss rural communities enjoyed greater autonomy and stronger corporate organization than those in most European regions, and many peasants had military experience. Additionally, the Swiss ideology of 'noble peasants resisting tyrannical aristocrats' could easily be turned against ambitious men like Waldmann. Finally, peasant subjects in Switzerland had only to look to their neighbours in Schwyz, Uri, and Unterwalden to see emancipated peasants who enjoyed substantial political rights. In April 1489, Zurich's peasant subjects marched against the city, where they joined dissatisfied citizens. In accord with the *Stanser Verkommnis*, the other cantons sent representatives to mediate, but the murder of a Waldmann henchman during the negotiations led to the collapse of his power; he was tortured, tried and publicly executed a few days later. A wave of further executions took place as various factions settled scores, while a large cash payment to the peasantry, together with repeal of Waldmann's new laws, convinced them to march home. No Swiss canton could ignore its rural population, despite the rise of urban and rural oligarchies.

Swiss consolidation at the end of the century ran in parallel with similar developments in the Empire of which Switzerland remained a part. Lawlessness, noble feuds and weak central government still flourished in the late 1400s. With the accession of a new Emperor, Maximilian, in 1493, widespread interest in an imperial public peace and new institutions to provide justice and order led (after much wrangling) to major reforms in 1495. The Confederacy did not participate in negotiating the reforms, however – which included new imperial courts and a universal tax – and insisted that their existing privileges superseded the new measures. The resulting political tensions were exacerbated by visible social and cultural rivalry: the southern German city of Constance, closely tied to the Thurgau and the Swiss but also a participant in German developments, often provided a flashpoint for rowdy clashes at markets and festivals. Meanwhile, the beginning of the Italian Wars, set off by the French invasion of Naples in 1494, increased the strategic value of both Swiss passes and Swiss mercenaries to the Empire, giving the Confederacy greater political leverage.

The multiple tensions between the Confederacy and the Empire provoked a last war between the House of Habsburg and the Swiss in 1499. A relatively minor border dispute between the Bishop of Chur, backed by the League of the House of God in the Grisons, and Habsburg administrators in the Tyrol set off the conflict. The Leagues had signed treaties for military cooperation with the Confederacy in 1497 and 1498, while Maximilian called on the Swabian League and on imperial forces to show the 'peasants' their place. Although

2.5 Battle of Calven, 1499. An early chronicle of the Swabian War used this generic image, with Christ watching the fighters, to illustrate the skirmish at the Calven, at the south-eastern margin of the III Leagues of the Grisons. A surprise attack from the rear by Grisons forces drove a Habsburg expeditionary force into retreat. The Battle of Calven became an iconic event for the Republic of the III Leagues, in parallel with Sempach's role for the Confederacy, with its own exemplary hero in the person of Benedikt Fontana.

Berne and Zurich sought to mediate, local skirmishes quickly accelerated into an open war along a front reaching from Basle to the Grisons. Much of the action revolved around raiding and looting (Grisons and Tyrolean mountaineers, in particular, seemed more interested in seizing their neighbours' cattle than in the legal issues that occupied the urban governments), but Swiss forces consistently prevailed in various largely impromptu battles, despite Maximilian's personal engagement. As the Habsburgs' military situation deteriorated, Maximilian declared imperial war on the Swiss and turned to propaganda, issuing a manifesto that evoked Leopold III, killed in 1386 'on his own, by his own, on account of his own', and characterized the Swiss as 'bad, coarse and disrespectful peasants'. General exhaustion, along with French advances in northern Italy, led to a truce and then a settlement favourable to the Swiss. At Swiss insistence, the Peace of Basle (22 September 1499) treated the conflict as a private feud between the Habsburgs and the Bishop of Chur and his subjects, not as a formally declared war. The imperial reform was not mentioned specifically, but the final clauses of the treaty blandly negated all suits regarding the Confederates, which provided *de facto* exemption from the new institutions. Although later historians spoke of Swiss independence after 1499, the Swiss negotiators were in fact intent on restoring their good standing in the Holy Roman Empire. In contemporary terms, the peace gave the Swiss Confederacy a status similar to the most important imperial princes – not least the Habsburgs themselves as Archdukes of Austria – by providing them with exemption from imperial courts and with the freedom to make alliances and wage war without imperial intervention.

THE SWISS AS A EUROPEAN FACTOR, 1499–1520

The history of Swiss military triumphs and increasingly aggressive foreign adventures peaked between 1490 and 1515, followed by a rapid withdrawal. The potency of the Swiss infantry had become frighteningly visible during the Burgundian war, and was confirmed in Italy after 1494 and in 1499. Involvement in northern Italy – part of a struggle for the Italian peninsula pitting Valois France against Habsburgs in Spain and Austria – dominated political life in the Confederacy from 1500 to 1520. Swiss mercenary companies became a hot commodity, and money flowed freely, both publicly and in private, to the cantons and their leaders. Huge numbers of Swiss men streamed south, pushed by the increasing scarcity of available land at home and pulled by generous pay and the promise of loot.

Several cantons and allies seized the opportunity to expand their own control further south into the Italian Alpine foothills, bringing the Valtellina and Ticino under Swiss control. Military successes by Swiss troops even raised the possibility that Milan – far larger and richer than any Swiss city – might become a tributary of the Confederacy. The conditions favouring the Swiss forces turned out to be temporary, however. Changing military tactics undermined the superiority of the Swiss infantry as decisively as the Swiss had undermined heavy noble cavalry. When the Habsburg, Valois and Trastámara dynasties emerged from their fifteenth-century weakness, moreover, they controlled funds and forces far beyond those available to the Confederacy.

Swiss participation in the Italian Wars moved large numbers of men to Italy's battlefields – where many died – and large amounts of money to the treasuries of the cantons and to military entrepreneurs. It also constituted the most important shared business among the cantons during the first two decades of the sixteenth century. Negotiations with foreign envoys and among the Diet's delegates over the best strategy to follow were frequent and often divisive. In addition to the existing tensions between the cities and the rural cantons and old divides such as the rivalry between Schwyz and Zurich came new divisions: Berne and Fribourg wanted support for expansion toward Vaud; the Inner Swiss, the Valais and Grisons wanted support for acquisitions in Italy; and Zurich and Schaffhausen sought peace with the Confederacy's neighbours, not least because they were trade and manufacturing centres.

The Diet provided a site for discussions of such problems, but negotiation also took place before the councils of individual cantons, or in secret with leading political figures. By 1500, the leaders of most cantons felt that they had lost control over military recruiting. This threatened the magistrates' monopoly over the means of violence within their own territories, and also meant that lucrative pensions and bribes might elude their grasp. Popular hostility to recruiting resulted from the many deaths in Italy, and from anger at the luxurious life of the military entrepreneurs. Magisterial and popular concerns came together in attacks on mercenaries and their recruiters. In 1503, these concerns motivated a new Confederate statute, the *Pensionenbrief*, which prohibited private military

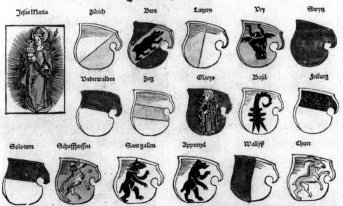

2.6 Song of the Battle of Novara outside Milan, 1513. The Swiss celebrated their repeated battlefield victories in Italy before 1515 through the new medium of print. The song here, which celebrated God's and the Virgin Mary's support of Swiss troops, carried the coats of arms of the XIII Confederates and their allies, along with the image of the Virgin with child that Pope Julius had awarded the Swiss for their military banners in 1512.

recruiting and required a majority of the Diet to approve troop agreements. It soon became clear that the cantons could not carry out their own decision, however, since new agreements with foreign recruiters continued.

Two major military decisions near Milan – an avoided battle and a lost one – illustrate the limits to Swiss participation on the European stage. At Novara in 1500, a French army consisting largely of Swiss mercenaries surrounded another Swiss force guarding Duke Ludovico Sforza of Milan, who sought to recapture his duchy from the French. The possibility that Swiss might fight Swiss on behalf of foreign princes led to negotiations that allowed the force employed by Sforza to withdraw. Sforza disguised himself among the Swiss to escape, but was betrayed by a soldier from Uri. Mercenary service, especially when not controlled by the Diet, had nearly caused a fratricidal disaster, and had brought dishonour for the Swiss. After another decade of battlefield victories, the Battle of Marignano in 1515 revealed the end of Swiss invincibility. The battle began after many of the Swiss regiments present had accepted 1 million French crowns to yield Milan to the new French king, François I. Other regiments decided to fight, however, and drew their compatriots back into the battle. The artillery that François deployed proved devastatingly effective against the massed Swiss infantry. Nearly half the Swiss on the field of Marignano lost their lives, provoking bitter debates about who was responsible for so many deaths. Never again did Swiss forces command European battlefields: weak central command and new military technologies made them unable to compete with the armies of the early modern period.

Swiss manpower remained interesting to the great powers, however, especially to France. Rather than suffering a collapse of its diplomatic interests after 1515, therefore, the Confederacy negotiated a lasting and profitable alignment with one power, France. Even after major losses, thousands of Swiss soldiers could be raised at very short notice. Only a year after the catastrophe at Marignano, for example, the French and the Habsburgs recruited nearly 25,000 troops from the Confederacy. Swiss men thus continued to perform military service outside Switzerland, mostly under a very favourable 1521 mercenary treaty with France that included all the cantons (except Zurich) along with the Grisons and Valais. The Swiss already received large reparations in 1516, and increased annual pensions went to every signing canton in 1521. Among other provisions, special tariff and toll privileges in Milan and France and privileged access to French salt markets had long-lasting consequences. In exchange, the French king gained the right to recruit up to 16,000 infantrymen for his campaigns. The Habsburgs and the Swiss also negotiated a permanent peace in 1511, the *Erbeinung*. By 1521, the Swiss had thus stabilized their relations with the two most powerful neighbouring rulers.

The structure of the Confederacy around 1500 – as a coherent network of allies that acted in concert – meant that new members remained a possibility. Notably, the successes of Swiss arms in Burgundy, Italy and Swabia encouraged the formation of pro-Swiss factions in many nearby cities. After the Swabian war, such a faction in Basle led the city away from its Alsatian allies and into the Confederacy in 1501. Schaffhausen, too, seized the moment to move from being an ally to a member of the Confederacy, even if its membership limited its ability to pursue independent policies. Mühlhausen, already allied with Solothurn, Berne and Basle, followed in 1515, accepting the status of an associate (*Zugewandter*) to strengthen its position as the Habsburgs consolidated their hold on the rest of Alsace.

Once Habsburg and the Valois controlled Alsace, Burgundy, Milan, Tyrol and Swabia, however, opportunities for adding either members or new subject territories diminished. Only the lands of the House of Savoy still offered opportunity, which culminated with Bernese seizure of the Vaud in 1536. Tellingly, the last full member to join the Confederacy, Appenzell, was not on the borders. Rather, its membership in 1513 merely clarified treaties going back to 1452, and reflected the participation of the Appenzeller as partners in Italy. Despite the objections of the Abbots and city of St Gallen, who remained mere associates, the Appenzellers joined under terms similar to those for Schaffhausen.

Encouraged by difficult economic circumstances and anger at 'corrupt' magistrates and arrogant mercenary entrepreneurs, popular unrest boiled over repeatedly in southern Germany and in the Confederacy in the early 1500s. Both regions were affected by military losses, and both experienced rising social conflicts over dues, rents and noble jurisdiction. Peasant unrest in Swabia took the form of conspiracies energetically suppressed by nobles and ruling cities, whereas rural subjects in Switzerland were more successful in gaining remedies. When the authorities ignored rural discontent after 1510, numerous Swiss peasant communes took action. Unhappy subjects of Berne stormed the city in 1513 after gathering at a church festival in Köniz, and demanded that alliances with foreign princes be subject to their approval. Similarly, Zurich's rural subjects marched into the city in late 1515, convinced that the Swiss defeat at Marignano had been brought about by French bribes. In both cases, the magistrates were forced to acknowledge their subjects' right to participate in decisions on war and peace, slowing the growing trend towards oligarchy that Switzerland shared with its neighbours.

A EUROPEAN NATION AND CULTURE

Events in the second half of the fifteenth century resulted in the emergence of a Swiss polity and Swiss nation, the Old Confederacy, which survived with few formal changes from 1513 to 1798. Military success in the early 1500s gave the Confederacy political weight, while Swiss participation in European culture and the emergence of a distinctive Swiss historical mythology helped form an identity, internally and externally, that set the Swiss apart from their neighbours and that increasingly shaped their choices and actions.

The key cultural development of fifteenth-century Europe was the intellectual movement we call the Renaissance. Beginning in Italy, Renaissance educational and historical thinking spread across the Continent, leaving traces in the Swiss region as well. Notably, Switzerland became a distinct region in the minds of Europeans owing to the efforts of Humanist geographers who reintroduced the old Roman designations Helvetia and Raetia to the region. The two Church councils held in the region – at Constance from 1414 to 1418 and in Basle from 1431 to 1449 – also increased Europeans' familiarity with Switzerland, while the growing prominence of Swiss mercenaries in various European wars led to a rather different picture, emphasizing the barbarity and effectiveness of Switzerland's soldiers.

Renaissance Humanism began to influence Swiss intellectuals late in the fifteenth century. Local writers mixed Humanist-style historiography and geography with more traditional forms of chronicle in

Das   XV   blat.

Von wilhelm Tellen dem frommen landt=
man der sinem eigen kind ein öpffel müst ab dem houpt schiessen
vnd wie es im ergieng.

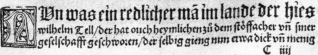
Vn was ein redlicher mã im lande der hies
wilhelm Tell/der hat ouch heymlichen zů dem stöffacher vñ siner
geselschafft geschworen/der selbig gieng num etwa dick vñ menig
C iiij

2.7 William Tell shooting the apple. The story of William Tell's
deeds emerged after 1470 to become a central point of reference
for Swiss identity. In the first printed chronicle of Swiss history
by Petermann Etterlin, Tell was depicted with the 'three
confederates' of the earlier chronicles, about to loose his quarrel
at his son. As in most versions, a second quarrel was ready in his
hood, intended for the evil bailiff Gessler should Tell's son be
harmed.

describing the Confederacy. Early on, Albrecht von Bonstetten praised the Confederacy in his *Superioris Germaniae Confoederationis Descriptio* of 1479, while later Swiss Humanists wrote in more refined Latin, notably the two Glarus scholars Heinrich Loriti ('Glareanus', 1484–1563) and Aegidius Tschudi, (1505–72). Tschudi compiled Classical references to the ancient Roman province of Raetia in his only published work, though he was equally interested in medieval charters, which he zealously copied in manuscript. Like many Swiss Humanists, Glareanus spent considerable time in Basle, the site of the first (and for a long time the only) Swiss university, founded in 1460. The confluence of Basle's printing industry and its university ensured that Basle became the only Swiss city where Humanism really flourished, illustrated most vividly by Erasmus of Rotterdam's decision to live there.

Renaissance thinking had little influence on the enduring cycle of myths and stories that explained the origins, legitimacy and virtues of the Swiss Confederacy, first to the Swiss and then to the rest of Europe. As a confederation of republics in a monarchical world, and as a polity based on corporate citizenship rather than feudal hierarchy, Switzerland was unusual in early modern Europe. The Swiss liberation saga wove the tale of the brave crossbowman William Tell together with that of the three virtuous 'oath comrades' (*drei Eidgenossen*) from Uri, Schwyz and Unterwalden, uniting anti-aristocratic themes, stories of brave sacrifice against tyrannical abuses and a running emphasis on God's support of the virtuous Swiss. The oldest surviving version of the Tell story – with most of its elements already in place – dates to 1470, when it was copied into a book of charters, the White Book of Saarnen, compiled in Obwalden. It described how after the death of the good king Rudolf in 1291, greedy bailiffs from the Thurgau and Aargau oppressed the inhabitants of Uri, Schwyz and Unterwalden by seizing their animals, abusing their wives and daughters, and threatening their sons. In response, the men of the valleys formed a secret conspiracy to protect their traditional liberty. Before they could act, the Uri bailiff Gessler placed his hat on a stake, demanding that every man bow to it as though he himself were present. The wild hunter Tell refused, and when he mocked Gessler after his arrest, was ordered to shoot an apple from his son's head. Gessler then reneged on his promise to leave Tell unharmed, but Tell escaped, and after lying in wait, killed Gessler with another arrow, triggering a general rebellion by the Confederates.

These stories, with added elements celebrating the battles at Morgarten and Sempach and the subsequent growth of the Confederacy, soon found their way into numerous songs and chronicles, and were available in print after 1507 in Petermann Etterlin's *Kronica von der loblichen Eydtgnoschaft* (Chronicle of the Praiseworthy Confederacy). Altogether, the medieval genre of the chronicle flourished to an extraordinary degree in Switzerland, especially after 1450, with elaborate illustrated chronicles sponsored by city councils recording the history – usually in very self-interested ways – of the cantons and their alliances. The myth of resistance against tyrannical nobles helped explain the autonomy of the Swiss, who were represented as enjoying liberties going back to Roman times that evil nobles sought to usurp. It also provided a counterpoint to the critical literature circulating after the 1440s that dismissed the Swiss as crude rebellious peasants, which appeared in everything from diplomatic correspondence to formal manifestos. Notably – and with considerable consequences for Swiss political culture – the debate over the legitimacy of the Confederacy tended to cast all of the Swiss as 'peasants', no matter their actual status or wealth.

Swiss engagement in Italy after 1494 also attracted attention from European thinkers, most notably Niccolò Machiavelli, who admired the Swiss combination of military effectiveness and republican government. In *The Prince*, he praised the Swiss with his observation that 'Rome and Sparta remained armed and free for many centuries; the Swiss are most armed, and thus most free.' In contrast to literary Humanism, the artistic impulses of the Renaissance found only a piecemeal reception in Switzerland. The most lasting influence occurred in the Italian valleys south of the Alps, where village churches and local palaces were decorated in popular versions of the Renaissance style. Elsewhere, the Late Gothic style of the north continued to predominate, although significant visual artists like Hans Holbein the Younger – also from Basle – and Urs Graf adopted Renaissance techniques in their work.

The Confederacy of the early 1500s possessed both a political system and a cultural and political identity that put it on a par with other princely states within the Holy Roman Empire. Despite growing social tensions, it enjoyed relative peace and internal stability, while its scholars proclaimed its virtues to the world. As Europe embarked on a period of accelerated change after 1500 – driven by the European encounter with the New World and Asia, by growing population and a dynamic economy, and not least by growing social tensions – the Confederacy seemed well placed to thrive. Instead, a thoroughly unexpected challenge to the unity of Western European Christianity made Switzerland a centre of change in entirely new ways, while testing its political and cultural coherence to the limit.

3

A divided Switzerland in Reformation Europe, 1515–1713

A dense web of political ties bound the Swiss Confederacy together by 1500. The Confederacy's emergence paralleled developments across Europe, which was increasingly dominated by coherent states – in the west, the new monarchies of Spain, France and England, and in the band from the Netherlands to Italy, a combination of sizeable princely states and a few important republics, including Venice, the Swiss Confederacy, and eventually the Dutch Republic. The trajectory of Swiss development took unexpected directions in the early sixteenth century, however, because of Swiss troops' declining potency and even more because of the Protestant Reformation and the resulting schism, which bitterly divided the Confederacy. Indeed, the Confederacy became an important centre for the development and spread of Protestant ideas with the preaching and church leadership of Ulrich Zwingli (1484–1531) and Heinrich Bullinger (1504–75) in Zurich, together with Jean Calvin (1509–64) in Geneva. In addition, the Anabaptist movement, predecessor of the modern Mennonite and Amish as well as many other community-based sectarian churches, had some of its earliest origins in Switzerland. Religious schism deeply divided the cantons, and brought institutional developments to a halt. Despite division, ironically, the national myths of the Swiss continued to evolve into the 1570s, and became widely disseminated.

The Thirty Years War (1618–48) was a cataclysmic struggle that devastated much of the Holy Roman Empire – but not Switzerland. Rather, despite internal religious division, the Confederacy remained neutral, although the associated Grisons were drawn into the war and suffered in consequence. At the end of the war, the overheated economy's decline, exacerbated by a corruptly executed devaluation of the coinage, triggered a massive peasant revolt in the midlands. The Swiss Peasants' War of 1653 briefly united peasants from across the Confederacy, whose 'parliament' unsuccessfully demanded a permanent voice in Swiss politics. Once social unrest had ebbed, religious tensions triggered another civil war between Catholics and Protestants that ended with Protestant defeat and the reaffirmation of the religious status quo in the Third Landfrieden of 1656. Although the intensity of religious disputes waned by 1700, the Landfrieden remained contentious because it regulated the condominiums. In 1712, disputes over religious issues, primarily in the Toggenburg, led to another short civil war. This time Zurich and Berne dominated, leading to a final, Fourth Landfrieden that strengthened the Reformed cantons' position in the condominiums, though leaving the Catholic cantons' territory and churches intact.

During this tumultuous period, Switzerland came to be viewed as a distinct nation in Europe. The Peace of Westphalia that ended the Thirty Years War brought Switzerland complete exemption from imperial law, completing a process of divergence from the Empire. After 1648, the Confederacy acted as a sovereign state in the European concert of nations. Economic growth accelerated, especially the rural manufacturing known as proto-industrialization, and a pre-Alpine cheese industry emerged that produced for distant markets. Culturally, Switzerland remained conservative and cautious after 1648. However, the rigid orthodoxy of the period faced growing challenges as Protestant and Catholic intellectuals participated in the opening of European culture through the early Enlightenment.

THE SHAPE OF THE OLD CONFEDERACY, 1536-1798

The arrangements among cities, rural cantons, abbeys, and other entities that made up the Confederacy were complex, but by the early 1500s, contemporaries simplified them into three categories – the cantons, the Associates (*Zugewandte*), and the condominiums (*Gemeine Herrschaften*, sometimes called Mandated Territories). After Berne's seizure of the Vaud in 1536, only minor changes in

Swiss Political Structures, 1536–1798

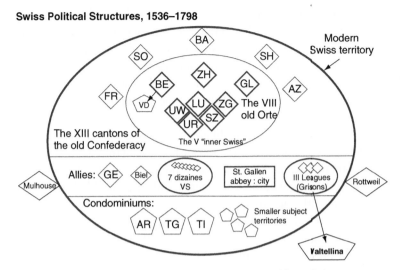

Figure 3.1 The constitutional structure of the Old Confederacy

territory took place until the French revolutionary period. The Swiss Confederacy as a political actor consisted of the thirteen cantons (known in German simply as *Orte*, 'places'), divided into the old VIII and the new V. The VIII old cantons included the three cities Zurich, Berne and Lucerne and the five rural cantons Uri, Schwyz, Unterwalden, Zug and Glarus. The VIII old cantons spoke in order of rank at frequent Diets, and ruled, in various combinations, over the Confederacy's condominiums. The V new cantons that became full members of the Confederacy after 1481 (Fribourg, Solothurn, Basle, Schaffhausen, Appenzell) all had long associations with the Confederacy, but had to defer to the old VIII in some matters.

The Associates included a heterogeneous array of communities and lordships united only by their associations with the Confederacy. The large communal confederations in Valais and Grisons participated in the Swiss campaigns in Italy, but only sporadically visited the Diet, and remained largely autonomous in their foreign and internal affairs. Relations with the Associates Biel, Neuchâtel, and the abbey and the city of St Gallen, in contrast, grew more intense and more unequal during the sixteenth century, something even more true for smaller rural Associates such as the Toggenburg, Gruyère and

Saanen. Close ties with the Confederacy offered these smaller regions protection and stability, but at the cost of autonomy. Finally, relations with the two most distant Associates, the imperial cities of Mulhouse and Rottweil, declined to insignificance by the seventeenth century.

Lowest in status, but pivotal for internal politics, were the condominiums in the Aargau, the Thurgau, the Ticino, the Rheintal above Lake Constance and the Sarganserland. Each came under the Confederacy's control in a different way, and was governed by a particular set of cantons. The strategic location of the condominiums – the Aargau linking Berne, Zurich and Lucerne, the Ticino south of the Gotthard pass, the Rhine valley and Sarganserland connecting the Swiss with the Grisons passes – made them important for the Confederacy's territorial integrity even if they produced little revenue. The rotating office of *Landvogt* or bailiff in each condominium brought prestige to its holders, while the need for oversight spurred regular meetings among each condominium's ruling cantons. Shared responsibility and frequent meetings spurred the Confederacy's institutional consolidation in the fifteenth century; after the Reformation, the condominiums became critical locations for struggles between the faiths, since they were ruled by cantons confessing different religions and emerged from the early Reformation with religiously divided populations.

Despite the Confederacy's internal complexity, more and more contemporaries began thinking of the Swiss as forming *one* republic with its own distinct identity. Within Switzerland, this identity found expression in stories about William Tell and the Confederacy's beginnings, which appeared both in official chronicles and in the arts and popular culture. This history became known across Europe when Zurich cleric Josias Simler integrated it into his best-selling 1576 guide to the Confederacy, the *De Republica Helvetiorum Libri Duo* (Two Books about the Republic of the Helvetians). Because Swiss unity was not defined by a single ruler or by natural boundaries, however, its nature remained contested until the doctrine of the sovereign state allowed its integration into the European state system after 1648. Around 1500, the Swiss Confederacy appeared to be potent and open, an active participant in European affairs that might expand by assimilation or conquest. By 1715, the Confederacy was a stably constituted minor power with clear limits.

Swiss political life took place on three separate but connected levels. The Confederacy participated in the European politics of dynastic rivalries and sovereign states. The cantons and Associates constituted a second political sphere, bound by solidarity that put limits on each one's freedom of action. Finally, each canton possessed an internal political life characterized by dynamic rivalries among factions, kin-groups, social classes and individuals. At each level, developments after 1500 echoed and amplified broader European trends toward caution, closure and the protection of vested interests. Across the Confederacy, privileged corporations, from local stockherders' associations to urban councils, closed themselves to new members. The growing formality and complexity of administration further favoured exclusion, as magistrates increasingly used written documents to manage property and politics. Still, the privilege of all male citizens of communes to participate in decision-making, which retained great legitimacy in the Confederacy, set the Swiss apart from aristocratic Europe. In Valais, Grisons and the cantons with annual *Landsgemeinden* (assemblies of members), communal members voted directly, and occasionally resorted to force if their views were ignored. In the urban cantons, magistrates continued to consult urban citizens and rural subjects at crucial moments well into the sixteenth century. Typically, an uneasy balance existed between a few families who usually dominated politics and the remaining citizens who sought to share in power through consultative institutions.

The almost complete exclusion of women from formal politics set Swiss practices apart from the aristocratic governance of other regions. Whereas kingdoms and lordships in this period experienced a number of important women rulers, the republican focus of Switzerland provided no such opening, especially after the Reformation led to the abolition of most Swiss convents. Until the 1520s, the abbess of the Fraumünster in Zurich was the nominal sovereign of the city, for example, but no similar figures appear later. The strong association between bearing arms and full citizenship in Swiss communes – symbolized by Appenzell's requirement that each voter at the Landsgemeinde bring his sword – blocked participation by women. Women also faced exclusion from guilds (even as the widows of guild masters) and economic life, though they did to appear as plaintiffs as well as defendants in the civil

3.1 After battle (drawing by Urs Graf). Widespread
participation in mercenary service made many Swiss aware of
the horrors of warfare. Basle artist Urs Graf, who himself took
part in a number of campaigns in Italy, captured the devastation
that followed battles in his drawings for private patrons.
Popular resentment at the suffering of soldiers was increased by
the ostentatious wealth that mercenary recruiters and the
Confederacy's political leaders gained from the soldiers'
hardships.

courts. While the wives of merchants and other wealthy men played
a role in household and business management, as has been shown
for the German imperial cities, the very scarcity of evidence about
women's lives in Switzerland reveals how a strong republican culture silenced their presence to an unusual degree.

The end of official Swiss participation in the Italian Wars after 1516
did not produce greater stability within the Confederacy. Thousands
of troops still entered foreign service, and private recruiters thrived. As
major defeats of Swiss regiments at Bicocca (1522) and Pavia (1525)
demonstrated, however, the era of Swiss military invincibility was
over. Anger at these losses combined with resentment of the wealthy
in an era of economic uncertainty to encourage reform of the entire
civic order. Even so, it was at just this moment that long-term relations

with Switzerland's two most powerful neighbours stabilized. Treaties in 1516 and 1521 made France the Confederacy's closest ally, offering generous pensions to cantons and individuals in exchange for the ability to recruit mercenaries – a relationship that was to last for nearly three centuries. Emperor Maximilian renewed and extended the older Habsburg agreements with the Confederacy in 1511, and he and his grandson Charles V sometimes sought Swiss military support for their ventures. A 1512 alliance with Pope Julius II gave Swiss troops the privilege of carrying the papal arms and an image of the Virgin Mary on their banners, a matter of great pride. In 1520, the Swiss future looked bright.

RELIGIOUS SCHISM AND THE DIVISION OF THE CONFEDERACY

A powerful movement for church reform spread across the Europe after 1517, set off by Martin Luther in Germany and expanded in Switzerland by Ulrich Zwingli. Ultimately, the disputes set off by Zwingli's prophetic preaching dominated political conflict in the Confederacy from the 1520s until the end of the seventeenth century. Not only spiritual issues were at stake: since religious orthodoxy and political legitimacy remained closely connected in European culture, the idea of sharing oaths and political identity with 'heretics' or 'idolaters' remained difficult on both sides of the schism. In practice, however, the Confederacy's shared interest in its condominiums and in European politics would force cooperation even when religious hostility was high.

In 1500, a single institutional church preached orthodox doctrine and practice and enjoyed support across Western Europe. In the Swiss lands, numerous parish foundings and church improvements around 1500 showed that peasants and townspeople alike desired better clerical services and a vibrant religious life. Many voices called for a *better* church, but few called for radical changes. By 1600, in contrast, Europe was divided among competing 'confessional' churches (that is, each adhering to its own confession of faith) whose clergies attacked their rivals as heretical servants of the Antichrist. In some Swiss cantons, along with England, Scotland, and the Netherlands, the Reformed movement originating in Zurich

CONVENIVNT FATIS NOMINA SAEPE SVIS.

3.2 Ulrich Zwingli in 1531. Zwingli came from the rural
hinterland of the Toggenburg, via Glarus and the abbey of
Einsiedeln, to serve as the main preacher in Zurich in 1519. His
blunt preaching, founded on experience as a military chaplain
and familiarity with the work of Erasmus and Luther, spoke to a
broad spectrum of Swiss, from urban patricians' sons to
handworkers. Zwingli's conviction that he had been appointed
to a prophetic mission helped bring about his death on the
battlefield of Kappel in 1531.

with Zwingli and continued by Jean Calvin in Geneva became the official church. The Roman Church, too, reformed its organization and teachings at the Council of Trent (1543–62), and reached out energetically after the 1550s to support Catholic Europeans, including the many Swiss who remained Catholic. Both churches in Switzerland claimed a monopoly on religious truth, and required obedience and public adherence to their tenets.

Born of an established Toggenburg family in 1484, Ulrich Zwingli exemplified a generation of intellectually ambitious clergymen. He attended Latin schools in Basle and Berne before studying in Vienna from 1499 to 1506. Zwingli's qualifications gained him a call to Glarus as parish priest, where he served for ten years. His duties included accompanying soldiers on their campaigns in Italy, including the battle at Marignano, which made him a vocal critic of mercenary service. A new position in Einsiedeln offered Zwingli the opportunity to concentrate on theological study after 1516, focusing on the Church Fathers. By the time he was selected as cathedral preacher in Zurich late in 1518, Martin Luther's works had upended the debate about church reform. Like Luther, Zwingli was a passionate preacher who did not hesitate to break from tradition about the meaning of the Gospel. His preaching found a ready audience, reaching leading men, guildsmen and their families, and Zurich's rural subjects. Importantly, several young men from prominent families, fervent supporters of Zwingli's teaching, persuaded their relatives on the city council to protect Zwingli from prosecution for his views.

A visible break with the old church took place in Zurich during Lent in 1522, when the printer Christoph Froschauer gave his workers sausage for supper. This act violated the Church's and the city's laws on fasting before Easter. Zwingli preached the following week on Christians' freedom from dietary regulations, making his defiance of church authority public, and the city council chose not to punish the violators. Zwingli's further sermons on clerical celibacy and the veneration of images widened the breach in 1522, making it clear that new religious ideas had spread into the Confederacy. Concerned, the Swiss Diet in 1522 issued a call to avoid 'innovation' in religion, but execution remained in the hands of the cantons. In Zurich, the magistrates responded by organizing a disputation that followed an agenda provided by Zwingli, after which they ordered that preaching should be 'according to the Gospel', thus taking Zwingli's position. Soon, the city ended celebration of the Mass, removed images from the city's churches, and took over church responsibilities such as poor relief and the supervision of marriages and morals.

3.3 First Zurich religious disputation, 1523: caught between the popular appeal of Zwingli's teaching and the dangers of challenging Europe's religious order, the Zurich magistrates staged a theological disputation in 1523. Although they invited their bishop to prove Zwingli's errors, Zwingli set the agenda, showing that the disputation's primary purpose was to consolidate support behind his ideas. The city council set the city on a clear path of religious change after the disputation, anchored in the city's self-government.

Although Luther, Zwingli and Calvin shared a common perspective on 'salvation by faith alone', they parted ways on the consequences of this principle for a Christian society. In contrast to Luther, Zwingli and, after him, Calvin maintained that a well-ordered Christian community, while flawed, could nevertheless guide its members towards a way of life pleasing to God. The strong community life of southern

Germany and Switzerland may have encouraged the relative optimism of this perspective, or the reformist spirit of Humanism may have affected Zwingli and Calvin more than the scholastically trained Luther. Zwingli, his successor Heinrich Bullinger and Calvin produced highly influential tracts that described how a Christian society should be organized and treat its members. These ideas, along with specific theological differences with Luther, resulted in a new church separate both from the Catholic tradition and from the Lutheran church emerging in Germany.

Although Zwingli rejected the old church, his willingness to defend practices such as tithes led some of his earliest followers to reject his ideas as excessively deferential to worldly concerns. These radicals, including both laypeople and trained clerics, questioned all existing arrangements in the church and in the world. Some pointed out that Jesus and his disciples had been baptized only as adults, and therefore argued that infant baptism was unbiblical, gaining them the epithet Anabaptists ('rebaptizers'). Others, citing Scripture, felt that Christians must refuse to take oaths, which were a fundamental element of social cohesion in early modern Europe. Traditionalists and reformers alike not only rejected the radicals' ideas, but also connected them with social unrest, especially after the German Peasants' War of 1525 revealed the potency of popular desire for religious change. Persecution of the Anabaptists began almost immediately, and continued on the part of both Catholic and Protestant authorities over the next two centuries.

Because Berne was the most populous canton in the Confederacy, its choices were particularly important for the future of the evangelical movement. Although considerable sympathy for evangelical ideas developed among the citizens, the city's leaders remained cautious. But popular opinion increasingly favoured the new teachings, and in 1528 the magistrates introduced the new church in Berne and imposed it on the more reluctant countryside. Basle and Schaffhausen also adopted the new ideas in the late 1520s, whereas Fribourg, Solothurn and most importantly Lucerne suppressed local evangelicals and stayed loyal to Catholicism. Most of the rural cantons also stayed Catholic, forming a solid bloc in central Switzerland; only Glarus and Appenzell had successful Zwinglian movements, which eventually led to bi-confessional governance in Glarus and division of the canton in

3.4 Iconoclasm in Stadelhofen. Zwingli's preaching in Zurich
inspired both urban and rural lay preachers to read and
interpret the Bible. Whereas Zwingli deferred to the city's
magistrates in political matters, and defended tithes and infant
baptism, some of his followers adopted a form of biblical
literalism that rejected oaths, baptism and all use of images in
religious services. The picture shows radicals tearing down a
cross in the Zurich village of Stadelhofen. Magistrates in
Reformed and Catholic regions alike punished such
'Anabaptists' harshly, but popular support allowed small
radical communities to survive for centuries.

Appenzell. The heterogeneous Associates experienced heterogeneous
outcomes, with strong Reformed movements in Grisons and Biel, but
adherence to the old church in Valais and Rottweil.

After 1523, the rapid spread of Zwinglian worship increasingly
occupied the Diet's agenda. Deeply held beliefs and practices on
both sides made compromise difficult, while the emergence of
radical positions made the new movement seem more threatening.
From 1525 to 1529, tensions rose every time another canton chose
to embrace or reject Zwinglian ideas. Zwingli himself continued to
publish works articulating his theological position, which gained
resonance well beyond the Confederacy. As his influence grew, so
did Zwingli's conviction of his calling as a prophet: the urgency
of his cause and the importance of reforming Christian society
led him to demand political as well as spiritual action to spread

his faith. His intransigence pushed the Confederacy closer to open conflict.

Events in 1525 added to the tensions from the growing religious schism. Just north of the Swiss border, hundreds of thousands of German peasants and townspeople took up arms against their lords, demanding both secular reform and free preaching of the Gospel. Local unrest broke out within the Confederacy, as well, beginning when peasants stormed and destroyed the Thurgau cloister of Ittingen in 1524. The Catholic cantons had to decide how to respond to such unrest, and to increasingly bold moves by the Zwinglians in the Confederacy. In February 1529, for example, the magistrates in St Gallen, with support from Zurich, seized the abbey as Abbot Franz von Gaisberg lay dying, and introduced Zwinglian worship in the abbey's rural territory. The Reformed cities also established a defensive alliance, which also included St Gallen, Constance and Mulhouse. In response, the Catholic cantons allied with the Habsburgs, who promised to defend the Catholics against attacks from Zurich in exchange for the right to recruit 6,000 troops.

In June 1529, Zurich's magistrates declared war on the Catholic cantons, and Zurich and Schwyz mobilized their troops near the village and cloister of Kappel on their border. Negotiations continued, however, since the rest of the Confederacy opposed a war. The troops probably fraternized, as well, and legend has it they shared a soup of milk and bread from a cauldron placed on the line between the two camps. On 26 June 1529, an agreement, the First Kappeler Landfrieden, was reached, and each side withdrew its forces. In the Landfrieden, all cantons agreed to avoid coercion in matters of faith, and allowed communities in the condominiums to choose by majority vote whether to keep the traditional church or accept the new teachings. The first Landfrieden of 1529 stabilized matters only briefly. The Zurich council and preachers used its favourable terms to encourage parishes in the Thurgau to accept the new church and to attach themselves politically to the city, while Catholic bailiffs in other condominiums pressured communities to retain the old church. Growing religious tension in the Empire also fed into Swiss events. Eventually, Catholic frustration and Zurich's pressure for further concessions triggered another, more violent confrontation. In May 1531, Zurich and its Reformed allies banned sales of grain from their markets to the

V Catholic cantons. After negotiations stalled, this existential threat provoked Schwyz to declare war and move its troops toward Zurich. The war brought a devastating defeat for Zurich and for Zwingli's supporters. Zwingli himself died at the Battle of Kappel on 11 October 1531, and the city experienced a second defeat on the Gubel on 24 October.

Since Berne and the other Reformed cantons refused to support further hostilities, the Second Kappeler Landfrieden negotiated between the parties and sealed on 20 November 1531 favoured the victorious Schwyzer and the religious traditionalists. The agreement recognized the existence of two faiths and set out guidelines for their coexistence, which rapidly became part of the Confederacy's fundamental laws. Crucially, each canton remained free to choose either the 'true undoubted Christian faith' of the Catholics or the 'faith' of the Zwinglians. While individual provisions as well as the document's tone privileged Catholicism, the peace was thus a moderate document. It was also an early example of the emerging principle that local sovereigns enjoyed a choice among Christian confessions, as established in 1555 for the entire Holy Roman Empire. The political damage to both belligerents was serious, however. Moreover, religious difference still divided the Confederacy, and religious civil war recurred first in 1656, then again in 1712. Some historians call this the 'confessional' era across Europe, after the rival faiths that helped shape politics and culture through their conflicts.

TERRITORIAL CLOSURE AND CONFESSIONAL POLITICS AFTER 1531

In the west, one last conflict broke through the Confederacy's increasingly passive stance in international affairs: the seizure of the Vaud from Savoy by Berne, Fribourg and Valais in 1536. The Bernese had long been both allies and rivals of the House of Savoy, and temporarily seized much of Vaud in 1475. Savoy's restored authority remained precarious, owing to the Dukes' many rivals. In Geneva, the pro-Confederacy faction grew rapidly after 1500, since the Dukes could neither protect Geneva's commercial interests nor preserve the peace. Tensions peaked in 1525 when Duke Charles III convened the city council in a room surrounded by armed soldiers, but this only encouraged the pro-Swiss 'Eidgenouts', who allied with Berne and Fribourg immediately after this incident. The subsequent Treaty of St Julien between Berne and the Duke in 1530 confirmed Savoy's weakness, since it authorized Berne to intervene and even to seize Vaud if the treaty were violated.

Berne's influence also helped Protestant preaching gain a foothold in the Vaud; by 1534, Guillame Farel and several other preachers had established themselves in Geneva. In January 1536, invoking the Peace of St Julien, Bernese troops marched into the Vaud, pillaging castles, taking oaths from the population, and occupying Geneva and Lausanne. Fribourg and the Valais also seized Savoyard territory, and French soldiers occupied the remainder of the duchy, which they held until 1559. The Bernese initially claimed Lausanne and Geneva by right of conquest. The Geneva council successfully resisted, aided by the other cantons, but Lausanne joined Vaud in subjection to the Berne. These last Swiss acquisitions of territory thus entered the Confederacy partly as one new Associate, Geneva, whose status was unaffected by the fact that it was Francophone, and partly as extensive new Bernese subject territories. These, like earlier conquests in Italy, were administered in their own language and not in German. With these acquisitions, the Confederacy reached its final early modern extent.

Europe was torn by war and religious conflict in this era. Open war between Valois France and the Habsburgs through the century – often involving Swiss mercenaries – halted only briefly with the 1559 Peace of Cateau-Cambrésis, while Protestant footholds emerged in England, the Netherlands and Eastern Europe. Despite the Confederacy's location directly between France and Austria, the Swiss did not become party to further wars. France valued the status quo in Switzerland because it provided a buffer for French-occupied Savoy and because the cantons sent regiments to serve the Kings of France. The Habsburgs, too, saw modest advantages in a neutralized Switzerland, while Emperor Charles V's many other concerns made it prudent to avoid intervening in the Confederacy. The Reformed cantons did not join the Schmalkaldic League formed by the Lutherans of Germany, in part for theological reasons, keeping the Swiss out of the Schmalkaldic Wars. The policy of caution and

Stillstehen that emerged in these years anticipated more formal expressions of Swiss neutrality in later European conflicts.

In Zurich, Zwingli's replacement Heinrich Bullinger, who remained in office for over forty years, shaped both the Swiss Reformed churches and the entire European Reformed movement. In over 12,000 letters to ministers and learned men across Europe, he advised, encouraged, and sometimes despaired as the tides of politics and religion swept back and forth. He was especially important for formulating a series of increasingly precise confessions, formal statements of Reformed doctrine that became the foundation of the Swiss Reformed church. During his long career, Bullinger turned his attention to a wide variety of matters, including influential treatises against the Anabaptists and in favour of prosecuting witches, and even popular dramas.

Geneva's exposed position and dependence on Berne propelled the question of religious change in the city with particular intensity. The rapid introduction of the Reformation, along with developments in France and the Confederacy, soon brought a figure of European significance to the city: Jean Calvin. Calvin was an educated Frenchman who encountered the evangelical movement while studying in Paris, Bourges and Orleans. When royal pressure on heretics increased in mid-1533, he followed the path of many refugees through Strasbourg to Basle, where he issued the first edition of his major work, the *Christianae Religionis Institutio*, in 1536. This book became a guide for Reformed theology over the following decades, and immediately made Calvin a recognized figure. Later that year, he returned briefly to France, but when forced to flee, he took up a clerical position in Geneva. For the next thirty years, Calvin struggled against opposition both clerical and political to build the church he had imagined in the *Institutio*. Calvin held positions on many theological issues that resembed those of Luther and Zwingli, along with some that diverged from both. During the 1540s and 1550s, he participated in Europe-wide efforts to find a religious compromise, including the Colloquy of Regensburg in 1541, but eventually moved into closer alignment with the Zurich church headed by Bullinger. Given Geneva's vulnerable location, such an alliance made political sense, but theological issues, especially over the real presence, also encouraged the formation of the unified Swiss Reformed church, preaching in German and French,

3.5 Jean Calvin. After Humanist studies in Paris, Calvin
adopted evangelical ideas in the early 1530s; the French crown's
persecution of the movement drove him into exile shortly
thereafter. After a stay in Strasbourg, he settled in Geneva,
where he became head of the Reformed church established after
the Bernese conquest of the Vaud in 1536. A powerful writer
and determined reformer, he allied the Genevan church with the
Reformed movement of German Switzerland. His theology and
writings on church organization had even greater influence in
Great Britain, France, Germany and eventually in the new
world.

which obtained its mature doctrinal form in Bullinger's Second Helvetic Confession of 1564. By building up a church on the border of France that energetically supported the evangelical movement there, and by shaping Reformed ideas about church governance into a coherent package, Calvin shaped the religious evolution of the entire continent and left a profound mark on the Reformed church across Switzerland as well.

Religious refugees from diverse origins provided crucial pathways for religious ideas to spread in this period – not just Calvin's, but also Anabaptist and other radical teachings. Evangelical refugees to Switzerland played an important role, particularly the wave of English Protestants fleeing the Catholicism of Queen Mary I in 1553. Radical refugees to the Confederacy fared less well. The most famous was the Spanish physician and anti-Trinitarian Michael Servetus, who escaped from a French Inquisition prison and fled to Geneva. Calvin adjudged his ideas blasphemous for denying the Trinity. Consequently, when Servetus was recognized attending church, the Genevan magistrates seized and executed him with Calvin's approval, triggering one of the first European debates over the use of coercion in religious matters. Many Anabaptists also fled *from* Switzerland for havens in Eastern Europe, and later in the New World.

The most dangerous part of Europe after 1560 was France, where a weakened monarchy faced powerful noble clans divided by religion. The Huguenot party maintained close ties with Geneva and the Reformed cities, while the strongly Catholic faction headed by the house of Guise relied on support from Spain, Savoy and the Catholic Swiss. Swiss mercenaries thus served on all sides of the French civil war that raged from 1561 to 1593. The war undermined the French alliance with the Confederacy as a whole, and threatened to bring Swiss troops face-to-face in battle again. Savoy's efforts to regain the Vaud, backed by ultra-Catholic Spain and pursued in part by shifting alliances with the Catholic cantons, also raised tensions in western Switzerland.

Growing religious polarization within the Confederacy reached a first peak in the 1580s. In addition to disputes about Geneva, the Bishop of Basle was at loggerheads with his city over rural territories, and tempers flared over a polemical book published in Fribourg with the encouragement of the Jesuit rector there, Peter Canisius. In 1586, the Catholic cantons established a new alliance among themselves known as the Golden League. Protestants immediately expressed anger at a clause that not only protected the Catholic religion, but also stated that 'no older or newer alliance, whether already established or established in the future, shall hinder us in such protection'. This provision seemed to override the existing alliances that constituted the Confederacy. In 1587, despite new protests from the Protestant cantons, the V cantons and Fribourg also agreed to a defensive and mercenary treaty with the King of Spain.

THE CONFESSIONAL CENTURY: RELIGION, POLITICS AND CULTURE IN THE 1600S

The Swiss Confederacy entered the seventeenth century bitterly divided along religious lines, in parallel with Europe and the Holy Roman Empire. Yet the latter were drawn into a devastating war from 1618 to 1648, whereas the Confederacy managed to remain internally at peace and externally neutral. The pattern of neutrality during European wars that was set during the Thirty Years War became a fixed part of Switzerland's interactions with its European neighbourhood, eventually reaching formal status at the Congress of Vienna in 1815. When the Thirty Years War ended, however, Switzerland soon experienced two major internal conflicts: the Peasants' War of 1653 and the First War of Villmergen in 1656. Understanding political developments after 1600 thus requires attention both to the confessional cultures that had emerged and to how the Confederacy's political network blunted the conflicts that these cultures provoked.

Separation and polarization driven by religious difference affected every aspect of life in seventeenth-century Switzerland, from politics to family life to reading habits. Local religious constellations ranged from sizeable blocs committed to a single confession, such as central cantons around Lucerne or the Bernese territories, to side-by-side Catholic and Reformed congregations in a single village and sharing a single church, as in some condominiums. Even in religiously homogeneous territories, however, contact across confessional lines was frequent because of economic and social ties. For clerical and secular authorities, the resulting mingling was a source of constant anxiety

3.6 The Escalade in Geneva, 1602. Religious and political
tension inside and around the Confederacy peaked around
1600, and included a failed coup sponsored by the Duke of
Savoy in 1602. Geneva's citizens succeeded in blocking the
entry of the full Savoyard force, and survived the attack.
Although the Catholic cantons prevented Geneva from
becoming a full member of the Confederacy, it remained safely
within the Swiss fold after this date, and represented an
important cultural and economic gateway to France.

as they struggled to teach and discipline the general population. Yet
it also meant that everyone in the Swiss lands had some experience
with people of differing religious persuasion, often at very close
range.

At moments of high tension, voices on each side demanded that
the bi-confessional Confederacy should be abandoned. After the
crisis over the Golden League of 1586, another set of struggles in
the 1620s developed between the Abbot of St Gallen and Reformed
villages in the condominiums; brought to the Diet, intransigence on
both sides led to deadlock. Each confessional party trumpeted
catalogues of 'abuses' perpetrated by the other, while refusing all
compromise. In the early 1630s, Schwyz even suggested dividing
the condominiums, rather than continuing joint control. Yet at

each juncture, other voices defended confederate traditions and the need for cooperation. Despite the clergy's misgivings, the Zurich and Berne councils sent a delegation to Lucerne in 1585 to argue for unity, and received a return delegation from the Catholic cantons. In 1632, an agreement on how to negotiate confessional issues in the condominiums was reached, though there was little progress on the ground. Constant tension between impulses to separation, on the one hand, and the desire to sustain unity, on the other, shaped Swiss confessional culture in this era.

The dangers of involvement in great power rivalries amplified by confessional division became shockingly visible in the Grisons from 1616 to 1636. Because of its strategic passes, the Grisons republic was courted by both the Habsburgs, interested in connections between their Milanese possessions and Austria, and by the Franco-Venetian alliance, which sought to block Habsburg mobility while moving German mercenaries to Venice. Rival factions within the Grisons, funded with bribes and pensions, struggled to control the republic through mass assemblies of the communal troops. When some Reformed pastors turned a 1618 assembly in Thusis to confessional ends, the backlash led first to invasion of the Valtellina by Milan (accompanied by a rebellion of Valtellina Catholics that included the slaughter of over 400 local Protestants), and then to an Austrian invasion of the Grisons. Rival armies brought looting, oppression and the plague throughout the 1620s and early 1630s, until the local elites united behind a Spanish alliance in 1639 and restored fragile order.

The chaos in the Grisons provided an object lesson on the virtues of neutrality to the XIII cantons and their subjects. The profits from sales of food and military materiel – above all horses – also made neutrality more attractive. A dangerous moment came in 1633, when Swedish troops marched through the Thurgau to encircle the Habsburg city of Constance. The Reformed captain of the territorial defence troops, Killian Kesselring, was accused of allowing the Swedish incursion, and the resulting trial nearly triggered another war between Zurich and Schwyz. Cooler heads prevailed, and Kesselring escaped with his life. Until the very end of the war, however, efforts towards a joint defence of Swiss borders failed because of confessional suspicions. Only in 1647 were the cantons able to agree on the modest *Defensionale* of Wil to patrol the north-eastern border.

When the weary warring parties of Europe gathered in Westphalia to negotiate a peace, the Swiss at first saw no need to attend. Johann Rudolf Wettstein, the mayor of Basle, recognized the importance of the negotiations, however, and went to Westphalia to represent Switzerland. Although he arrived without credentials from the Diet, he succeeded in having the peace clarify the Confederacy's legal and political status. Article VI declared the cantons 'to be in possession of a quasi-full Liberty and Exemption from the Empire, and so in no way subject to the Tribunals and Sentences of the said Empire'. Although short of explicit sovereignty, this formula confirmed that Switzerland was a separate entity on the international stage. The treaty was silent on the status of the Associates, but in practice, they gained the same privilege under the Swiss umbrella. The stability the Swiss had enjoyed, especially during the destructive 1630s, left a deep impression on contemporaries, and is celebrated in Grimmelshausen's famous novel of the war, *Simplicissimus*.

Paradoxically, peace in Europe reignited conflict in the Confederacy. The war years had caused a boom in Swiss agriculture. Well-off peasants invested to meet German demand by taking on credit, even as a deteriorating climate and growing population made overall productivity decline. This local boom also disguised the frequent degradation of the petty coinage used in everyday transactions, caused by urban mints' skimping on precious metal so as to increase state income for defence works and similar projects. The early 1650s reversed all these conditions: prices for grain and horses fell, putting the heavily leveraged upper peasantry into difficulty, while the harsher climate pressured the poor. When several Swiss cities suddenly devalued their coins while protecting urban investors at the cost of other regions, rebellion ensued. Protests began in the Entlebuch valley belonging to Lucerne: the leading peasants were hard hit by devaluation of Bernese coinage and by demands for taxes, and rose up to demand restoration of their 'ancient privileges'. The revolt spread rapidly into Berne, Solothurn, and Basle's rural districts as well.

In a series of negotiations intensified by the threat of violence, the peasants' goals rapidly expanded beyond economic issues and the 'old law' they originally sought to restore. Instead, in three increasingly radical manifestos they sought to create a separate alliance among the entire Swiss peasantry, both Catholic and Protestant, 'since the authorities also ally themselves'. The peasant leaders justified their actions by calling on William Tell, the founder (as they believed) of the Confederacy:

> Oh William Tell, I beseech you,
> Wake up from your sleep:
> The bailiffs want to have it all,
> Horses, cows, calves and sheep.

Here we see the historical mythology of the late fifteenth century reformulated to support the rebels' claims that they, not the urban elites that ruled them, were the true William Tells of their generation. The rebels also ignored divisions between Catholic and Protestant regions in organizing their revolutionary alliance; in parallel, Lucerne, Zurich and Berne cooperated across religious boundaries in suppressing the revolt. Intense negotiations under great pressure eventually fragmented the peasant front and led to a series of local agreements that restored order. Once the peasants had disbanded their militias, the authorities, especially in Berne, repudiated the negotiated amnesties and punished the rebellion's leaders harshly.

With the existing magistrates firmly in charge again, the political stalemate between the Catholic and Protestant cantons once again came to the fore. The Catholic majority at the Diet was aided by the unequal terms of the 1531 Landfrieden, which gave them disproportionate influence in the condominiums and on other issues, which they used to stall or resist complaints from their Reformed confederates. If one looked at population or wealth, in contrast, the Reformed cantons significantly outweighed the Catholic ones. The result was a dangerous brew of fear and resentment. When a conflict over a group of crypto-Protestants in the village of Arth broke out between perennial rivals Zurich and Schwyz late in 1655, this brew boiled over into a short confessional war, the First War of Villmergen. Zurich struck first early in 1656 by seizing the Thurgau and besieging the town of Rapperswil, but its assault quickly stalled. Meanwhile, a supporting contingent from Berne was defeated in a battle with Lucerne troops near the Aargau village of Villmergen on 24 January, with losses of some 600 men. After some further skirmishing, France and Savoy initiated negotiations that largely restored the status quo in March through a Third Landfrieden. Even in the troubled 1650s, neither the accumulated resentments of the peasantry nor the reignition of religious disputes sufficed to bring about significant changes in the Confederacy's structure. The bitterness of the division, however, encouraged both Catholic and Protestant cantons to develop the practice of meeting separately, leading to the emergence of *de facto* Catholic and Protestant Diets, as well as the common Diets in Baden.

Although the 1656 civil war showed that religion still divided the Confederacy, the emergence of more flexible religious ideas, especially on the Reformed side, caused the clergy growing concern. The rapid spread of René Descartes's ideas among university professors undermined orthodox Protestant theology, while the teachings of the pastor Louis Tronchin and his students in Geneva offered a less dogmatic approach to religion that respected individual liberty of conscience. This so-called Enlightened Orthodoxy brought forth a vigorous response from conservative Protestant leaders in Switzerland, who imposed a new, rigidly orthodox *Formula Consensus* on teachers and pastors in 1675. Despite official approval by the Protestant Diet, signatures to the *Formula* came slowly, and an increasing number of leading figures refused to sign, especially in Basle. By 1706, the city no longer supported this effort to bolster orthodox religion, reflecting the growing influence of the early Enlightenment and the ongoing transformation of European intellectual culture.

Confessional divisions – entangled, as always, with political issues – nevertheless triggered one more civil war in Switzerland, the Second War of Villmergen in 1712. Behind this conflict lay decades of hostility between the Prince-Abbot of St Gallen and his largely Reformed subjects in the Toggenburg, who enjoyed substantial liberties and joint oversight by four of the Swiss cantons. The Abbot turned to the Habsburgs for support, while the Toggenburg population, which set up its own regime in 1707 after expelling the abbot's bailiffs, looked to Zurich and Berne. In a calculated move, the two Reformed cities sent troops to the abbot's lands in St Gallen as well as to the critical territorial link between Zurich and Berne in the Aargau in summer 1712. In contrast to 1656, the urban troops of the Reformed cities were well organized and professionally led – more than a match for the popular militias on which the Catholic cantons still relied. Recognizing the poor odds, the Catholic cantons approved a settlement that would have weakened Catholic privileges in the condominiums. This humiliating concession, however, triggered a popular uprising in Lucerne's rural domains, supported by Uri, Schwyz and Unterwalden. Led by Catholic priests and their supporters among the village elites, the protests briefly rekindled the war against Zurich and Berne. Events quickly dashed the rebels' hopes. When the armies met, again at the village of Villmergen, the Catholic forces suffered a devastating defeat with nearly 3,000 dead.

The political shape of Switzerland for the rest of the eighteenth century was set in the Fourth Landfrieden, promulgated August 1712 in the Peace of Aarau. Zurich and Berne used their dominant position to force substantial changes in the Confederacy's constitution, although without impinging on the territory or autonomy of the existing cantons. The Catholic cantons were excluded from the administration of much of the Aargau, and Berne was added to the rulers of the Thurgau. Strict parity in religious affairs in the condominiums was legislated in detail, ending the disadvantages that the Reformed congregations had faced under the previous Landfrieden. The Abbot of St Gallen regained his lordship over the Toggenburg under conditions that protected the Reformed majority there in worship and daily administration. The settlement generated great bitterness among the losers, but it also removed many of the petty irritants that had produced deadlock at the Confederacy's Diet.

By 1715, the Confederacy was again pacified internally, and its external neutrality and sovereignty were widely recognized. The messy network of pacts, agreements, treaties and habits that controlled its governance might be hard to describe and often ineffective, but they provided stability and continued to evolve, so that the system as a whole functioned. The growing divisions between rich and poor found an echo in the continuing trend towards oligarchy in rural as well as urban cantons: a few powerful families benefited the most from the established order, as was the case all over Europe.

THE MATERIAL WORLD, 1500–1700

Material life in Switzerland from 1500 to 1700 changed only incrementally, and patterns of production, reproduction and consumption remained similar. In 1600 as in 1500, Switzerland had a primarily agrarian economy, crafts took place largely in towns and cities and almost all labour relied on animal or human muscles for power. Water turned mills, and burning wood heated forges, bath-houses and residences, completing the range of energy sources. Yet slow but important changes took place in many aspects of material life, including the climate, population, trade and manufactures. By 1700, the spread of rural manufacturing of textiles and other goods circumvented the urban guilds and increased the commercialization of the countryside, as did the flourishing cheese industry, even as the pass trade declined in relative importance. Throughout the period, the financial strength of the urban cantons grew, making them important sources of credit and encouraging the rise of banking.

Some of these changes helped define Switzerland as a lucky region in a violent continent; others made life harder for most Swiss men and women as the period went on. Reduced by the great epidemics of the fourteenth and fifteenth centuries, the population expanded steadily until about 1600, despite occasional setbacks. After that, a less favourable climate and the disruptions of warfare slowed growth of both population and the economy. Still, Switzerland was one of the few regions in Europe to benefit from war after 1500: by avoiding warfare themselves while selling military services, Swiss cities and military entrepreneurs accumulated capital and brought prosperity to elites and moderate taxes for their subjects. The fragmented political system also made it easier for rural manufacturing to spread, challenging the traditional urban domination of the skilled crafts.

By the late sixteenth century, signs of increased pressure and shrink-ing opportunities became common. With few exceptions, urban man-ufacturing declined in importance, while a rising population closed off opportunities for social ascent that had existed earlier. As a result, migration (seasonal and permanent) increased, while the underprivi-leged non-citizen population of cities and in the country became more numerous and more impoverished. Changes in landholding patterns and family structure reinforced social differences at the village level, changing relations not only between the rich and poor, but also between men and women, elder and younger children, and those with or without access to patronage. These trends accelerated when a deteriorating climate, especially in the 1570s and 1650s, brought about repeated agrarian crises. The worst years were 1571/2, when midland lakes froze owing to extreme cold in the winter, and 1587/8, when snow fell in the midlands well into the summer. A larger population and more frequent crop failures reinforced the advantages of landlords and employers over peasants and labourers, and stimulated the use of credit by peasants and townspeople.

Some half-million people inhabited the territory of modern Switzerland in 1500, not counting the densely populated Italian valleys of the Valtellina and Val d'Aosta. A few rural regions had surprisingly dense populations, such as Appenzell. By 1600, this had increased to about 900,000, with the midlands growing faster than the Alpine regions. Growth slowed sharply from 1600 to 1650, but returned for the remainder of the seventeenth century, leading to a total population of about 1.2 million by 1700, by which time only one-third of the population lived in the Alps. The population data confirms the picture of slow change and vulnerability to crises caused by epidemics and poor weather.

One sign that rural population was beginning to exceed the demands of agrarian labour was the ready availability of young men for mercenary service. At the end of the sixteenth century, some 50,000 Swiss men may have served in foreign regiments, or 5 per cent of the total population. Many did not return. Emigration took other forms, too, corresponding both to the supply and skills of Swiss men and women, and to labour demand in neighbouring regions. Much emigration was seasonal, such as harvest workers, though such work left few records. Where emigrants had specific skills, like the families of artists from the Ticino who established dynasties in Italy, prospects were brighter. The Serodine family, for example, craftsmen and painters from Ascona, found employment in Rome and elsewhere in Italy. Other Ticinese craftsmen practised the craft of stucco sculpture as far away as Hungary and Spain.

Like the rural economy, the economy of the Swiss cities changed only incrementally during the sixteenth century. By 1500, most of the textile manufacturing that had brought prosperity to medieval Zurich, Fribourg and other cities had declined, with the exception of the St Gallen linen industry. The trans-European fairs that drove Geneva's growth before 1500 shifted to Lyons, leaving a diminished city. Local and regional markets brought some business, and the growing revenue from pensions and mercenary operations kept most city treasuries in balance, but the sixteenth century saw few

3.7 Town of St Gallen with linen bleaching fields. North-eastern Switzerland was an early outpost of large-scale textile production in Switzerland. Already in the fifteenth and sixteenth centuries, flax grown in Appenzell or around Lake Constance was turned into quality linen cloth on an industrial scale. The spread of proto-industry in the seventeenth century moved more production out to rural areas with low labour costs, which ultimately undermined towns' monopoly on craft production.

new manufactures. The major exception was printing, which attracted skilled personnel: Basle became an international printing centre, while smaller shops appeared in Zurich and Geneva. On the whole, though, the political functions of the cities supported their economies: as the site where taxes were gathered, officers appointed and policies negotiated, and as the seat of wealthy families, the cities gained economic advantage through their political centrality.

In the seventeenth century, a new phenomenon spread: manufacture of lower-quality goods, mostly textiles, in the countryside though the putting-out system. In many cases, urban entrepreneurs provided raw materials and basic tools to poorer peasant households, who had surplus labour after they tended their often modest fields and gardens. The products of their farming subsidized their wage labour, making such manufacturing profitable, even as the meagre wages they earned enabled families to survive on smaller plots of land. By allowing more families to form, rural manufacturing also led to a higher birth rate, which drove down the cost of labour further and increased the gap between landed peasants and rural labourers. This system, sometimes called proto-industrialization, built on predecessors such as the St Gallen linen trade, which also combined rural and urban labour, and spread steadily across the midlands.

Commercialized cheese production for distant markets also took off. The Alpine regions had switched to cattle-raising in the late Middle Ages, but in the seventeenth century, specialized cheese-producers appeared in the pre-Alps and midlands. Such 'brands' as Emmentaler and Gruyère cheese emerged for export to European cities. Producing cheese on an industrial basis required substantial capital, and was promoted by a small number of successful entre-preneurs who owned substantial herds and meadows, and who bought milk from many farmers. The cheese trade further commer-cialized the countryside through cash purchases and wages, while concentrating wealth in fewer hands. A few new specialized urban manufactures emerged, as well. In Geneva, for example, Huguenot refugees brought both the capital and expertise to launch a silk industry in the 1580s and 1590s.

The economy of the region diverged from its neighbours from 1500 to 1700 in a few significant ways. The key difference was fiscal: because the cantons and Associates did not bear the enormous costs of warfare, modest economic growth generated new capital in public and private hands. Instead of paying for troops and fortifica-tions, the cantons drew in pensions from French, Spanish, Austrian and Venetian agents. Low costs and outside income allowed the Swiss cities to end the wealth taxes they had previously levied, since consumption taxes on markets and dues from their rural subjects provided enough revenue to grow urban treasuries. The cities thus became sources of credit both within and outside the Confederacy. Basle operated a very successful public bank, and Geneva began developing private banking toward the end of the sixteenth century, often in connection with Huguenot refugees from France. The accumulation of capital in public and private hands created a pool for further investments that became crucial when rural industrialization took off after 1700.

Slow change in the Swiss economy affected social relations as well. Perhaps the most important was the economic closure of communities of all kinds to new members, in parallel to the political closing of councils and citizenship. In a society for which membership in a commune was a central marker of identity, this closure was of great importance. The phenomenon is most visible in the cities, where a shrinking group of families, the *Ratsfähige*, monopolized political life and economic opportunities. In Lucerne, members of some forty-eight families sat in the council between 1510 and 1520, but of only thirty between 1590 and 1600. In the fifteenth century, new families had found it easy to move into urban councils and guilds as they gained in wealth, but after 1500, this flow came to a nearly complete halt. The fees charged to new citizens rose rapidly, especially after the 1550s, and the number of new full citizens dropped sharply. The result was what some historians call 'aristo-democracy', while others call it oligarchy.

Spurred in part by the Reformation, the period after 1500 also brought about important changes in marriage, the most important formal relationship linking women and men, for Catholics as well as Protestants. These changes did not end the legal advantages that men enjoyed – indeed, these tended to intensify during the sixteenth century – but they did transform how gender relations were represented and understood. Zwinglians rejected the Catholic conception of marriage as a sacrament, and denied church courts jurisdiction over marriages, adultery and fornication. Instead, the evangelical cities established civil courts to regulate both marriages and morals. These allowed separations or even divorce in a few cases, but refused to recognize marriages made by couples themselves, demanding instead that parents and pastors give permission. Catholic and Reformed authorities alike sought to discipline individual behaviour and encourage sexual and social propriety by limiting carnivals, festivals and lavish wedding feasts in the name of spiritual values.

Fear of female power also increased across Europe in this period, and contributed to more frequent prosecution of people – mostly rural women – for practising evil magic. Some of the earliest prosecutions of this kind took place in the western Alps, including the Valais and the diocese of Lausanne, in the fifteenth century. Witches were prosecuted in many parts of Switzerland for harmful magic (*maleficia*) in the early sixteenth century, often in connection with local quarrels involving sickly infants or hail damage in the fields. The pattern of witch hunting in Switzerland changed sharply after 1550 as magistrates inspired by the notorious *Malleus Maleficarum* carried out more prosecutions for Devil-worship. The latest evidence counts over 1700 trials in the Vaud, and at least 1,000 trials in the Grisons between 1580 and 1655, the peak years of the witch craze. Where magistrates had firmer control, witch trials were much less common: in the same period, only eighty persons were prosecuted in Zurich's territory. Still, the rural areas of Switzerland continued to see occasional prosecutions for witchcraft long after governments elsewhere had abandoned the 'crime' entirely, enabled by Switzerland's loose structure and social conservatism.

After the crises of the 1520s and the spread of the Protestant Reformation, Switzerland settled into a pattern of local contention but overall caution and conservatism. In the war-torn early modern period, this stance served the Swiss well, leaving them more prosperous and more peaceful than their neighbours, and reinforcing their sense of distinctiveness. Change slowed further after 1656, and became less visible: the institutions of the Confederacy, for all their complexity, seemed permanent and unchangeable. Managed by a patriarchal and increasingly patrician elite, these institutions still left room for a prosperous class of burghers and for a stable peasantry, though one that was vulnerable and increasingly included many impoverished day-labourers. However, these were still better off than peasants elsewhere. Change continued slowly after 1713, but both internal reformers and outside observers generally regarded the Confederacy as ossified and archaic.

4

The Ancien Régime, 1713–1798

The Peace of Aarau and the fourth Landfrieden revised the religious balance in Switzerland to the benefit of the Protestant cantons, but left undisturbed the rigid patrician oligarchies within the cantons. As outsiders noted, the country remained as stable and as complicated a European fixture as ever, but, while other Western states were modernizing their armies and governance, the Swiss political class did not follow suit, and so became increasingly passive participants in international affairs and less flexible and accommodating at home. In fact, the peace enabled the patricians to consolidate what can be called the Swiss Ancien Régime: a congeries of stable urban and rural oligarchies, relatively prosperous but increasingly inflexible and repressive. All this encouraged stasis.

Stasis intensified despite the fact that the oligarchic regimes experienced repeated challenges, often from ordinary people who felt the patricians were breaking older conventions and undertakings, but also from within patrician circles by those influenced by Enlightenment thinking, which was one of many European trends in which the cantons shared. Slow but steady internal change – often pushed by members of elite families or by ambitious individuals from the edges of the elite – also threatened the existing order. And, despite growing oligarchical resistance to change from the 1770s, economic growth over the following two decades generated further pressures at the very time that the French Revolution encouraged new forms of protest. Ultimately, the Ancien Régime's increasing rigidities and its promotion of cantonal over confederal interests made it impossible for the old Confederacy to survive in the face of French invasion.

STABILITY AND CHALLENGES

In the immediate aftermath of the Villmergen War, it was not at all certain that the Peace would hold. Although relatively moderate, it was bitterly opposed by the Catholic cantons because, along with giving Berne and Zurich a more proportionate share in the administration of the condominiums of Aargau and Thurgau, it also formalized religious parity for the Confederacy's subjects. Instead of interfering with rights of worship, it provided new processes for mediation of disputes. The Peace also ended the practice of dual Diets, although the Catholics refused to meet in Baden, from which they had just been excluded. Thereafter the Diet met in Frauenfeld with each faith providing its own secretary to draw up its acts.

The new settlement was soon secretly challenged when, in May 1715, the Catholic cantons renewed their old Golden League alliance and their treaty with France. To the latter was added a secret protocol, kept hidden in a trunk – hence its nickname of the *Trücklibund* – in which France promised to mediate in case of disputes with Protestants so as to assist the Catholics to restore their lost prerogatives. While this was never acted on, it symbolized Catholic resentments, feelings that lingered into the 1770s. Yet these never threatened to break up the Confederacy, partly because the surrounding powers did not want this, and partly because the old order was consistently held together by the collective self-interest of its elites, which cut across the religious divide.

Persistent resentments helped, in other words, to prevent any rapid change to the ramshackle constitutional structures of the Confederacy and its subject territories. It remained a contractual system based on a network of treaties, respect for the established order and multiple layers of privilege. Hence the Diet was little more than a symbol and a means of socialization, lacking army, finance and a proper administration as it did. Indeed, if anything, the Diet became even less active at this time because of the need to meet in private and refer all decisions back to the cantons. The joke circulated that the Diet would not agree that snow fell in winter without asking for instructions. Even when decisions were finally reached, cantons were not obliged to act on them.

Certainly there was never sufficient agreement to admit Geneva as a full member, as suggested in 1734, or to modernize the Confederacy as was occasionally proposed. Religious disagreements also prevented renewal of the 1663 alliance with France, because the Protestant cantons refused French persuasion and were less active in supplying mercenaries, making room for more regiments from Catholic cantons like Zug and Solothurn. Nonetheless, France remained a dominant influence in Swiss politics throughout the century, further curtailing the role of confederal decision-making, and encouraging both sides to hold on to authority in their cantons. The French link thus helped to consolidate stability and rigidity as well as power.

In both confessional camps, power remained firmly in the hands of the one group, the so-called patriciates, who through their control of supposedly representative institutions enjoyed monopolies over mercenary recruitment, economic activity, land and office. In fact the patriciates became even more restrictive, closing off access to economic opportunities as well as to citizenship and public office and consolidating oligarchical regimes. In Fribourg only three families were allowed to join the patriciate between 1627 and 1782. By 1734, a third of the Genevan Conseil des Deux Cents came from just ten families, while the Bernese *Gnädige Herren* (Gracious Lords), as they were known, became increasingly cut off from their growing and hard-pressed rural population. The successful investments that the *Gnädige Herren* made in British shares and government funds, together with their monopoly of the fifty lucrative posts as bailiffs in the subject territories, meant that they were decreasingly reliant on taxes for state income. Increasingly, the elites of cities like Berne and Lucerne came to think of their rule as equivalent to the self-governing cities of the ancient world, while they also took on the role of the heirs of William Tell. Their self-regard is evident in both the palatial country mansions they erected and the imposing, albeit self-satisfied portraits that grace those houses. Such regimes became increasingly acquisitive, bureaucratic and monopolistic. Thus, the Etats de Vaud met for the last time in 1739, just as elections were being phased out in the Inner Rhoden of Appenzell and in Neuchâtel.

This trend did not go unchallenged. In fact the oligarchies were often suspected of abusing their powers and breaking what were

4.1 Waldegg Castle. The Chateau in the Catholic canton of Solothurn is a magnificent example of patrician display belonging to the Besenval family, the richest and most powerful in the canton in the eighteenth century. Their wealth and power came from the pensions provided by service in the French *Gardes Suisses* and a salt monopoly. The family was one of the leaders of the French party in Switzerland, being intimately connected to the French royal family and its wars.

popularly seen as the old established rules as they sought to intensify their control and extraction of resources from the population. At the beginning of the eighteenth century, the government of Zurich thus found itself at loggerheads both with its guilds, who objected to the failure to consult them over the decision to go to war at Villmergen, and with the town of Winterthur. The latter objected to new restrictions on its economic activities, as did Wilchingen when Schaffhausen imposed a city monopoly on inns on its territory. In Glarus, a stand-off between the authorities and the bailiwick of Werdenberg arose when the former cancelled peasant rights to forest use and pasturage. The locals demanded to see the documents on which the authorities based their claim. Peasants and subjects too looked back to the past and, like the elites, thought in terms of traditional privileges rather than modern rights.

The most unusual episode came in the Bernese subject territory of the Vaud in late March 1723. Abraham Davel, a 53-year-old notary and major commanding the Lavaux region, ordered his militiamen to march on Lausanne and demand an end to Bernese domination. He objected to the way Berne sold church positions and forced the rigidly conservative *Formula Consensus* of 1675 on unwilling Vaudois clergy. Being naïve, he was tricked into surrendering and hastily executed. The authorities tried to conceal his list of demands but these, along with his stoicism on the scaffold, made him something of a hero in the longer term.

More commonly, conflicts of the 1720s and 1730s arose from factional struggles within the elite for control over the sinews of oligarchic power. Appenzell Outer Rhoden and Zug saw bitter struggles between the 'hards' – or opposition parties – and the governing 'softs'. In the former, the Wetter family of Herisau ousted the 'softs', the previously dominant aristocratic clan headed by the Zellwegers of Trogen. The latter were then prosecuted because of their stance over customs disputes with St Gallen and the powers of the Landsgemeinde. At issue in Zug was control of the French pensions paid to mercenary officers. The Schumacher family and the 'hards' made an abortive attempt to end the monopoly on pensions and salt supply enjoyed by the Francophile Zurlaubens and their 'soft' faction. With considerable sums of money at stake, the conflict nearly led to civil war, and cost one Schumacher his life.

The divide between the elite and the masses was at its sharpest in the allied city of Geneva. Authority there was in the hands of the 'citizens' or 'nobles', a select group distinct from the ordinary bourgeois who increasingly monopolized both political power and access to the professions. Their attempts to refortify the city against threats which no longer seemed real triggered a revolt in the 1730s, because this meant new tax burdens on the already downtrodden 'habitants', mainly post-Revocation arrivals for whom access to the bourgeoisie was no longer possible. At best their offspring, if born in the city, could become 'natifs', who had few rights but were allowed to share the tax burden. Although by the 1720s habitants made up 50 per cent of the population, their situation was increasingly difficult and politically deprived. In fact, prior to 1767 only ninety people were admitted to citizenship, and then only after paying large sums.

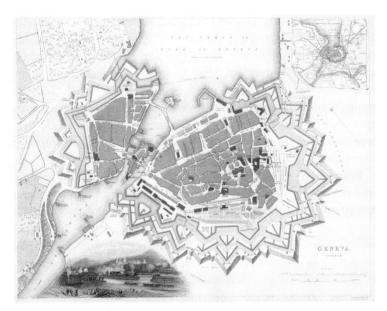

4.2 Fortifications of Geneva. Because of its geographical and
political position, on the borders of Savoy and France and only
an ally, not a full member, of the Confederacy, the city was
always at risk of attack. Hence by 1727 it had erected these very
strong defences, modelled on the ideas of Vauban. Later
proposals to extend the fortifications played a part in
developing internal Genevan dissensions.

The actual complaint behind the 1730s troubles was that the new
levies had not been submitted for approval to the Conseil Général,
the open assembly of the entire bourgeoisie. This break in traditional
republican practice caused both protests from the bourgeoisie and
popular agitation. When the oligarchs found their troops being dis-
armed by the bourgeois militia, Berne, Zurich and France had to send
in troops and impose the French-guaranteed Mediation of 1738.
This, at the cost of minor changes, allowed the 'citizen' oligarchy to
maintain its position over the next twenty years. The oligarchy, in
fact, was willing to accept virtual French domination as long as its
own powers were not threatened. This reflected the way they were
increasingly becoming a European elite.

Similarly, in the Bishopric of Basle, trouble began after 1726 when
the Bishop attempted to end the peasantry's rights of free pasturage

while also increasing taxation. The resulting tax strike and disorders forced the Bishop, who could get neither Berne nor the Catholic cantons to bail him out, to sign a secret treaty with France, whose troops intervened in the 1740s to put down the revolt. As well as a defence of traditional social privileges against enclosures and economic modernization, the revolt was also a challenge to established episcopal authority. When Pierre Péquinat, one of the ringleaders, was executed in 1740, he too eventually became a symbol of liberation.

Before then, Switzerland as a whole was affected by the series of mid-century European wars. In 1734, the Protestant cantons offered troops to guard the frontiers when the War of Polish Succession threatened the Rhine. During the War of Austrian Succession, when neutrality was formally declared, troops had to be provided to defend Geneva when it was threatened by Spanish forces campaigning nearby. Such large-scale wars also affected the mercenary business. Combatant states demanded more control and more training for Swiss troops, so as to make use of new technologies. In 1734 this forced the Swiss to revise their regulations concerning mercenary capitulations. The rising death rate at battles such as Laufeld in 1747, together with poor rates of pay and harsher discipline, made mercenary service less attractive. It became harder to recruit outside the poorest regions, and desertion was not uncommon. This meant Swiss military entrepreneurs' profits began to fall. The French, in particular, baulked at paying a premium for Swiss regiments especially if, as was often the case, 30 per cent of their strength was not actually Swiss.

The declining appeal of mercenary service also reflected the country's growing prosperity. The recovery of population growth after the end of the so-called Little Ice Age *c.* 1730, accelerated by better hygiene and the better diet provided by the increasing use of the potato, was a key factor. It pushed the number of Swiss well beyond the 1.2 million of the beginning of the century. The construction of new roads, notably by the Bernese, helped to break down subsistence economies and create a more effective market. Another factor was the spread of cotton spinning and weaving, often initially introduced to help the poor, which became well entrenched in Geneva and Zurich. From the latter, new textile manufactures spread into

4.3 The execution of Samuel Henzi. Writer, teacher, soldier, librarian and administrator, Henzi was one of those who challenged the Swiss Ancien Régime. He was put to death with two others outside the city on 17 July 1749 for his part in a conspiracy against the Bernese oligarchy. His execution was symbolic both of patrician regimes' refusal to countenance any criticism of the status quo, and of the way in which such executions could strengthen opposition forces.

Glarus and other parts of eastern Switzerland. Organized on the putting-out system – in which merchants took materials to contracted households to be spun or woven and then collected, made up and sold on as finished products – rural manufacturing began to provide significant income for peasant families. In the same period, watch manufacturing began to spread out of Geneva, where it had usurped the place of silk, and into the Jura region.

Yet economic recovery did not end political challenges. In Berne, the heart of the Ancien Régime, some of the artisanal families who had increasingly been excluded from power began to publish pamphlets demanding restoration of the rights of guilds and people, as laid down in 1384, leading to some of them being exiled in 1744. On returning from exile in 1749, one of them, Samuel Henzi, whose military career had already been hindered because he was not an aristocrat, lost out to an unqualified young patrician for the position of state librarian. This led him to join a plot to overthrow the regime by force and replace it with a guild system. The plan was quickly betrayed and Henzi and others were executed. Many more were exiled and stripped of their civic rights, which discouraged the discontented from further challenges. However, Lessing wrote a play about the incident, and a posthumous play by Henzi, based on the Tell legend, was published, ensuring that the affair was not forgotten.

Six years later, in the Leventina Valley, the Uri authorities' efforts to reform the corrupt but much-used system of wardships caused a considerable commotion. While the protestors wanted to negotiate, news of the trouble had already reached Uri, which with its allies mobilized 2,000 troops and sent them south. In face of such pressure, the dissidence subsided peacefully. The leaders were nonetheless executed and the locals were forced to take a new oath of allegiance. Though this affair later became a symbol of Ticinese liberty, it seems to have been as much a matter of poor communications as of revolt. Certainly it did not discourage the Ticinesi from supporting their trans-Alpine masters in the 1790s. Indeed, generally speaking the conservative early-century challenges were fended off without too much difficulty.

INTELLECTUAL CHANGE AND PATRIOTIC AWAKENING

However, the general conservatism of the Swiss elites did not always apply to their intellectual pursuits, either generally or in thinking about Swiss history. Hence the country took a growing, if ambiguous, cultural role in Europe. It also developed a nascent national movement, parallel to that emerging in other parts of Europe. In fact, despite a successful willingness to repress, the ruling elites of eighteenth-century Switzerland were surprisingly open to intellectual change – though this was to prove subversive of the social and cantonal status quo. Many patricians were highly educated and cultured, even though Switzerland had only one university, meaning that many were forced to look to Germany for higher education. They were often advanced thinkers and very much in the European mainstream. Swiss savants took leading positions in fields such as theology, philosophy, natural science, medicine, international law and historiography. Basle was strong in mathematics with the Bernoulli brothers and Euler. Zurich could boast of Johann Kaspar

Lavater, who was to become one of the fathers of modern psychology, and of Breitinger and Bodmer, two leading figures in German literature and history. In 1734, Bodmer published Tschudi's *Chronicles* and argued against the idea that Switzerland had been a revolutionary creation. Two years earlier, Albrecht von Haller, a Bernese polymath, published his ground-breaking poem on the Alps, which was to stimulate admiration of mountains and the lifestyle they produced.

All this helped to develop political awareness across Swiss society. With censorship beginning to ebb, newspapers like the *Mercure Suisse* of 1732 began to emerge. Colporteurs travelled the countryside with pamphlets, while towns saw a growing number of reading societies, coffee houses, salons and schools, all of which helped stimulate public debate. Even more important were the growing number of learned societies, such as that of Public Utility, founded in 1737, the Economic and Statistical Society of 1760 and a number of Agricultural Societies.

These developments helped Switzerland become something of an entrepôt for English ideas and a required stage on the Grand Tour, especially as Swiss intellectual life was less anti-clerical than that in France. It was partly for such reasons that Edward Gibbon was sent to Lausanne in the 1750s. Another intellectual dynamic came from the ideas of Jean-Jacques Rousseau, who was both a citizen of Geneva and had many contacts with Neuchâtel. Voltaire also became an admirer of things Swiss, and took up residence on the borders of Geneva, where many of his works were published. As a result, the country found itself at the heart of new religious and intellectual controversies. The printing of the *Encyclopédie*, along with much other Enlightenment literature, at Yverdon in the 1770s meant that the country played a major part in disseminating French ideas as well. Geneva, Lausanne and Neuchâtel also became important publishing centres. Increasingly Switzerland mattered intellectually to Europe while many Britons, like Gibbon, were attracted by its political arrangements.

In the later eighteenth century, Swiss society became more tolerant, with executions for heresy and witchcraft gradually ceasing and torture coming under attack. This tolerance was often helpful to women, who became more able to contribute to social life. In fact, the first Swiss school for women was set up in Zurich in 1774, suggesting that attitudes were becoming marginally less restrictive than in the past. Lower-class women may also have benefited from new opportunities in the putting-out industries.

However, neither this tolerance nor their cultural interests stopped patricians from seeking to quash ideas that they considered subversive – and much of the Enlightenment was indeed corrosive of the foundations of oligarchical rule. Hence, those who were felt to have stepped out of line, like the Neuchâtel pastor Ferdinand-Olivier Petitpierre, who in 1755 preached that damnation might not be eternal, were sacked and forced into exile. In 1762 Petitpierre was joined in England by the noted artist Henry Fuseli, who was forced to leave Zurich after joining with Lavater and Johann Heinrich Pestalozzi, the well-known educational theorist, in criticism of a corrupt bailiff. A few years later, Pastor Christoph Müller was forced to flee the city after publicly defending Genevan-style democracy.

When, in 1761, Pastor Freudenberg showed that, as many had suspected, the legend of Tell shooting the apple off his son's head had originated in Denmark, his book was burnt by outraged Uri authorities. They did not like any challenge to their Tell founding myth, as Gibbon was well aware when he decided to set aside his planned history of Switzerland. Johannes von Müller had to pretend that his highly influential romantic *History of Switzerland*, which circulated from the 1780s and talked about Tell, was published in Massachusetts in order to avert criticism from Bernese officials who saw Tell as a revolutionary. Nonetheless, Freudenberg's discovery prompted a real debate and a search for proof. In contrast, the rediscovery in 1758 of the 1291 compact by Johann Heinrich Gleser, a young lecturer turned baker, had little impact on historical thinking until later. Most Swiss followed the liberation saga as set out in the fifteenth-century chronicles.

Despite the hazards, many Swiss intellectuals were drawn towards thinking about their own Swiss identity and asking what held them together despite their linguistic and religious differences. The late 1750s saw the publication of a number of introspective writings, such the *Patriotic Dreams* of both Franz Urs Balthasar from Lucerne and Isaak Iselin from Basle. The latter was historian, philosopher and critic both of Rousseau and of Switzerland's mercantile and aristocratic spirit. Balthasar and others were even more critical of the state of the Confederacy, the former proposing a federal college, a unified army and a confederal tax to remedy its weaknesses. More than in previous centuries, intellectuals now thought of Switzerland as a single nation, though one sorely lacking in political unity. Folk songs and the increasing interest in the mountains helped to further the idea of distinct Swiss and Alpine identity.

From the early 1760s, such thinking was focused on the Helvetic Society, which began meeting at Schinznach in Aargau in 1762. Inspired by Iselin, the society sought to bring the cantons together and to overcome the religious divide by appealing to Swiss patriotism through a glorification of Swiss exploits in the Middle Ages. Attracting some 400 members, mainly professional men but even including a few women, the society was mostly critical of the Ancien Régime, since its members sought to modernize Switzerland and see it profit from general European economic growth on physiocratic lines. Politically, Iselin saw Switzerland as a free state, but one in need of unification. Hence, like Balthasar before him in 1744, he drafted a model Swiss constitution. The Society's failure to offer unblemished support for the existing order meant it also faced attacks from conservative elites. Hence, after 1766, it was forced to moderate its tone and become less critical. More dramatically, the Bernese Economic Society, which was critical of mercenary service for corrupting the country and limiting population growth and agriculture, was forced to shut down by the authorities. Nonetheless, Helvetianism remained a significance intellectual force and, in time, was to help call the Ancien Régime into question and provide a basis for more national thinking, in part by encouraging people to look to Swiss history as a basis for unity.

CONTRADICTORY TRENDS AT MID-CENTURY

Around this time, the Ancien Régime was also shaken by economic disruption and the way that questions related to mercenary service caused internal conflicts and new tensions with France. While a new treaty eventually emerged, none of this encouraged the Confederacy to modernize, despite the example offered by enlightened despotism in neighbouring countries. As with cultural developments,

4.4 Fabrique Neuve de Cortaillod in Neuchâtel. The factory
opened in 1752 in this elegant classical building, replacing an
earlier cotton workshop. In its time, it was the country's biggest
and most modern textile factory, employing 700 workers.
Powered by water, it produced 45,000 cloths a year, which it
sold throughout Europe. Although badly hit by the British
blockade during the Napoleonic Wars, it remained in operation
until 1854.

Switzerland's mid-century political difficulties clearly owed much to
accelerating economic change, which in turn began to threaten the
social basis of the Ancien Régime. In fact, agricultural development
accelerated as land became more expensive, leading to more intensive
and commercial farming; artificial fertilizers came in by the 1770s,
along with new root crops. Commercial cheese production for distant
markets spread further into the midlands, leading some peasants to
switch from cereals into dairying; cheese sales made some quite
wealthy, despite their increasing dependence on the market. More
and more Swiss peasants also came to own their own land, especially
in the mountains.

The growing population also provided labour for the growing
domestic industries in the smaller towns and villages of German-
speaking Switzerland. The year 1750 also saw the opening of the
Fabrique Neuve de Cortaillod in Neuchâtel, one of the biggest textile

centres in the country. Growth was encouraged by the expanding trade with France after the 1740s. Geneva merchants also increased their involvement in colonial trade, something that helped to encourage bankers such as Necker, whose firm flourished after the Seven Years War had ended. These developments began to create and spread wealth, allowing for its display at a more popular level, despite continuing sumptuary legislation by the big-city elites. Indeed, by the 1770s, concerns about pauperism began to fade. Only in the Ticinese hills and the Engadine did substantial numbers still have to resort to seasonal migration.

Prosperity did not prevent further political disorders around mid-century. The most significant troubles came in Geneva after 1762, when the government ordered the burning of Rousseau's *Émile* and *The Social Contract* because they were subversive. Intellectuals and many locals objected and, in 1763, a formal 'representation' or address to the authorities was made, complaining that neither Rousseau nor the Consistory had been heard before the burning. The government refused either to accept the representation or to allow it to be taken to the Conseil Général. Hence, many of the middling classes began to demand the legal right to present such petitions, creating a new opposition movement, nicknamed the 'Representants'. A pamphlet war with the patricians ensued, to which Voltaire began to contribute. A mediation attempt by Berne and other cantons was rejected by the Conseil Général because it wholly backed the patricians, whose theatre was burned in protest. Although an Edict of Conciliation allowing the Representants new rights was agreed on in 1768, following a French blockade, their unsuccessful resort to further violence led to its revocation two years later and forced some opposition leaders into exile.

In Neuchâtel, problems began in the mid-1750s, caused by Frederick II of Prussia's attempts to apply some of the dictums of Enlightened Despotism to his far-off principality, notably selling off tax collection rights to the highest-bidding group of so-called tax farmers. In 1766, this attracted real anger when, following a failure to attract bids, the authorities tried to sell off state lands, which the locals saw as a breach of promises made to them in 1707. Frederick then appealed to Berne, which found in his favour and, when unrest persisted, mobilized 9,000 men, apparently cowing the city into submission. But when Frederick nominated Claude Gaudot – his main defender but formerly a member of the opposition – as lieutenant governor, anger flared up again, and Gaudot was murdered in April 1768. The town was then reduced to obedience.

In the Catholic and Landsgemeinde cantons, questions of foreign policy and mercenary service generated numerous internal disputes. In the Inner Rhoden of Appenzell in 1760, a popular innkeeper called Suter was elected *Vogt*, but soon fell out with the moneyed elites and the monasteries. Exiled in 1775, he was executed in 1784 for challenging the big families' control of the Landsgemeinde. In Lucerne, as part of the long-running struggle between the Meyer and Schumacher families, Placide Schumacher, the cantonal Registrar, was executed in 1764 for alleged treason. He had tried to raise a popular revolt after his relatives had been condemned for malversation. He also opposed both the Trücklibund and reform of mercenary service. A member of the aristocratic Meyer family was also exiled, and his writings burnt, because he sought to limit the power of the Church.

In Schwyz, trouble sprang from the way in which the Duc de Choiseul, French foreign minister after the disasters of the Seven Years War and Colonel-General of the Swiss, had, for reasons of economy, cut the number of Swiss-supplied regiments. When his actions provoked opposition, he disbanded the Schwyz regiments and withheld vital supplies of salt. Disorder also arose over tax questions in the outlying March and Einsiedeln districts. Lieutenant-General Josef Nazar Reding brought the disbanded troops home and unsuccessfully sought to mediate. He was seen as too favourable to the French, however, and was forced to flee. Choiseul's changes also caused trouble in Zug, where a 'soft' leader was forced to flee after opposition developed to his attempts to monopolize the mercenary and salt trades. Not till 1764 did all cantons accept the new French rules, allowing Reding to return safely to office.

Little of this political strife really involved the Diet, which remained an impotent bystander, unable to take decisions because Berne and Zurich were still resolutely opposed to French mercenary contacts. This changed only in the mid-1770s when Joseph II of Austria emerged as a worse threat than France, since Joseph's participation in the First Partition of Poland seemed to suggest he might want to reclaim the long-lost Habsburg territories of Aargau and Thurgau. Positions also shifted with the arrival of a new and more trusted King, in Louis XVI, whose ministers finally realized that the Protestant cantons could not be separated. A new fifty-year deal was signed on 28 May 1777, allowing France to go on recruiting mercenaries, but implicitly annulling the Trücklibund and nominally replacing French mediation by domestic agreements. A Plan of Protection was drawn up to enable the latter to be negotiated, but was never implemented, so strong were local particularisms and religious suspicions.

Equally, the Diet refused to respond to the demands for military reform made by the Helvetic Military Society in 1779. Reforms were clearly necessary, given the way that military exercises had to be cancelled in Fribourg in 1762 after incompetent gunners set their own roofs on fire. The Confederacy thus remained a weak body, lacking a constitution, an army and a reliable tax-based income. Far from being a state comparable to its more powerful reforming neighbours, it remained self-satisfiedly dependent on an implicit French guarantee, which in turn depended on a balance of power that had turned against France following its defeats in the Seven Years War. Hence the suggestion made by Johann Georg Stokar, a chairman of the Helvetic Society, that the country needed to unify and accept equal rights for all, was ignored. Indeed, things were already going in the opposite direction.

OLIGARCHIC REACTION AND ECONOMIC TRANSFORMATION

Faced with such emerging challenges, the patriciate ignored them and sought to move in a reactionary direction, in line with what some historians think was happening in France. While this was initially successful, it failed to cope with intensifying internal troubles or with the increasing socio-economic power of the politically excluded. In fact, the Swiss patriciate after 1770 seems to have been moving away from a mainly defensive stance towards more purposive efforts to fortify their position. Refusing ideas of unification was, in other words, symptomatic of the oligarchies' approach in the 1770s and

1780s. Going beyond immediate challenges, the oligarchs sought aggressively to entrench their positions and interests at the expense of lesser breeds, something that prompted very significant risings in Geneva and Fribourg. At the same time, proto-industrialization was expanding rapidly, enough that some scholars see this period as the beginning of the Swiss economic 'take-off' surge. Rural manufactures were often organized by political outsiders and took place outside the capital cities, making the political weight of the countryside increasingly significant. The hegemony of the restricted urban elites was at stake.

The epitome of the new oligarchical push was the 1773 decision in Lucerne to reduce the number of ruling families to twenty-nine. Only if one family actually died out, henceforth, could another be brought in. At the same time, the Meyer faction was banished because it sought an end to confessional politics. In Uri, the powers of the Landsgemeinde were curbed to the benefit of three major families, who also arrogated to themselves a monopoly over the vital transit trade. In Berne, the number of ruling families dwindled to sixty-eight, while only 3,600 out of a total population of 200,000 could play any part in politics, compared to 5,700 of 215,000 in Zurich, where only eighty-six families could hold office. In Basle, though there were many citizens, real power was limited to fifty-eight families, three more than in Solothurn. Overall, the patriciate in the late eighteenth century numbered some 10,000, in a population of about 1.7 million.

As the patriciates shrank, they also became more aristocratic. In Berne and Fribourg, families were allowed to use the particle 'von', which denoted noble status, while in Thurgau and elsewhere, the patricians redefined themselves as noble. Many elites also sought to tighten their control over their *Hintersassen*, the non-citizen subjects, by restricting crafts to urban artisans, by limiting the putting-out system and by rescinding rurals' ability to enroll in mercenary and other services. Although oligarchs also refused political rights to the lower orders in the capital cities, they were able to keep them satisfied by granting them economic privileges. This increasing discrimination was to have a lasting and destabilizing effect on Swiss politics over the next fifty years.

The first signs of instability came in May 1781 in Fribourg, when the government tried to cut twenty-seven feast days, shut down a monastery notable for helping the poor and sought to tax livestock. Dissatisfaction amongst sharecroppers was channelled by Pierre-Nicolas Chenaux, a charismatic but ruined farmer-cum-businessman from the Gruyère region, who had been denied promotion in the militia because he was not a patrician. He joined in a plot being hatched in Bulle to march on and occupy the capital. Though the government got wind of this, Chenaux was still able to raise 3,000 men and advance on Fribourg. His attempts at negotiation failed when Bernese military assistance arrived. Most of the rebels surrendered without a fight, while Chenaux himself was killed by another rebel turned bounty hunter. Although even Berne urged concessions, fierce repression followed. However, the countryside was invited to make known its complaints, mainly about taxation, while the urban middle classes called for change. But the only changes carried out actually relaxed the restrictions on noble families by allowing their children to hold office, along with a slight widening of the patriciate. Many of those who protested were forced into exile in 1783.

In Geneva, a further wave of troubles resulted from a new offensive by the most reactionary amongst the elite, the so-called 'Constitutionnaires', who had never accepted the reforms of 1768. Having gained a majority in the governing councils at the end of the 1770s, they were able to block the codification of the city's numerous laws that the 1768 agreement required. This greatly annoyed the 'Representants'. Both sides began to pamphlet and mobilize their followers, causing street scuffles. The reformers gained the upper hand early in 1781 and passed the Bienfaisant Edict, which bestowed new rights on the *natifs*, committed the city to regular acceptance of new citizens and abolished some feudal dues. The unhappy mediating powers ordered that elections should not be held, but the government ignored them. It did annul the Bienfaisant Edict, however, prompting a massive popular rising in April 1782, followed by an opposition purge of the Councils and the government. But, when the powers responded by investing the city, the radical leaders had to yield. Many of them fled abroad, allowing France and Savoy to institute a White Terror of their own.

Such victories won the patriciates a few more years of unchallenged peace, but these were not used to institute reforms that could have helped them cope with rapidly changing circumstances at home and abroad. The authoritarian oligarchs continued to see no need to adapt. They preferred to rely for their legitimacy on custom, heredity and closeness to an established church. Indeed, they saw themselves as a divinely ordained elite at the peak of a hierarchical society. In this they eschewed the newer representative ideas emerging in the Anglo-American world in favour of continental traditions of the seventeenth century.

Yet Swiss society was itself changing fast. From about 1780 Switzerland underwent what Rappard and others have called a real industrial revolution, based at first on the putting-out system but quickly expanding into factory production. By 1790, a quarter of the population, which would soon reach 1.7 million, was dependent on manufacturing, three quarters of these in the textile industry, which already employed 90,000. Although Sonderegger introduced mechanized spinning to Herisau in the early 1780s, mechanization accelerated after 1795, as competition from British mechanized textile production made itself felt. Output grew enormously, both in cotton and in watches, of which some 50,000 a year were being turned out in Geneva alone. Neuchâtel had some 3,500 watchmakers by the end of the century. Much of the expansion in textiles was financed by master weavers, not by banks, showing that the new economy was making some employers increasingly wealthy. However, bankers also saw the attractiveness of textiles and began to invest in the sector. Trade also flourished and moved into new areas, with some Swiss even engaged in the slave trade. The midlands and its new cheesemakers increasingly dominated agriculture.

This transformation created a dual challenge to the patriciates. On the one hand, economic dynamism was moving away from capital cities, where the oligarchs were mainly based, to rural areas and outlying towns. The latter grew rapidly in size and number, so that at least forty-two towns reached a population of over 2000 by the end of the 1790s. Outlying areas thus counted for much more than in the past. On the other hand, industrialization produced and promoted new middle classes who were better off, more educated and increasingly politically aware. Some were large-scale commercial farmers, others textile entrepreneurs, and many more were hand workers. Their emergence had increasing political effects, such as movements against corruption in Zug and Zurich. The latter also saw the foundation of a critical newspaper, the *Züricher Zeitung*, in 1780. Seven years later the *Journal de Genève* was founded. Exiles in Paris also remained vocally critical of the Swiss Ancien Régime.

Even though the resulting social dissent left the old order exposed, the system continued to hold together, and the endemic violence of the century rather died away. This temporary stability owed much to the intransigence of patrician leaders. The very complexity of the Ancien Régime's structures was a further strength, providing it with multiple bases, including the support of France, the advantages of neutrality and the availability of military aid. The fact that the regime usually provided relatively good governance, prosperity and openings through military service and low taxes also helped, as did the fact that opposition was both fragmented and traditionalist, even if Chenaux's rebels did try to invoke the American War of Independence in their rhetoric. However, the outbreak of the French Revolution in 1789 added a dangerous new dimension to dissent. Even though many of the resulting challenges remained quite traditionalist, calling for remedial and local reforms, the elites' own past success in resisting change made it hard for them to make concessions. Successfully putting down popular outbursts had helped to strengthen their rule, so it is not surprising that they rejected revolutionary-era challenges in just the same way. Ultimately, internal pressures were unlikely to have led to regime change, but the oligarchs' failure to provide real remedies, notably where feudal dues and representation were involved, allowed intellectuals and extremists to facilitate the French aggression that brought down the Old Confederacy. The patrician reaction thus proved counter-productive even if challenges to it for long remained localized and traditionalist.

THE SPREADING SHADOW OF THE FRENCH REVOLUTION

Given their geographical position, the Swiss cantons could not escape the effect of events in France. The French Revolution in fact cast a long shadow over Switzerland, thanks to its ideas, the disruptive effects of disturbances on Swiss borders, its impact on economically rising groups and, in the end, its military power. Initially the oligarchies were able to control the resulting intellectual ferment, but the increasingly extreme developments in France overshadowed the country, encouraging troubles that often meshed with industrial take-off and the appeal of the traditional liberation saga. The Diet, however, was too reactionary and divided to take the quasi-revolutionary steps that might have forestalled the overthrow of the Ancien Régime.

News of the Revolution led to the establishment of new reading societies, led by schoolmasters and rural clergy, which began to spring up in peripheral towns like Wädenswil, Stäfa and in the valley of Glatt in Zurich, encouraging peasant political awakening. Nonetheless, while the early Revolution fed into the disaffection latent in much of the Confederacy, no real groundswell of resistance to the existing order appeared. Very often, opposition was created as much by the intransigence of governments as by deep-seated political divisions. A growing number of intellectual dissidents were active, whether the exiles in Paris who created the Club Helvétique in 1790, or the Swiss pamphleteers outside the country, but they lacked the means to act. Prominent amongst the dissidents was Frédéric César de La Harpe, a lawyer from Vaud who had left his homeland because he could not stand the way it was governed by their Gracious Lords of Berne. He ended up serving as tutor to the grandsons of Catharine the Great of Russia. From St Petersburg he wrote articles in the *London Chronicle* demanding freedom for Vaud. The Bernese authorities immediately proscribed him, even though he was in Russia. Cantonal governments also sought to censor the press and guard the frontiers, but such intellectuals and exiles still created a good deal of pressure, especially in western Switzerland and in the secondary towns. The Vaudois peasantry, in contrast, had no rebellious traditions and often favoured the Bernese regime.

The first signs of internal protest came in Unter-Hallau which, in early 1790, refused to take an oath of allegiance to Schaffhausen and issued a memorandum demanding the restoration of its old rights as a free town. This was followed later in the year by unrest at Monthey in the Valais and the so-called 'crochets' conspiracy in the Chablais

4.5 Nineteenth-century painting by Karl Jauslin depicting the open-air political banquet held at Jordils, near Ouchy, to celebrate the second anniversary of the storming of the Bastille. Local notables are shown wearing revolutionary cockades, toasting the French Revolution and generally having a good time. Attracting more than 150 people, the actual banquet involved toasts to liberty and the États de Vaud. This and other banquets, notably at Rolle the following day, moved the Bernese oligarchy to crack down, banning such meetings and forcing the Vaudois to seek a formal pardon, thereby worsening relations with their Francophone subjects. Hence many see the banquets as stepping stones to the independence of Vaud at the end of the decade.

district in 1791. Berne sent in troops to restore order, but some districts began to buy back the feudal dues to which they were subject. By then, provocative banquets celebrating events in France had also begun in Vevey, Rolle and Ouchy. Demonstrators and banqueters were sharply warned by Berne, as troops and examining magistrates were sent in. La Harpe's soldier cousin, Amedée de La Harpe, was condemned in absentia for subversion because of his active participation in a banquet. But none of this prevented new petitions for change and tax cuts. The magistrates' response to these was uncoordinated and somewhat passive. Attempts by the Bernese after 1790 to impose censorship, halt movement and block talk of 'rights' – which had spread following the dissemination of pamphlets from France – proved unavailing, since the new press followed events in Paris closely. Attempts at repression in Vaud in 1791 and in Zurich a few years later proved ineffective. Indeed, the proscription of the La Harpes merely strengthened the opposition to Bernese rule, leading to riots in Lausanne.

Subject areas, whether inside cantons or in the condominiums, were particularly vulnerable to unrest. In the Bishopric of Basle, where the Bishop, following the example of Basle city, had tried to head off trouble in 1790 by abolishing serfdom, the emerging political clubs transformed much of the principality into the Rauracienne Republic. When religious dissent and the Bishop's call for Austrian support forced the French to invade in 1793, the bishopric became the French department of Mont Terrible. Abbot Beda of St Gallen also abolished feudalism in 1795, but two years later his successor reneged on this, and called in the Swiss to try to preserve his principality. But his peasants simply refused to pay the reimposed tithes.

In the Suisse Romande the oppressed French-speaking subjects in the Lower Valais demonstrated their unhappiness with their subjection after 1791. Elsewhere in the region there was trouble in Neuchâtel and Geneva. In 1792–3, the former saw clashes between Jacobin Clubs in Le Locle and La Chaux and government supporters. Geneva, being so close to France, was especially affected. As early as 1789, the 1782 settlement was repealed and the exiles were allowed to return. Food shortages also encouraged militancy, and very soon citizenship was made generally available. The new regime appealed to France for support, but Zurich and Berne blocked a French take-over in early 1792. However, by November of that year, Swiss troops were withdrawn in accord with the Swiss declaration of neutrality after the outbreak of the War of the First Coalition. Geneva soon followed Paris down the road to revolution, setting up an extremist regime that began to purge the old elite and established a new revolutionary constitution in 1794. The effects of the Thermidorian Reaction in France ended the local radicals' dominance, and by 1798 the city was integrated into the one and indivisible French Republic. The annexation of Geneva was only one example of how

French expansionism put the old Confederacy and its treaties under great pressure.

The idea of change became especially appealing in the late 1790s, because competition from mechanically produced English textiles was beginning to deprive the textile industry of its markets. In German-speaking cantons, dissent over economic controls emerged in Aargau, but the most significant development came from the Stäfa district of Zurich in 1794, where trouble was sparked by a Memorandum from the local Reading Society demanding more rights. The authorities offered to act if it could be proved that the district's rights had been violated; the locals then circulated a recently rediscovered charter issued after the fall of Hans Waldmann on the rights of the rural areas. The charter seemed to show that the area had enjoyed much more freedom in the late Middle Ages. When the government refused to confirm the charter, a more radical committee formed and began negotiating with the city. The Zurich government responded harshly, accusing Stäfa of rebellion and using troops from Zurich's farming regions and from other cantons (but not from areas of proto-industrialization) to occupy the town, although Lavater persuaded the magistrates not to execute a large number of the protesters. The Stäfa affair illustrates how local issues were increasingly becoming entwined with echoes of the revolution. The peasantry also became restive elsewhere, planting liberty trees in strongly patriotic Basle and St Gallen. Excitement was increased when Napoleon crossed Switzerland after his Italian campaigns, receiving a hero's welcome from those favourable to change.

Even after these developments, most cantonal governments resisted any changes to their structures that would reflect the way the balance of power was shifting in favour of outlying regions. This hesitation recapitulated their earlier failure to capitalize on the general revulsion over the massacre of the Swiss Guards in the Tuileries in Paris on 10 August 1792, which alarmed reformers as well as conservatives. Only minor adjustments occurred: Zug freed its outlying bailiwicks from subjection, and Berne offered to allow a few Vaudois into the charmed circle of political rights in order to sustain the elite's numbers (though only their children and grandchildren would be entitled to hold offices). Basle also moved a little towards social reform. Unfortunately for the oligarchs, this was all much too little and too late. Nobody was willing to follow von Müller and Pestalozzi, who urged the sacrifice of privileges in order to survive. Resistance and counter-propaganda remained the regimes' preferred strategy at the cantonal level.

At the confederal level, the inherent weakness of the system became all too apparent after Schwyz in 1789 refused to agree to a renewal of the *Defensionale*, which coordinated joint efforts for defence of the borders. Likewise, the St Gallen politician Müller-Friedberg's call for a new charter between all the cantons and allies had no effect. Such continuing preference for local over general interests made it almost impossible for the Confederacy to muster sufficient political and military force to resist French encroachments. It remained an assemblage of self-interested rural and urban communities. As a result, the Diet failed to agree on any emphatic measures until very late in the day, because disagreements and traditional arrogance continued to dominate, even though passive stability was no longer enough.

The French Revolution's radical turn late in 1792 greatly influenced Swiss responses, since the Confederacy's push towards conservatism forced the country to break with France, which had been its most important ally for nearly three centuries. The link with France as a revolutionary republic now threatened to undermine, rather than support, the Ancien Régime. When European war broke out in 1792, the Diet declared its neutrality, in line with Zurich's thinking, although the Bernese leadership wanted to join the Allies. In consequence, the Swiss troops who had moved into Geneva agreed to retire. However, Spain and the other Allies were allowed to recruit mercenaries freely, something made possible once the Diet withdrew its regiments from French service following the massacre of the Swiss Guards. The Diet also sanctioned the regiments in French royal service that rebelled because they were unpaid. These actions pushed the Confederacy firmly into the counter-revolutionary camp, as did the enthusiastic way Fribourg and other western cantons subsequently welcomed hundreds of French nobles and others who were forced to emigrate after the abolition of the monarchy and under the Terror. The link with France had become a weakness, rather than a means of strengthening the Ancien Régime. The intervention of Britain through William Wickham, its envoy in

Switzerland, provided little real balance and merely annoyed the French. Basle especially found itself in trouble, because its bankers had lent generously to the now hated monarchy. Nonetheless, once France signed the Peace of Basle with Prussia in 1795 and negotiations at Rastatt with Austria had started, a majority of cantonal regimes assumed that the crisis had passed. They were unaware that, with the Thermidorian Reaction and the rise of the Directory, France was looking beyond its frontiers. Especially after Napoleon's victories in Italy and the coup of 18 Fructidor in 1797, the French regime began to covet Swiss land, resources and routes, partly because these provided a vital link to Italy, and partly because the new regime was aggressively imperialist.

The idea of intervention in Switzerland arose in discussions between the Director Reubell, an Alsatian, and Swiss radicals led by La Harpe and Peter Ochs of Basle. La Harpe had been forced to leave Russia in 1795, and after a stay in the Genevan village of Genthod had moved to Paris. His hostility to Berne had been intensified by his unsuccessful attempt to recover the goods and reputation of his cousin Amedée, who had been killed in action in French service. In 1796–7 he produced a forceful essay on the Vaudois constitution, which had considerable impact in his homeland. Ochs, a Basle lawyer and administrator, had long been a supporter of the Enlightenment, having been influenced by Iselin. Town clerk of Basle from 1790, he became head of the guilds in 1796. The following year he was invited back to Paris by Napoleon, who had apparently decided to set up a unitary and pro-French state in Switzerland, believing that unification was the only way to block the oligarchs and allow the French to control the country. The French were aware that they could easily exploit Swiss divisions. Indeed, Ochs was persuaded to help organize a pacific revolution in Switzerland. By then Mulhouse, a long-term ally of the Confederacy, was slipping towards integration with France while the Valtellina, having been refused recognition as a fourth league of the Grisons, was lost to France's Cisalpine satellite.

Despite the worsening situation, little was done to modernize cantonal militias in response to the Revolution. Even the Bernese forces were in great need of reform, partly because the canton was, for once, in financial difficulties. In fact, despite the use of spies, censorship, repression and counter-propaganda, the situation in Switzerland became very fragile. The oligarchs' traditions and the way circumstances had pushed them into the arms of the counter-Revolution made them obvious targets for French hostility. Yet even as La Harpe was petitioning the French on 9 December 1797 to invade and free Vaud, and Ochs in Paris was talking constitutions with the Directory, all the Diet did was launch an effort to renew the old alliances, which had not been done since the sixteenth century. Even this symbolic act was almost too much for the confederal assembly and took a month to manage, such was the distrust amongst the cantons. The Confederacy was too stagnant to be able to respond to the influence of the Revolution before this took on a military form.

By then, in fact, the French army was poised on the frontiers, having warned Berne and Fribourg on 28 December 1797 that Vaud was under its protection. On 25 January 1798 the Diet broke up, having made no military preparations despite the French menace. When the French occupied Vaud a few days later, however, many western patrician regimes finally bowed to circumstances and yielded up many of their prerogatives. A month later the French army moved eastward, forcing the Bernese government to appeal for military aid from the other cantons, but very little support materialized. In early March, the Bernese regime also yielded after allowing their troops – which were continuing the fight – to be needlessly defeated at Grauholz. Once the city was occupied, many leading Bernese patricians went into exile, while most of western and central Switzerland fell under French control. Only in the mountains of central Switzerland did the Ancien Régime continue, intermittently, to resist.

The old order thus effectively abdicated in 1798, both nationally and at the cantonal level. The very success of the oligarchs in cementing their position up to that point, moreover, meant that no convincing new political forces had been able to develop which might have supported them. The late eighteenth-century push to strengthen the Ancien Régime had apparently succeeded but, in fact, the cantonal oligarchies were too rigid and too divided to adapt to new challenges or develop the national military or political organizations that might have saved them. Tellingly, the Catholic cantons had continued to refuse to be bound by the *Defensionale*. The Confederacy's passive strength, even with a changed religious balance, was no match for French military dynamism as this emerged from the shadow of the Revolution. Moreover, the deference that had helped sustain oligarchical rule was swept away cataclysmically in the 1790s, as the patricians paid the price for not using their earlier successes to create a more balanced regime. In the end, Swiss stability proved illusory. Hence the complete collapse of the old order in Switzerland after 1797 opened the way for a half-century of troubled attempts to create a new political order.

5

Revolution and contention,
1798–1848

The French invasion of 1798 unleashed both a political revolution in Switzerland and a half-century of contention over the validity and nature of the new polity that then emerged. This contention, more-over, took place much more within a single Swiss political arena than had been the case before, so that increasingly it becomes possible to look at Switzerland in terms of a single narrative. This began in 1798 when the old order was overthrown by a combination of its own weaknesses, the work of a nationally minded minority and French military muscle. Together, the possibility of armed intervention and the clear impotence and bad faith of the Ancien Régime liberated the enthusiasm of patriot forces. Because of French military backing, the country had to accept the replacement of the old order by a new centralized Helvetic Republic, which however found itself plagued by contention over its nature, its powers and even its very existence. Consequently, although it superficially united the country and ended the old Confederacy, the Helvetic regime never succeeded in creating a stable state. Much conflict and argument over the precise nature of the new polity was to follow before this was finally achieved in 1848.

Indeed, the Helvetic Republic very soon descended into civil war, which allowed Napoleon to impose a compromise solution that earned the Swiss a few years of relative stability and prosperity. But with his fall came the resurgence of older forces. In 1815 the Great Powers managed to temper the cantons' reactionary aspirations to some extent when they endowed the country with a conservative Confederal Charter. However, the post-war regime was then challenged by the Holy Alliance and by disgruntled liberal supporters of the post-1798 reforms. Aided by the increasing pace of industrialization the liberals broke through in 1830 and 'regenerated' the constitutions of most cantons, ending all hopes of a return to an Ancien Régime dominated by capital cities and their elites. Some wished to end change there, others to take it further, although the latter's aspirations for a national and social solution conflicted with both conservative and Catholic leanings. Diverging visions eventually led to a civil war, won by radical forces and leading to Switzerland becoming, for the first time, a real federal state. In all this, Switzerland was very much part of Europe's emerging national movement.

THE HELVETIC PERIOD: REVOLUTION, RESISTANCE AND CONSTITUTIONAL EXPERIMENTS

The initial Swiss revolution of 1798 began among self-proclaimed 'patriots' in Basle and Vaud. Under often violent pressure from the previously oppressed countryside, Basle gave its countryside equality with the city, drafted a new constitution and, in early February 1798, set up a National Assembly, the first modern representative parliament in Switzerland. In Vaud, the patriots seized the chateau of Chillon while local leaders in Lausanne set up new committees to try to steer the unrest in the town in more moderate directions. But enthusiasm triumphed and, on 23–4 January, a whole forest of liberty trees – often crowned by a Phrygian bonnet or a Green 'Tell' cap – was erected and a Lemanic Republic was proclaimed. These developments were mainly the work of La Harpe and other patriots who wanted to succeed where heroes like Davel, Henzi and Péquinat had failed, but change would not have been possible without French support. In fact, the French Resident in Geneva publicly incited the Vaudois to rise and, when they did, their revolutions were underwritten by the French army. Its commander, General Guillaume Brune, used an incident at Thierrens, when Vaudois gendarmes fired on French soldiers escorting a French envoy, killing one of them, as an excuse to invade and occupy Vaud. As a result, local enthusiasm was overtaken by French power politics, which first determined the shape of the new order and then thrust Switzerland into a damaging new war. This intervention helped

Ceremonie de la Plantation de l'Arbre de la Liberte
sur la Place de la Cathedrale a Basle
...

Feyerliche Pflanzung des Freiheits Baums
auf dem Munster Platz zu Basel
...

5.1 Liberty tree in Basle, 1798. The city, a stronghold of
patriotic reformism, copied the French revolutionary habit of
erecting these symbols of liberty, a practice replacing the
traditional use of maypoles. Liberty trees were often crowned
with a Tell cap and used for important political acts. Opponents
saw them as suggesting foreign domination. Hence they
vanished with the fall of the Helvetic Republic, only to make a
partial return in 1830–1.

to undermine the new Swiss order, which deteriorated to such a point
that Napoleon had to set it aside.

Initially, however, events in Basle and Vaud liberated revolutionary enthusiasm elsewhere. Thousands of liberty trees went up across
Switzerland, and many mass meetings demanded reform, notably at
Weinfelden in Thurgau, as subjects of the old cantons rebelled
against their overlords in the name of economic freedom and a fair
share in political decision-making. Several little local republics briefly
emerged. A number of patrician regimes, notably Zurich, rapidly
took the double hint and began to allow former subjects to share
power. Fribourg, too, drafted a new constitution and admitted non-
citizens to its councils. Even though change was also underway in

Berne and Solothurn, Brune nevertheless marched eastward in late February, calling on the Swiss to unite into one state as he did so. Fribourg and Solothurn immediately capitulated, and when the Bernese authorities received little aid from their allies, they too yielded in early March. Once Berne was occupied, the city treasury was stripped, its arsenal taken over and its bears shipped to Paris, while most of western and central Switzerland fell under direct French control.

The patriots had started by reforming their own localities, but French pressure and the legacy of the Helvetian thinking earlier in the century meant that there was bound to be change at the national level. In fact, when Napoleon declined to produce a confederal rule-book himself, Ochs produced a draft constitution which he discussed with the new Basle Assembly. A more conservative rewrite by the Directory in Paris quickly overtook his efforts, and was immediately printed and, in early February, circulated in western Switzerland. Although a number of cantons approved the revised Basle draft, the French refused to be shifted from their text, and simply decreed that acceptance of the Basle project constituted support for their own version. Thus, at Aarau on 12 April 1798, the French-drafted text was formally proclaimed and the new unitary Helvetic Republic inaugurated. This was the first time that the country had been treated as a single polity, let alone endowed with a single constitutional document. The political nation was also expanded by giving full cantonal status to most of the former subject territories. Aargau, Thurgau and Vaud became cantons more or less as they are today, while the Italian territories and what was to become St Gallen were also included, though not yet in their modern forms.

The French army swiftly completed its occupation of the country. It moved on Lucerne and Zurich in late April and, despite being checked at Rothenturm, eventually defeated forces from Schwyz led by a former mercenary officer, Alois Reding. Such continued resistance revealed that, although the Ancien Régime was overthrown in 1798, its supporters did not go away. Rather, they continued to oppose the French-dominated regimes that followed, sometimes in arms, at other times politically. They were thus intimately involved in the long series of short-lived constitutional experiments that followed.

In any case, by late May 1798, the country was largely subdued and could be dragooned into applying the Helvetic structures. On paper the Helvetic Republic was a strongly unitary state with a powerful five-man Directorate as the executive. A Senate of four members per canton, an indirectly elected Grand Council, a High Court and a volunteer army completed the government. The cantons were downgraded to mere administrative units, subject to a Prefect and no longer able to claim sovereignty or to create barriers against the centre. Their structure was frequently revised, moreover, with the fractious Urschweiz cantons

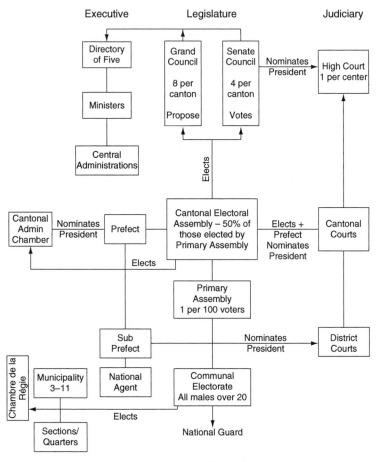

Figure 5.1 The organization of the Helvetic Republic

sometimes unwillingly merged into a new Waldstätten canton, and the Bernese Oberland given autonomous status so as to weaken the influence of Berne. Some of the new cantons were also divided and renamed so as to reduce their influence.

The new constitution was intended as much as a means of ensuring French control and an extension of its *la grande nation* policy as a way of creating a Swiss democracy. When some of the original Helvetic Directors dared to challenge Paris, they were ousted and replaced by La Harpe and Ochs. In reality, the Helvetic Republic was anything but one and indivisible, and was resisted by an amalgam of supporters of the Ancien Régime, a populace hostile to new impositions and Catholics antagonized by the anti-religious nature of the revolution. It proved hard for the newly installed Directory to implement the new unitarian order, both because it lacked the manpower and the resources to do this and because it was also continually challenged by the resentful cantons. Both resistance to new central taxes and the Directory's association with secularizing France – along with the depredations of French soldiery – spurred resistance. The government was also forced to sign an offensive and defensive alliance with France, which signalled the end of neutrality. In mid-August 1798, when the people of Nidwalden were asked to take an oath of allegiance to the new constitution – locally derided as 'an infernal brochure' because of its lack of any invocation of the Almighty – they revolted. They arrested patriots and officials and mobilized their forces, only to be crushed with heavy losses. Pestalozzi set up his famous orphanage in Stans to care for and educate the many orphans left by the conflict.

Partly because the rebels had hoped for Austrian military aid, the French launched the War of the Second Coalition in February 1799. The war hit the country extremely hard, and not merely because the French tried to call up the 18,000 Swiss soldiers promised them by the new treaty. Switzerland was also subject to innumerable requisitions, while its lands were laid waste by battle and its agriculture was crippled by loss of livestock and an inability to plant. Hunger became rife in the winter of 1799–1800. The war started well for France, with Masséna occupying the Grisons and turning it into a new, full canton. When the French began losing ground in Italy, Masséna fell back north-westwards, only to be defeated at the First

Battle of Zurich on 4 June. Although he was able to retreat further to a defensive position on the left bank of the Limmat, most of eastern and southern Switzerland fell under the control of the Austrians, supported by English finance and political activity. Counter-revolution raised its head in Zug, while the Bernese diplomat and administrator Karl Ludwig von Haller, the son of Albrecht von Haller, broke with reform and began to assail the new order through his newspaper, *The Annals of Helvetia*, helping to develop an ideological challenge to revolutionary patriotism.

Things became even more threatening for the French when Russian troops under Korsakov pushed up from Italy to relieve the hard-pressed Austrians. However, the Russians were out-generaled and heavily defeated by Masséna at the Second Battle of Zurich on 25–6 September 1799. Another Russian force under Suvorov tried to relieve Korsakov, but was unable to force its way through the Gotthard, which forced it to make a harrowing retreat through the Alps. By the end of 1799 the devastated country was again free of Allied troops.

The government had been severely weakened during the war, and had to retreat from Lucerne to Berne. Yet La Harpe still chose to force Ochs out on the grounds that he was too pro-French. The regime also sought to abolish tithes and feudal dues, but never had the resources to provide the needed compensation. Ultimately, La Harpe tried to imitate Napoleon and stage his own coup to strengthen the regime. But the First Consul found him too idealistic and too independent for his more conservative taste, and lent his weight to moderate republicans in the Councils, led by Paul Usteri, a distinguished scientist and journalist from Zurich, who purged La Harpe on 8 January 1800, sending him into long-term exile. These events broke the existing rules, thus adding to instability, especially as the new leadership itself lasted only to August 1800, when it was in turn purged by other moderates and replaced by a nominated legislative council, pending a new constitution. Abortive attempts to buy out feudal dues, despite their failure, triggered a crop of separatist risings in the east of the country amongst opponents of the new order, while the endless constitutional tinkering which followed 1798 provoked opposition from Schwyz and other traditionalist areas.

Meanwhile, Napoleon himself had grown tired of the wrangling over the Swiss constitution, and decided to endorse a new draft at Malmaison on 29 May 1801. His proposal restored recognition of the cantons as self-determining, while still keeping a single national polity. Swiss politicians largely ignored Napoleon's efforts, and in the Vaud half the electorate petitioned for a return to Bernese rule. A further coup then brought to power federalists who believed in cantonal independence, if they did not hope for restoration of the Ancien Régime as a whole. Their leader was Reding, who flirted with Austria and opposed detaching Valais from the Confederacy, thereby arousing Napoleon's ire. After a failed constitutional referendum, Reding's government was ousted on 17 April 1802 by the Unitarians, supporters of the Helvetic Republic, under the pro-French Johann Rudolf Dolder of Aargau. The following month a new constitution, based on Malmaison and including a strong executive, was submitted to a referendum. Although it garnered only 72,900 votes in its favour, 20,000 less than those objecting, it was declared passed on the grounds that the 167,000 abstentions were effectively votes for the new order. But the reality was that it was rejected at the local level, so strong was the continuing resistance to change.

This was merely one of the Unitarian government's problems. Additionally, it was going bankrupt and was facing massive social dissidence. In Vaud the 'Bourla-Papey' movement was burning tithe records in protest against the high cost of redeeming feudal dues, forcing the authorities to abolish them without any compensation at all. Generally, the country seemed to be slipping into multipolar civil war, which gave a disillusioned Napoleon the chance to bring the Swiss to their senses. He withdrew French troops and left the regime to its fate. Federalist revolts broke out, focused on Lucerne where Reding tried to summon the old Diet. Attempts by the Unitarian government to repress the rising failed abysmally, but stimulated aggrieved peasants in the north-east to take to the field, armed with stakes and agricultural implements – hence the nickname of *Stecklikrieg*. In the end, the Unitarian army was chased back into Vaud and defeated at Faoug on 3 October 1802.

Such chaos proved Napoleon's contention that the Swiss could not govern themselves. The restored Diet had never met, allowing

Napoleon to impose a ceasefire, send French troops back into Switzerland to prevent the federalists wreaking vengeance on the Unitarians, and coerce most of the Swiss elite to attend a Consulta in St Cloud to draft a lasting settlement. Most of the Swiss delegates realized that the alternative was another crushing military offensive. Composed largely of federalists, the Consulta proceeded through discussions with three French aides who were well acquainted with Switzerland. On the basis of these talks, and Napoleon's own belief that the country could be governed only with the cantons and not against them (as the Helvetic Republic had tried to do), a draft was produced, submitted to Napoleon and then revised before being promulgated on 19 February 1803.

Three weeks later the Helvetic Republic dissolved, having had its day. It had given Switzerland unity, symbols, institutions and national citizenship as well as expanding the number of cantons, a term it used formally for the first time. But it was unable to create a lasting balance between nation and cantons, nor had it ever acquired legitimacy or stable mass support. Because it was tied so closely to France, it had failed to implant either a sense of national identity or even a willingness to tolerate its existence. As a failed state, even its liberating economic stance was contested.

MEDIATION: STABILITY ON SUFFERANCE

If the next ten years were to be rather happier ones for the Swiss, their calm and stability rested on shallow foundations, as events after the Battle of Leipzig in 1813 were to show. This was partly because the regime's stability depended on French military success, and partly because support for a return to the Ancien Régime had not been eliminated, but merely obscured, by the Mediation settlement. This made concessions to the forces of resistance but, because it maintained the new-style Switzerland, it left conservatives unhappy. Hence on the fall of Napoleon the Allies had to step in to restrain them and ensure that moderation continued.

The Mediation Act, on which the 1803–14 regime was based, consisted of a Preamble stressing the country's federalist character, nineteen cantonal constitutions – including Grisons, St Gallen and Ticino, which were established within their modern borders – and a

5.2 Louis Auguste Philippe d'Affry. A former soldier in French service and a leading figure in Swiss politics, d'Affry was well known to Napoleon, so the latter chose him in 1803 as the Mediation's first Landammann, reflecting also the fact that the Diet met in his home town of Fribourg. His ability led to his reappointment in 1809. The way he is pictured here with the new constitution suggests a desire to encourage the association of the new regime with the old elite, thus reassuring conservatives about a settlement that they accepted only on sufferance.

confederal charter. Despite the new equality among the cantons, their individual constitutions varied greatly. The Catholic cantons maintained a narrow franchise and restricted rights, while the new creations were more democratic. Nonetheless, in all cases it was the cantons that provided sovereignty. The fact that the confederal constitution came at the end was symptomatic of this. The new regime was chaired by a rotating directing canton, known as the Vorort, whose head was the Landammann of the new executive, a body with rather limited powers. In a partial return to the Ancien Régime model of Switzerland as a congeries of cantons, the Mediation allowed landowners, patricians and aristocrats back into power. All this was in line with Napoleon's claim that the new settlement meant the end of the revolution for Switzerland. More significantly, Switzerland remained a protectorate of France, which controlled the Swiss through the new military alliance of 27 September 1803. This allowed France to raise 16,000 troops from Switzerland, and to summon the Diet on its own authority, despite Napoleon's affirmation that there should be 'no chains on the children of Tell'. Napoleon's rhetoric reflected the way in which the Tell myth had been adopted by the French Revolution and, after the publication of Schiller's play in 1804, by much of Europe. Ironically, Schiller appears not to have believed in the historicity of Tell and saw him as a symbol of the human condition, but his play was to have great resonance inside Switzerland. For example, it forced Müller to revise his history to highlight the Tell story.

Although the new regime started life on 4 July 1803 amidst a new wave of rural revolts, as Zurich peasant columns marched on their capital demanding the restoration of the political rights they had enjoyed since 1798, the Mediation era proved to be a better time for Switzerland. Thanks to peace and to the protection offered by Napoleon's Continental System after 1806, the economy grew. The system cut off competitive English imports of textiles, and encouraged the Swiss to mechanize their own production. Encouraged by the government, a Vaudois entrepreneur called Pellis had set up the first mechanized cotton spinning works in St Gallen in 1801. The experiment rapidly caught on in Appenzell and Zurich, so that by 1814 there were 1,700 mechanized mills in Switzerland with more opening every year, taking Swiss power supplies beyond men and horses for the first time. Metallurgy and chocolate also began to mechanize. As well as developing the Swiss industrial revolution, the period also saw progress in agriculture as tithes were bought out. The Mediation governments also encouraged public works, such as the construction of a new Simplon road and the taming of the river Linth in Glarus. Despite crises in 1803–6 and 1811–12, social problems eased and population growth resumed.

The period also did more to develop national feeling at a popular level than had the Helvetic interlude, mainly through the creation of new national associations such as the reformed Helvetic Society in 1807, the Swiss Public Utility Society in 1810 and the Swiss Society for Historical Research in 1813. Renewed historical interest was reflected in the success of Johannes von Müller's history of medieval Switzerland, the fourth and fifth volumes of which were published in 1805 and 1808. More popular activities thrived, such as the successful Unspunnen folk games in Interlaken in 1805 and 1808, featuring wrestling, flag-throwing and yodelling. Johan-Rudolf Wyss, from the family of the author of *The Swiss Family Robinson*, wrote 'When you call, my Fatherland' (*Rufst du Mein Vaterland*), which (set to the tune of 'God Save the King') was to serve as a national anthem for many years. National feeling was clearly developing across society and not just amongst the elite.

French pressure ensured a darker side to the period, as well. The country had to accept conscription, which was not always popular. Some 30,500 Swiss served in the Grand Army, some of them even as marines on board ship at Trafalgar, and some in the front line at Borodino during the Russian campaign; few returned. Neutrality was ignored and Swiss independence remained at risk, since Napoleon considered annexing the country. This did not happen, but Neuchâtel was turned into a principality for Berthier, his chief-of-staff, Valais became a French département to guard the Simplon Pass and Ticino was occupied in 1810. Such losses helped ensure that the regime never won broad support, even amongst the federalists whom Napoleon had returned to power. In the end, the Mediation depended on French military power: when Napoleon suffered a major defeat at Leipzig on 16–19 October 1813, it began to subside, both nationally and at the cantonal level, where previously quiescent political aspirations began to reassert themselves. Nationally, the

Diet reasserted its sovereignty dramatically by sending a delegation to Napoleon to inform him that Switzerland would henceforward be neutral, something he now welcomed as it offered a guarantee of his south-east flank. The Diet also raised 10,000 men to guard the Rhine. However, its attempt to reassert neutrality was resisted at home by reactionaries, who looked to Allied aid, and was ignored by Austrian General Bubna and his 130,00-strong army, which marched across Switzerland from Aargau to Geneva, which he liberated in December. Ironically, Bubna used his influence to prevent Berne from repossessing Aargau and Vaud, and Geneva from going back to the 1770s. He, more than the old oligarchs, was aware that such moves were a recipe for renewed civil war.

On 29 December 1813 the Diet declared the Mediation regime dead and set about trying to convene a new Diet. The conservative cantons, which wanted to reconvene the Ancien Régime Diet in Lucerne, at first opposed this move. Their resistance reflected the way the old patrician regimes had re-emerged from the shadows, seized power and reasserted their old privileges, beginning in Berne in December and continuing in Lucerne – where there was an armed coup in mid-February 1814 –Solothurn, Fribourg, Lucerne, Schaffhausen and Valais. These developments showed that, despite the gains it had brought to Switzerland, the Mediation had been accepted only on sufferance. The hearts of many Swiss remained with the old order. However, this revived counter-revolution provoked alarmed peasants in Thurgau to march on Frauenfeld to preserve their recently won rights. The country was, in fact, on the verge of civil war, and it was only with great difficulty, and owing to foreign pressure, that the conservatives were persuaded to go to Zurich in April and take part in what became known as the Long Diet.

The Great Powers, notably the Russian envoy Capo d'Istria, made the Diet work on a new constitution, for which traditionalists saw no need. The Allies, however, insisted on the preservation of the new cantons the French had created out of the former subject territories and allies and added Geneva, Neuchâtel and Valais to their number. A draft was approved in February, but was then pruned by the Allies meeting in the Congress of Vienna. In fact it took considerable Allied pressure to force a new compromise regime on the Swiss, many of whom sought to return to the Ancien Régime.

The Swiss delegates to the Allies were also involved in difficult negotiations over their borders. The military wanted considerable extensions so as to create defensible frontiers, but was largely unsuccessful, being blocked by the French. Equally, the Valtellina was not restored to the Grisons. Berne did receive compensation for its 'colonial' losses by the acquisition of the former Bishopric of Basle's lands in the Jura. The final deal, which left the country slightly larger and stronger than before, was approved in March 1815. Meanwhile, the new Charter had been approved by the Allies on 7 September 1814, after the Diet formally voted to accept Geneva, Neuchâtel and Valais as cantons, showing that the Swiss were willing to accept the impact of the revolution and new national desires.

None of this was upset by the Hundred Days, although Napoleon's return prompted the Diet to show even more determination, rashly declaring war and sending 20,000 men under General von Bachmann into Franche Comté to hold the frontier and support the Swiss claim to the Jura. Unfortunately, this proved to be one of the most inglorious episodes in Swiss military history, since many of the ill-supplied soldiers mutinied, refusing to serve outside Switzerland. In any case, Austrian forces preparing to invade France took no notice and crossed the country anyway. Nonetheless, in mid-August 1815, the new constitution was promulgated by the departing Long Diet. Previously, on 9 June, Pictet de Rochemont, a senior Genevan representative, had persuaded the Allies to recognize that Swiss neutrality was in the general interest of Europe. This claim was formally confirmed by an Allied Declaration of 20 November 1815.

The new Charter was essentially a treaty amongst sovereign cantonal states. The cantons mutually guaranteed their own security and constitutions – often quite backward-looking – and sent representatives to the Diet under strict mandates. The Charter did not provide for a Landammann, a national judiciary or separation of powers. Nonetheless, it represented a step beyond the Mediation and towards a Swiss Confederation, the term being formally used for the first time. It contained a commitment to a common fatherland and gave the Confederation new powers. Significantly, the Diet could make binding decisions by a two-thirds majority. Cantons were banned from creating leagues amongst themselves, and the Diet gained responsibility for upholding confederal decisions, a new power, as well as for trade, diplomacy and defence. For the first time, a national army was established, even if it was made up of cantonal contingents.

RESTORATION, LIBERALISM AND 'REGENERATION', 1815–1831

Unfortunately the settlement did not end contention about who should control the new order. This was one of the dominating themes of the next fifteen years or so, because the events of the revolutionary era had had lasting effects on progressive public opinion, producing a new patriotic and anti-conservative movement. Such supporters of change developed a new liberal creed and ultimately broke through the forces of resistance in 1829–31, bringing to an end the hopes of those who wanted to restore the Ancien Régime. Such a counter-revolutionary restoration had seemed quite possible in 1814–15, since, profiting from the chaos of the times, the patricians had been able to rebuild much of their old control. Indeed, Fribourg simply reappointed the seventy-five members of the Grand Council still surviving from 1789. The old elite also regained control of mercenary contracts. Their stance was underwritten by the new ideology advocated by Haller in his 1816 *Restauration der Staatswissenschaften*, which claimed that legitimacy lay only in historic privilege and communal liberties. Despite the share they had had in devising the new order, the Great Powers did not refrain from intervening in Swiss politics, believing that neutrality allowed this. Switzerland was forced first to express an ambiguous adhesion to the Holy Alliance in 1817, and then, six years later, to pass a 'Conclusum' on the Press and Refugees. These measures responded to the Allies' dislike of Swiss tolerance of a free press and political exiles, and led to increased censorship and some expulsions. In practice, however, many cantons usually chose to evade extradition requests.

The new conditions challenged those who had benefited from the Helvetic and Mediation regimes: intellectuals, rural and small-town middle classes and peasants. Reversion to the old forms of privilege for corporate entities, territories and enterprises cost them dearly, and also clashed with their own emerging ideology. Stressing rights, representative government and education, the new liberalism (as it came to be known) found focus in the work of the Vaudois Benjamin Constant, then a member of the French Chamber of Deputies. In his 1816 book, *The Liberty of the Ancients Compared with that of the Moderns*, he argued that Europe should follow English precedents. Although liberalism at first failed to influence the restored regimes, it ensured that the country remained riven by political and intellectual contention well into the nineteenth century.

Conflict was often underwritten by the economic problems of the times. After a brief post-war boom, a major slump followed in 1816–18. This came about partly because of the return of English textile competition, which hit hand workers very badly. But the country also suffered what was to be its last harvest crisis, producing starvation and significant emigration, notably to the unsuccessful colony of Novo Friburgo in Brazil. Printers in Aarau responded by setting up their own sickness and invalidity scheme. While some entrepreneurs, such as the founders of the first chemical plant in Utikon, thrived, governments seemed helpless. Conditions were exacerbated because the Restoration regimes had brought back guilds, internal customs and tolls. Some 400 toll stations forced goods to be unloaded from packhorses, checked and reloaded, which was an immense disincentive to trade. Cantons also refused to grant rights of free settlement to Swiss from other cantons. Those who suffered from this protested, as in a tax strike in Schaffhausen in 1820.

The European revolutions of 1821 further encouraged the emergence of a new crop of voluntary bodies, which eventually provided the foundations for a liberal and national movement. These included student associations, like the Zofingen association of 1819, the historically focused Sempacher Verein of 1821, and the Sharpshooters of 1824. The revived Helvetic Society also played an increasingly political role. Historical thinking played a continuing part in political movements, as demonstrated by the Lion of Lucerne monument celebrating the massacre of the Swiss Guards in the Tuileries in 1792. National feeling was also strengthened by the new Confederation's main achievement, the development of the army with new regulations and, from 1818, a training school in Thun, financed by a levy on customs revenues. In the 1820s the army, under Guilliaume-Henri Dufour – a soldier and engineer who had served in the armies of Napoleon before helping to set up the War College – began producing its pioneering maps of Switzerland, seen as one of the few Swiss projects prior to 1848.

Liberalism was also both cause and effect of politically committed newspapers such as the *Aarauer Zeitung* and the revived *Neue Zürcher Zeitung* in 1821, and the *Appenzeller Zeitung* seven years later. In the West, Philhellenism, encouraged by the Greek uprising against the Turks, had an important impact on Swiss national feeling as well. The establishment's hold on Swiss politics was also weakened by the religious *Reveil* or 'Awakening' that began to challenge the hold of established Protestant Churches, notably in Geneva and Vaud, through renewed stress on the Bible, personal piety and systematic observance. At the same time the Catholic Church also felt the impact of Illuminism and mysticism, as well as of the recall of the Jesuits and the reorganization both of its bishoprics and its links with the state.

Opposition to the post-war regime increased as the economy grew strongly in the late 1820s. The population rose, reaching 2.1 million by 1830. An increasing number of peasants became landowners growing cereals, as the midlands became the driving force in Swiss agriculture. Even so, the country could not feed itself, and needed to export manufactures to Eastern Europe to generate the monies needed to buy food. This ensured that Switzerland remained committed to free trade, though in 1822 it was only the mountain cantons that prevented retaliation against French protectionism. As mechanization progressed, Switzerland came to account for 23 per cent of all mechanized cotton textile production, and exported textile products globally. For many of those involved in this growth, the restrictions and humiliations of the Restoration regime became increasingly hard to bear. Indeed opposition to mechanized weaving was to lead to the destruction of a much-resented pioneering factory in Uster in 1832, something encouraged by the growing movement for political change at the time.

Growing dissatisfaction became visible in an intensification of liberal activism, seen in the planting of liberty trees in the Bernese Jura and Lower Valais. Constitutional changes in Schaffhausen and Lucerne strengthened parliaments and gave more weight to the rural population, while Geneva also made timid alterations in procedure after a series of petitions. Even where similar liberal petitions in Vaud and Valais were rejected, pressure was clearly becoming harder to resist. In 1828 Glarus abolished censorship, reflecting the rise of a market for a liberal press. The Diet followed suit in 1829 by formally revoking the Conclusum. That same year, more evidence of growing liberal ferment came with unrest in Aargau over the excessive length of some official tenures, and in Basle and Zurich, where rural craftsmen protested against economic restraints. There were also violent disturbances in the Inner Rhoden of Appenzell that forced the Diet to intervene, leading to a constitutional reform that limited the power of the old families, which had been manoeuvring to go back to the Ancien Régime. In Vaud, further large-scale petitioning for reform panicked the government into a pre-emptive constitutional reform, only to find that its limited terms actually fuelled popular annoyance.

By then, events in the Ticino had led to the first real constitutional breakthrough. In May 1829, personal rivalries in the elite led former Landammann Maggi to propose reforms to enfranchise the outlying areas. Although rejected out of hand by local dictator Gian Battista Quadri, the idea gathered great support, especially when publicized by a young teacher and intellectual, Stefano Franscini, in his January 1830 pamphlet *Della Riforma della Costituzione Ticinese*. This generated sufficient pressure to force the elite to disown Quadri and pass a reform package in late June, a decision conformed by referendum on 4 July, well ahead of the July Days in Paris, and still known as 'the first love of the Ticinese people'.

Thus, thunder can be said to have been in the air that July, and the news from Paris – from which Swiss mercenaries were rapidly withdrawn – accelerated an ongoing process across the country of petitioning and protest. Although the Vorort on 22 September counselled calm and resistance to change, it was already too late. By then, the delaying tactics used against calls for reform in Aargau had already triggered an electoral strike and the threat of a popular march on Aarau. In October, both Thurgau and Zurich saw massive pressure for change, encouraged by pamphleteers such as Pastor Thomas Bornhauser and German exile Ludwig Snell, who attracted thousands to popular meetings. These forced the calling of constituent assemblies, which led to new constitutions. In Aargau, Fribourg, Lucerne and Vaud, popular marches on the cantonal capital brought similar changes. Faced with popular mobilization, the Diet changed its mind and, on 27 December, recognized the sovereign right of the cantons to change their constitutions; cantonal governments then gave way in Basle, Berne, Lucerne, Schaffhausen, Solothurn and St Gallen. Even cantons like Geneva and Neuchâtel, which were not directly affected by the movement, thought it wise to make adjustments. Only the cantons of Urschweiz, along with Grisons and Valais, held out against the trend, which saw a majority of cantons undergoing a set of liberalizing constitutional changes which, following Snell, historians now call the Regeneration.

The Regeneration was a clear victory for peasants and the middle classes of smaller towns, who had long suffered discrimination at the hands of cantonal capitals. It brought them new social, political and individual rights. To begin with, it did away with feudal privileges and the economic restraints reintroduced in 1815. Interestingly, city walls also started to be pulled down around this time, as capitals opened up to their surrounding countryside. Regeneration also reformed institutions, especially by giving more power to legislatures and making them more representative. In Zurich, for example, the countryside got two-thirds of the seats in the reformed body. The reforms also increased the separation of powers, limited office-holding terms and created collegial governments. Not only were most of the constitutions approved by popular vote, something which became *de rigueur*, but they also introduced new direct-democratic rights, such as the popular veto or the right to challenge new legislation, established in St Gallen and Basle Country. Even where there were no new constitutions, many cantons carried out partial revisions. Lastly the Regeneration ended censorship and greatly boosted both the press and education. These changes wrote finis to any remaining hopes of returning to the Ancien Régime, thereby creating a new kind of politics.

THE FAILURES OF LIBERALISM AND NATIONALISM

Like the 1815 settlement before it, the victory of liberalism around 1830 did not end contention. Indeed, it often intensified it, partly because even though cantonal constitutions had been modernized, it proved impossible either to take such modernization further or to transfer the Regeneration to the national level. Many liberals were satisfied with the new status quo and did not want to see social change or the creation of a more unified Confederation, which might sap their newly found self-determination. It was also partly because not all cantons were willing to redress the old territorial imbalances in the way implied by the Regeneration. Thus in the early 1830s in Basle, the rural population, led by the young lawyer Stefan Gutzwiller, felt it had to push both for fair representation in the Grand Council of the regenerated canton and for free access to the city markets. When their New Year's Day demands were not immediately accepted, the rurals set up a Provisional Governing Assembly of their own in Liestal, which was suppressed by the cantonal military. In response, the rurals refused to accept the revised Constitution – which offered only parity in representation – and continued their agitation. The city forces again attacked Liestal in August 1831, only to be driven off ignominiously, leaving thirteen dead behind them. The Diet then intervened with 4,000 troops to keep the two sides apart, thereby allowing the creation of a new Basle Country half-canton. The city refused to give up, and attempted a night attack on 6–7 April 1832, only to be defeated again at Gelterkinden. Ultimately, the Diet tacitly recognized separation, and withdrew its troops in the autumn of 1832. But the city remained intransigent, making a final military attempt to retain all its territories and privileges, only to be driven off with the loss of sixty-five militiamen at Pratteln and Liestal in early August 1833. All sides thereafter accepted the inevitability of having two half-cantons, and the city began revising its constitution accordingly.

Territorial discrimination had been even more institutionalized in Schwyz, with the so-called Outer Districts being allowed only a third of seats in the Grand Council. Encouraged by the example of Basle, the latter established their own Landsgemeinde and created their own political entity, which was accepted as a half-canton by the Diet. When forces from the inner territories of Schwyz occupied Küssnacht in July 1833, the Diet intervened and sent 8,000 men to stop them. This, and a general dislike of splitting the canton, led the old territories to make concessions. Since the conservatives under Alois Ab Yberg, the canton's largest landowner, remained in power,

5.3 The Uster Fire of November 1832. The building seen
burning down here was a mechanized weaving factory owned
by Corrodi and Pfister in Oberuster in canton Zurich, the first of
its kind there. There fire was started by local opponents of the
mechanization of weaving, showing the social pressures
underlying the Regeneration. Popular anger also owed
something to the prevailing general reformist surge. The fire and
the following proscription failed to prevent mechanized
weaving from developing in the area which, by 1850, had the
highest density of factories in Switzerland.

conflict continued throughout the 1830s. These two attempts at
resisting change led seven of the reformed cantons to form a defensive alliance, the so-called *Siebnerkoncordat*, in May 1832. In
response, on 16 November, five conservative cantons formed their
own *Sarnerbund* in opposition, since they felt half-cantons were
unconstitutional and probably impious as well. But after the failure
of the conservative cause in Basle and Schwyz, the Diet was able to
dissolve the special alliances. Nonetheless, hostility between the
liberal and conservative camps persisted.

5.4 Stephan Gutzwiller chairing the Basle Country Constituent Assembly in 1831. The assembly met outdoors amid an enthusiastic crowd because the new half-canton had no premises. A thirty-year-old lawyer from Therwil, Gutzwiller was one of the dominant figures in the Regeneration in Basle, his support for equal rights helping to precipitate the rural segment's secession. A reforming leader into the 1840s, he later became a leader of the conservative resistance to the democratic surge of the 1860s as supporters of reform split into radicals and moderates.

Moreover, at the same time a new division was emerging amongst supporters of the Regeneration as to whether its changes were the beginning or the end of the process of reform. Many of the new liberal regimes preferred to sit on their laurels, believing that ending absolutism was enough. They felt that any further change should be evolutionary, and should not involve the state intervening in the economy or providing social aid. Many among the liberals saw further democratization as a threat. Others sought further political progress through direct democracy and universal male suffrage, economic action to improve living standards and more secular education. Known as 'advanced liberals' or *Freisinnige* or free thinkers, or more commonly as Radicals, their movement took on a limited organizational form thanks to the creation of the quasi-military Schützenzenverein in 1831, a secession from the Helvetic Society, and the 1835 National Association. Their educational ideas brought them into particular conflict with Catholic cantons, where the Church controlled schools and where conservatives quickly set up defensive organizations of their own to defend Catholic interests.

These developing conflicts fed into emerging contention over the nature of the new Confederation. National feeling had been much encouraged by the Regeneration, and early on, the Thurgau delegation to the Diet demanded a stronger government and judiciary. In July 1832 the idea was referred to a committee under Pellegrino Rossi, an exiled Italian academic. Its report suggested a modest step forward by creating a government with more resources and enhanced powers, while leaving cantonal sovereignty unchanged. This proved too extreme for conservatives, and even for some regenerated liberal governments like Vaud, but it was also too timid for radicals. Only nine cantons endorsed the proposals, and by October 1833, they were effectively dead. Nonetheless, the desire for a stronger national government and more muscular resistance to foreign intervention was far from dying.

Concern over foreign intervention in Swiss politics reflected the fact that despite army reforms and the appointment of Guillaume-Henri Dufour as Chief of Staff, Switzerland was subject to renewed external pressure. For example, Mazzini's abortive radical invasion of Savoy in February 1834 prompted a blockade of Ticino. Later in the 1830s, fear of a French invasion arose when the Swiss refused to expel Louis-Napoleon, then an officer in the Thurgau militia, as demanded by the Orleanist monarchy. Foreign governments, spurred by the conservative forces gathered around the Austrian Chancellor Metternich, also called for tighter censorship and the expulsion of refugees from conservative repression. Resentment of such pressures helps to explain the formation of the Swiss Officers' Society in 1833, and provided the impetus for further military reform. National feeling was also underwritten by the creation of national gymnastic and singing associations in 1832 and 1843. It was symptomatic that in 1841, Alberik Zwyssig from Uri wrote the 'Swiss hymn', which was eventually to replace Wyss's composition as a national anthem. Such developments did not create an easy road to building a new nation and state, however. New factors were required to make good the failures of the liberalism and patriotism of the 1830s.

RELIGION, RADICALISM AND CIVIL WAR

In fact, from the 1830s, all these conflicts, like those over political reform, became increasingly entwined with religious questions. Rather than seeking a return to the Ancien Régime, conservatism became increasingly concerned with defending the rights of reviving Catholicism in face of the increasing strength of radicalism and nationalism. Since each side was willing to use violence to advance its cause, Catholic resistance first helped to tip the country into civil war, while its defeat in 1847 opened the way to the creation of Switzerland as a real federal state, rather than a loose Confederation.

The religious dimension first really came to the fore in 1834 when six regenerated cantons – ironically including Catholic cantons led by liberals – agreed to the Articles of Baden, which, in a search for an autonomous Swiss Catholic Church, laid down new rules on seminaries, marriages and feast days. Although the provisions were similar to those in many other Catholic countries, they were bitterly resisted in Switzerland because they conflicted with the increasingly fervent and political nature of conservative Swiss Catholicism and its proselytizing clergy. A symbol of this was Theodor Ab Yberg's 1836 recall of the Jesuits and the papal nunciature to Schwyz.

Three years later, an even more dramatic expression of religious concern broke out in Protestant Zurich when peasants marched on the capital in the belief that 'religion was in danger'. They were reacting to the liberal government's appointment to a chair of theology of David Strauss, a German theologian who was known to doubt the divinity of Christ. The march, during which fourteen people died, brought about the downfall of the government, which was replaced by a resolutely anti-radical government under Johann Caspar Bluntschli. The Strauss affair also reinforced Catholic concerns about the direction the country was taking. Catholic activists were led by Joseph Leu of Ebersoll in Lucerne, a fervent and charismatic

Catholic layman who pushed for the rejection of the Baden Articles and also for the recall of the Jesuits. He founded a Catholic Brotherhood to defend the Church's control of education, and helped to influence a new cantonal Constitution of 1841 in Lucerne that banned Protestantism. Catholic conservatives also moved against radical reforms in Valais and Ticino. A few in Lucerne, encouraged by the publications of Joseph Eutych Kopp, even began to doubt the legitimacy of Tell because he had been hostile to Austria, from where they hoped support would now come. However, generally speaking, both sides continued to paint themselves as his successors.

The looming confrontation was given an additional edge by the economic downturn of the 1840s, exacerbated in Switzerland by French protectionism and the creation of the German Customs Union (Zollverein). By 1843, there were 750,000 spindles in 150 firms, and mechanization was extending into ribbons, watches and cheese. Textile manufacture also stimulated development in chemicals and machine tools. These industries were concentrated in Schaffhausen and Zurich, while textiles dominated in the triangle between Aargau, Appenzell and Glarus. Agricultural improvement and the creation of technical schools also supported more intense manufactures. A quarter of the population came to be employed in industry, and Swiss achievements were much admired by John Bowring in his 1838 *Report to Parliament*. As prosperity increased, savings banks and assurance firms also multiplied. The 1840s downturn hit exports of cotton fabric very badly. The decline caused pauperism and other social problems, which in turn stimulated the first cooperatives and quasi-trade unions, such as the 1838 Grütlianer educational body, and it also reinforced radical ideas of interventionism and even early socialist ideas. The downturn also encouraged business to think of creating its own Zollverein and a government that could establish a proper railway policy. In 1847, only one line existed from Zurich to Baden (the so-called Spanisch-Brötli Bahn, or Spanish Rolls Railway), which whisked soft fresh bread from Baden bakers to Zurich customers.

Although economic tensions were important, it was religious issues that drove political contention and the final establishment of national unity. The trigger for the critical events of 1847–8 was provided by Augustin Keller, a liberal Catholic from Aargau who believed that a Catholic Church subject to the Vatican could not be free. He and the cantonal government rewrote the cantonal constitution in 1841 in a way that exacerbated the minority position of the Catholics in the Freiamt and elsewhere. They responded with a peasant march on Aarau, the capital, which the cantonal government forcibly blocked at Villmergen. In retaliation, the government ordered the closure of the eight convents in the canton, which they suspected of having fomented revolt, even though these enjoyed specific guarantees in the 1815 Charter. Understandably, the monks' expulsion and the state's seizure of their property led to protests. Although the Diet helped get four nunneries restored, some Catholic leaders started talking about leaving the Confederation. In fact, the Catholic leadership held talks in September 1843 about organizing themselves militarily and disassociating themselves from cantons like Aargau that broke the Charter. Extremists like Leu also used the moment to push through the recall of the Jesuits to Lucerne.

Such Catholic actions served as a red rag to the radical bull, especially when, after a civil struggle, the Valais conservatives imposed a new constitution that excluded French-speakers from power and banned Protestantism. A major radical mobilization followed, allowing new regimes to come to power in many cantons. In 1845 Henri Druey, the firebrand head of the National Association, and the radicals overthrew the liberal Vaudois regime because it was too weak on the Jesuit question. In Ticino Radicals saw off a conservative onslaught and introduced a new constitution restricting the rights of the Church. And in Zurich and Berne, conservative regimes were also voted out and more radical ones installed, with a new constitution in the latter in July 1846. Geneva also came under pressure from the 3 March movement of James Fazy, which used the Jesuit question as a lever. By the time the Aargau government demanded that the Diet ban the Jesuits, the whole country was divided.

The radicals also tried to overthrow the conservative regime in Lucerne from within, but failed. As a result, they and their allies resorted to violence: 1,000 volunteers or *Freischaren* from Aargau, Basle Country and Solothurn marched on Lucerne. Failing to attract

5.5 The second Freischarenzug (or Free Corps raid) defeated in
Lucerne, 31 March 1845: 3,500 anti-clerical free-corps activists
under Ulrich Ochsenbein of Berne set out from Zofingen and
Huttwil and, despite a check at Emmenbrücke, reached the
walls of Lucerne. But they failed to push on and take the town,
allowing local forces to pick them off with heavy losses. The
attack envenomed relations between radicals and conservatives,
helping to encourage armed Catholic resistance to change.

much support, they retreated, even though they had defeated a
federal force sent to stop them. A second onslaught by 3,500 volunteers under Ulrich Ochsenbein of Berne in late March 1845 was even
more unsuccessful, being outmanoeuvred and crushed with the loss
of 100 dead and 1,800 prisoners. The resort to violence proved
counter-productive, since the Ultramontanes, or enthusiasts for
papal power, came to power in Lucerne elections so that tensions
only increased.

Four months later a former *Freischaren* trooper murdered Leu, possibly at Radical instigation. This caused panic in Catholic ranks. Not merely did Gallus Baumgartner of St Gallen found a Catholic Association, ostensibly to defend the 1815 Charter, but in December, seven cantons – Fribourg, Lucerne, Schwyz, Unterwalden, Uri, Valais and Zug – signed a security pact establishing a war council and making contacts with friendly Great Powers. Implicitly, they were also signing up to Siegwart-Müller's ideas of manufacturing a new built-in majority for (enlarged) Catholic cantons. The existence of this so-called Sonderbund (or special alliance) was revealed during ratification debates in Fribourg the following June.

Shortly after it became public, ten cantons called for the dissolution of the Sonderbund. This was short of the necessary cantonal majority in the Diet, but after Fazy overthrew the liberal regime in Geneva in May 1847, and St Gallen, 'the canton of destiny', unexpectedly voted in a Radical legislature, the majority at the Diet was achieved. When the Diet met again on 5 July, Ochsenbein, the former leader of the *Freischaren* then chairing the Diet, made it clear the Radicals were intent on a stronger Swiss state and firmer resistance to the Great Powers. On 20 July, the Diet formally called for the disbanding of the Sonderbund and the expulsion of the Jesuits, and set up a committee to oversee the problem. It also decided to revise the Charter.

Rather than accept such changes, the Sonderbund began organizing for war, appointing the reluctant Johann-Ulrich von Salis-Soglio, a Grisons Protestant, as its commander. Unfortunately for them, arms supplied by France and the Italian states were intercepted, while Austria held back its support, whereas Britain supported the Diet. Several attempts at peace negotiations failed, and on 24 October 1847, the Diet took the decision to dissolve the Sonderbund by force, and ordered the mobilization of 50,000 men under Dufour. In fact 100,000 rallied to the flag, despite some Catholic mutinies. Dufour kept close control of strategy, whereas the Sonderbund, with less than half the troops, allowed its War Council to overrule Salis-Soglio by going on the offensive both in the Freiamt, where they were rapidly defeated on 12 November, and on the Gotthard, where initial gains were not followed up, partly because the Catholic troops did not like fighting outside their own cantons.

Dufour ignored these distractions and struck first at Fribourg, which capitulated after a few skirmishes on 14 November. He then moved on Zug, which fell on 21 November. This allowed him to concentrate on Lucerne, the heart of the Sonderbund. Although the latter's forces defeated Dufour's army at Gislikon and Meierskappell, they were eventually broken by his artillery, allowing Lucerne to be invested. With this, the Sonderbund collapsed. As in Fribourg, new radical governments were installed in Zug, Lucerne and Valais. In all the hostilities, some 130 were killed and 300 wounded. Significantly, the fighting ended before the Great Powers managed to intervene or 'mediate'. Only in January 1848 did they demand that the Diet respect the Charter, but British influence and the outbreak of revolution in Paris, Vienna and Berlin that spring blocked any further action. Taking advantage of the disruptions elsewhere, the republicans in Neuchâtel were thus able to eject their Prussian rulers in early March 1848.

The Diet made the Sonderbund cantons pay the 20 million francs the war had cost, and pressed on with constitutional revisions, which it had suspended during the civil war. Refusing merely to revise the Charter, the Diet went back to the Rossi draft to facilitate a fresh start. Its committee, with Druey and Johann Konrad Kern, the dominant politician in Thurgau, drafting the French and German texts, made rapid progress and produced a text in April. This was amended by the Diet over the next few weeks and accepted on 27 June, with only three and a half cantons dissenting. What the Diet produced, essentially as a result of military victory, was a real constitution that set up a federal state, even though it used the term Confederation. Central to the new constitution was the creation of an effective national government, although the bicameral legislature and the requirement for a double majority on important votes sought to reconcile national aspirations with cantonal sovereignty and the unease of the Catholic cantons.

Most cantons approved the new text by referendum, and by late September, fifteen and a half cantons had ratified it, against six and a half that rejected: in votes, the tally was 146,000 votes to 54,300. This margin was narrower than it appears, given that abstentions were again sometimes counted as votes in favour. The Diet proceeded to elect the first government, and dissolved itself. The new

constitution was a clear victory for Radical views and the culmina-
tion of a real revolution. Even so, while Switzerland was perhaps the
only place in Europe where 1848 did lead to the creation of a
successful radical-democratic state, the Swiss were still left facing
many challenging problems, including how to deal with the
Catholic question and the new form of contention it involved.

6

Forging the new nation,
1848–1914

Immediately after 1848, the new Switzerland seemed to pose a great threat to Metternich and other conservative statesmen. They were alarmed by Switzerland's propensity to offer asylum, and sometimes support, to opponents of monarchy, and saw it as 'a revolutionary turntable' intimately linked to events elsewhere in Europe. Reality was somewhat different because, although the Radicals dominated the new Swiss state, they were less extreme and proceeded more cautiously than the continental powers expected in starting to forge a new, democratic and restrained nation. Their moderation was aided by the willingness of the internal opposition to use the newly created democratic processes, which came to define Switzerland. In the 1860s, however, a new democratic dynamic within the cantons ultimately led to a revised and more centralized constitution. This allowed the country to cope with the social and religious difficulties that emerged as it encountered economic depression. In fact, both state and the party system in Switzerland were able to develop considerably before, around the end of the century, a new conservative turn took place which helped both to consolidate and to redirect the developing national identity that had emerged in parallel with 1848's state-building. The leaders of the new state were able to forge a new nation based on political will and the key institutions of direct democracy, federalism and neutrality.

ESTABLISHING THE NEW STATE

Though the Sonderbund War led to the creation of a state, the constitution really provided only its outline. It remained to fill this out

6.1 The first Swiss Federal Council, elected on 16 November 1848. One of many such presentations, this shows: top: Wilhelm Matthias Naeff (St Gallen); middle (from left to right) Ulrich Ochsenbein (Berne); Josef Furrer (Zurich); Henri Druey (Vaud); and bottom: Martin Josef Munzinger (Solothurn); Stefano Franscini (Ticino); and Friedrich Frey-Herosé (Aargau). The relatively modest positioning of Furrer, the first President, emphasizes the collegial nature of the government.

domestically with implementing legislation and to ensure that doubters were kept on board. Externally, Switzerland's new situation meant standing up to the doubting neighbouring powers and devising a more positive neutral role. Immediately after 1847, these tasks fell to the

Radicals – the party which had most strongly opposed the Sonderbund and which monopolized the new government and Parliament. This enabled them to activate the new constitution and establish a limited but functioning state. Radical dominance began when the outgoing Diet appointed seven Radicals to make up the new government, led by Jonas Furrer, the leader of anti-liberal forces in Zurich and one of the architects of the new constitution. Thanks to a certain amount of gerrymandering, the movement also held 95 of the 111 seats in the National Council and 38 of the 44 seats in the *Ständerat*. The remaining seats were held by conservative Catholics, led by Philip Segesser of Lucerne, a journalist and cantonal administrator who became one of the dominant figures of the Swiss Catholic world.

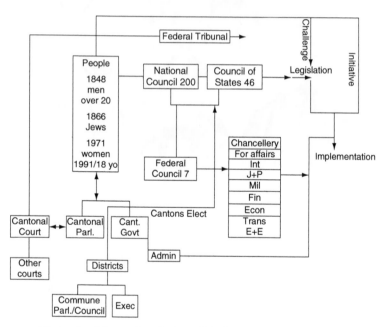

Figure 6.1 The modern Swiss political process

Yet the Radicals were actually more of a family, or a movement like the US 'Tea Party', than an integrated force. United by their support of the new unified state, liberal institutions and a free economy, they were divided by personalities, region and ideological leanings. On the right were free traders led by Alfred Escher of

Zurich, in the centre French-speaking federalists and moderates like Ochsenbein, who lost his place on the Federal Council to fellow Bernese Jakob Stämpfli in 1854. The latter represented the left wing of the movement, along with the *Neue Zürcher Zeitung* and politicians like Druey, who wished both to develop a state railway system and to support liberation movements in other countries. For Druey, there could be no neutrality in the struggle between princes and peoples. However, Escher was able to build up a following of nearly fifty MPs, often nicknamed the *Bundesbarone* ('Federal Barons') because of their influence, who blunted the left's influence. Given that most of the new MPs came either from the entrepreneurial classes or from the ranks of cantonal magistrates, and often held their seats for long periods, the Federal parliament ultimately imposed cautious rather than extreme governance on the country.

Because of such growing restraint, no real purge of Sonderbund supporters took place. Rather, by taking measures against the Jesuits and a few Sonderbund leaders, the new government gave the impression that the war had been a plot by outsiders in which the Catholic population at large was not involved. Given this attempt at conciliation, Catholic opposition to the new order was rarely violent, save in Fribourg and Ticino, where the federal government quashed elections and helped the Radicals hold on to power. Catholics either pragmatically took part in the new order or retreated into a politically inert ghetto, defending their position by the establishment of bodies like the Piusverein of 1857. They showed little desire to undo the verdict of 1847–8 or to plot with foreign powers against the new regime. Their leaders also faced pressure to use 'national' rhetoric, even though the *Urschweiz* cantons stayed out of celebrations such as the 500th anniversary of Zurich's entry into the Confederation in 1857. Nevertheless, conservatives of all kinds had to accept the modernization of the cantons, notably in the Grisons, where the principle of communal autonomy expressed through leagues was suppressed, because it was felt too illiberal and old-fashioned for the new government. Similarly, in Schwyz and Zug the Landsgemeinden were abolished.

The new government proceeded carefully in dealing with the frequent cantonal refusals to follow new rules, sending in commissioners and threatening to withdraw subsidies. Moreover, although it devoted much energy to building the new state's institutions, it held back from developing an educational and cultural policy, which could have forced Catholic conservatives into outright opposition. In any case, conservative forces came back into power in the early 1850s, notably in Berne and Fribourg. In the latter canton, armed risings against the carpetbagger regime paved the way for its electoral defeat in December 1856. By then the conservatives had also strengthened their position in Geneva, Ticino and Valais. All this made it harder, as well as unwise, for the new government to resort to extreme policies.

Hence, as part of a policy of limited centralization, the new government left the cantons with considerable revenues, although it was now able to draw on customs levies to fund its activities. Importantly, the new state issued its own currency. By 1852 the 65 million or so coins then circulating, issued by up to eighty authorities, had been withdrawn and replaced by a new franc, of equivalent value to the French franc and not to the South German guilder, as some had wanted. The government also took over border security, gunpowder, and posts and telegraphs, together with weights and measures. The Constitution also allowed for the creation of a national university, but linguistic fears and cantonal rivalries blocked any progress: only a polytechnic was created in Zurich. An even more important function was national defence. In May 1850, a new law set up a three-tier militia, based on the universal male obligation to serve in cantonal contingents. The army was the Federation's major expense.

Conversely, railway development, after a bitter debate that focused on what the role of the state should be, was very largely left to private interests. This reflected both the cantons' desire not to increase central authority, and the power of Escher and his faction, which felt that a state railway, as envisioned by Stämpfli and Druey, would be socialistic and un-republican. However, the policy slowed economic development and led to financial difficulties, despite the establishment in 1856 of the Credit Suisse bank in Zurich, which was set up to counter the arrival there of German banks and to finance the building of new lines. The bank eventually made Zurich, rather than Basle, the richest city in Switzerland. Rivalry between the two cities was reflected in a major conflict between Escher's North-eastern Railway and the Basle-based Central Railway.

Nonetheless, the new state successfully revived economic growth by eliminating tolls and other barriers to trade, as well as bringing in free establishment for business enterprises so as to create a real internal market for goods and labour. It also signed Switzerland's first free trade treaties, including with Britain, an important step since the domestic market remained small. The government encouraged industrialization, including experiments in water power and in the food sector, where the first condensed milk factory opened at Cham in Zug in 1866, a year before the predecessor of the Nestlé corporation was founded. Industry proved able to absorb both natural population growth and peasants left behind as agriculture was restructured around dairying, livestock and wine, all of which were less labour intensive than cereals. As a result, emigration did not greatly increase, although urbanization did. These economic changes had significant social implications, with the first trade unions emerging in the late 1850s. The foundation of the Alpine Club in 1857 also demonstrated the increasing importance of mountaineering and tourism.

External events also imposed further caution on the new government, because the great powers still saw Switzerland as a revolutionary state, which was understandable, given the way many Swiss sympathized with various national liberation movements. Indeed, the country provided a base for German revolutionaries' raids on the Grand Duchy of Baden, and for Ticinese involvement in the Italian war of 1849. In 1852 the expulsion of Capuchins from the canton led to a very damaging blockade and the expulsion of 6,000 Ticinese who were working in Lombardy. Nonetheless, although the country accepted some 9,000 foreign refugees, the government, encouraged by Escher's faction, sought to maintain a policy of neutrality.

This proved most difficult to sustain in 1856, when republican forces ejected a group of pro-Prussian royalists who had seized the citadel in Neuchâtel city in an attempt to return the principality to full Prussian rule. Prussia mobilized 160,000 men on the Rhine and threatened to overrun Switzerland in response. But the Swiss government refused to yield, even though its forces were outnumbered more than five to one. Its resistance bought time for Napoleon III to negotiate a settlement in which the King of Prussia gave up his claims, allowing Neuchâtel to become a full Swiss canton. At the same time, the government signed a treaty of friendship with the United Kingdom, which provided support for Swiss independence and neutrality.

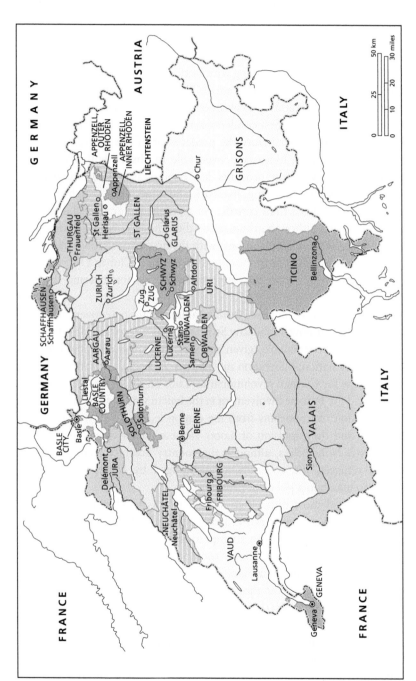

Map 6.1 The modern 26-canton Switzerland

Neutrality came into play again in 1859–60, when the government prevented radical elements from invading Savoy to take advantage of France's preoccupation with its war with Austria over Italian independence. The government also refused Napoleon III's subsequent offer to sell Chablais and Faucigny to Switzerland. The government feared both the cost and the effects on the religious balance of incorporating large numbers of Catholics. Likewise, the government refused to accept Stämpfli's idea of invading Savoy to stop it from falling into French hands. However, it did secure the creation of customs-free zones round Geneva and a satisfactory division of the disputed Valley of Dappes in the Jura. To underline Swiss neutrality, the last remaining mercenary regiments, in Italy, were formally disbanded, leaving only the Vatican Guard.

Swiss caution in the 1850s paved the way for the country to adopt a new role as Helvetia Mediatrix in the 1860s. An important step was taking over control of the infant Red Cross, in which Dufour played a large part along with Henri Dunant. The offer of mediation became a tool of Swiss foreign policy, which encouraged other powers to take Swiss neutrality more seriously. This they did after the Franco-Prussian War of 1870–1, when the Swiss provided good offices for some German states and sent welfare relief to besieged Strasbourg. More significantly, Swiss forces were responsible for disarming and interning the 87,000 men of Bourbaki's French Army of the East after its harrowing retreat through the Jura hills into Switzerland. Increasingly the country came to be seen as an unthreatening haven that also provided services in the interest of Europe, such mediating between Great Britain and the United States during the 1872 negotiations over the damage caused by the Confederate privateer *Alabama*, which had been illegally fitted out in Birkenhead. By this time foreign fears about the threat from Switzerland had largely dissipated, which further strengthened the position of the new state.

DEMOCRATIZATION AND CONSTITUTIONAL REFORM

This was fortunate, because the 1860s also saw a new surge of popular activism at home, leading to democratization and constitutional reform first at cantonal level and then nationally, with constitutional revision leading to the transformation of Switzerland into a developed federation. Such developments might have caused international alarm, especially as they involved new friction with the Catholic authorities and community, but by then the country had proved it was no threat to Europe. However, from the 1860s the government's cautious strategy faced domestic challenges, because it was at odds with the more militant democratic aspirations unleashed in the 1840s. Many supporters of change objected to the arrogant rule of the Radical *Bundesbarone* and started campaigning against them, demanding more participation and real control of cantonal governments and parliaments. They also resented the continuing economic disadvantages suffered by outside districts, which were responsible for spurring emigration in the 1850s. These forces turned to direct democracy as their weapon, building on a programme launched in the 1850s by a Zurich journalist and enthusiast for cooperatives, J. J. Treichler. Zurich introduced the legislative initiative, and Neuchâtel the financial referendum, which required a popular vote before any large capital expenditure. Under democratic pressure, Schwyz also did away with the remaining discrimination against the external districts.

The democratic movement really boiled over in the 1860s, starting with opposition to Berne's railway policy and to Fazy's autocratic rule in Geneva. However, the real pathfinder was the new half-canton of Basle Country. There, a Liestal teacher called Christoph Rolle led a fierce campaign for a constituent assembly to draft a new democratic constitution, something which, after some complications, was achieved. The new cantonal constitution subjected all legislation to an obligatory popular challenge, and allowed 1,500 citizens to propose new legislation. Direct election (and recall) of executives and judiciary was also introduced. From Basle, the movement spread to Aargau, Berne, Lucerne, Solothurn and most significantly to Escher's fief in Zurich, where a Winterthur-based movement to bolster parliamentary governance by direct democracy got under way. After a series of mass meetings, revision was agreed in December 1867, and a new constitution came into effect in 1869. It introduced legislative and constitutional initiatives, obligatory referenda on all major expenditures, a reduction of Grand Council powers and the direct election of the government. A cantonal bank and progressive taxation were also established. Politically this meant the end of Escher's influence, not just in Zurich but also in the country at large.

The democratic trend continued to spread beyond Zurich, and progressive constitutional reforms were pushed through in several more cantons. Such local reforms enabled the cantons to develop a new dynamism that helped to balance the overall trend towards centralization in the later nineteenth century. Moreover, the first calls for political rights for women were heard, leading to the establishment of an International Women's Movement in Geneva. The social pressures behind the movement also spurred important social legislation during the 1860s, with a Seventy-Two Hours Act and a Factory Act in Glarus forced through by the Landsgemeinde, and similar legislation in other cantons. Cantonal banks were also widely established, crafts given freedom from guild regulation, bankruptcy laws changed and indirect taxes whittled away, moves which helped hard-pressed craftsmen, peasants, shopkeepers and minor professionals. In 1864, trade unions were legalized nationally, followed by strikes the next year.

Although no single new democratic party emerged, the process did have an impact at the federal level. The issue of popular rights gained resonance through Protestant and liberal responses to the 1864 papal 'Syllabus of Errors', which condemned most modern ideas out of hand. In response, the Bernese administration introduced new restrictions on Catholic organization in the Jura district. Catholic feelings were also aroused by an 1864 trade treaty with France that gave French Jews more rights than those enjoyed by Swiss Jews. A constitutional amendment was needed to remedy the discrimination and give all Swiss citizens full rights of establishment anywhere in the country, though this offended a latent strain of anti-Semitism in Swiss society. The amendment on free movement was linked to several other suggested constitutional revisions, including on freedom of belief. But only the new equality provision and an endorsement of the metric system were accepted, showing that despite democratization – or because of it – Swiss voters remained doubtful about change.

Popular resistance to new measures became very clear in the early 1870s, after the experiences of war had shown the country's military organization to be ill suited to a long mobilization because of its dependence on cantonal contingents. Led by Emil Welti, an Aargau Radical and from 1867 the party's dominating personality, the Federal Council decided to include army reform – replacing cantonal contingents by central control and provision – in a larger programme of constitutional reform, described as 'one law, one army'. The initiative involved fifty mainly centralizing changes to laws that had been poorly handled in 1848, new policy powers for the centre, including over marriage, and wider political rights. These included the introduction both of a popular legislative challenge by 50,000 voters, plus legislative initiative and repeal. Overall, the constitutional revision offered a pithier document that was less concerned with cantonal rights than its predecessor.

Such changes were too much for many. One moderate federal councillor, Jakob Dubs, who had been the government's leading light before Welti had been elected in 1867, resigned to fight the changes. Another, Jean-Jacques Challet-Vernet, was later voted out in favour of a known supporter of the changes. Radical opponents of revision were able to draw on Catholic opposition, led by Segesser, to changes in marriage and church laws, and in cantonal rights. Traditional liberals were also unhappy about centralization and the effects of legal and military unification. Suisse Romande cantons feared that in a closer federation, French-speakers would be dominated by the German-speaking cantons, marking the emergence of language as a salient political divide for the first time since the expansion of the Confederation after 1799 had brought in non-German-speaking cantons. Over the next hundred years and beyond the language issue was to become increasingly important. In the plebiscite of May 1872, hostile votes in Geneva, Vaud and the Urschweiz were particularly significant in the narrow defeat of the package by 260,000 votes (13 cantons) to 256,000 (9 cantons).

However, Welti and the progressive Radicals in government did not give up, and continued to work for constitutional reform, claiming that 'Revision is dead, long live revision'. They now sought to divide and rule the opposition by responding to French-speaking

6.2 One of several souvenir lithographs celebrating the successful reform of the Federal Constitution in 1874. Flanked by the shields of the cantons it shows Helvetia standing on a plinth detailing the acceptances and rejections. The fact that there were nearly 200,000 of the latter, drawn especially from the German-speaking Inner Swiss cantons, points to the continuing difficulties the new republic was to have with Catholic conservative dissidence. However, the poster surrounds Helvetia with reminders of the main achievements of the new Confederation, including unified law; protection for workers and children; free establishment; federal support for marriage and freedom of thought.

concerns and ignoring those of the Catholics, with whom their relations were declining. As they put it, 'We need the *Welsche*' (as French-speakers were nicknamed in the east of the country). The package was redesigned by slimming down the legal and military changes and restoring some cantonal rights. The legislative initiative was withdrawn, but the number of signatures needed for a challenge was reduced to 30,000. The draft was also more overtly anti-clerical than its predecessors, banning the creation of new bishoprics and the introduction of religious orders. The Radicals' strategy worked, winning over people like Dubs, so that the package was comfortably carried in May 1874 by 340,000 (14½ cantons) to 198,000 (7½). As a result, Switzerland became even more of a more thoroughly federal state, more powerful and legitimate, under a constitution which was to prove surprisingly long-lasting.

The anti-Catholic tone of the new constitution was one aspect of a recrudescence of religious conflict in the early 1870s, a phenomenon known as the *Kulturkampf*. Division had its roots in liberal responses to the growing Catholic ultramontanism visible after the First Vatican Council and the 1871 declaration of papal infallibility. Many Catholics were unhappy about these moves, and many Protestants were absolutely horrified. When, in 1872, Bishop Lachat of Basle ignored advice from his colleagues and not only promulgated the decree, but also excommunicated clerics in the Bernese Jura who opposed it, an explosion of anger ripped through non-Catholic Switzerland. After the majority of Jurassian clergy supported the Bishop, the Bernese authorities intervened harshly, using troops to close churches and arrest clergy, who were often replaced by outside clerics. State support also went to a group of dissenting liberal Catholic clerics who seceded and set up a new Christian Catholic Church, which refused to accept the Vatican Decrees. Pope Pius IX added to the conflict by denouncing the *Kulturkampf* and appointing, without any consultation, the aggressive ultramontane Gaspard Mermillod as Apostolic Vicar of Geneva. The Federal Council responded by expelling both Mermillod and the papal nuncio and then breaking off diplomatic relations with the Vatican. Moreover, even as the democratic movement and the new constitution revived a latent division, other major problems were also beginning to press in on the country.

AN AGE OF DEPRESSION AND STRESS

The divisive relationship between successive Radical governments and the Catholic Church was in fact considerably complicated by an economic downturn that began in 1873 and led to other destabilizing social divisions. Most notably the crisis promoted trade unions and socialism, which became a threat not just to the Radicals but also to Catholics. The latter saw them as a real danger to their beliefs and position, forcing them to draw nearer to the new state. They were helped in this by the fact that they could use the new instruments of direct democracy to block legislation of which they disapproved. As a result they reinforced the country's emerging sense of identity and unity.

In the 1860s, the economy had continued to grow and mechanize, notably in cotton, watches and machine tools. In part, growth fed on the railway boom, even though many lines remained in debt. The upward cycle also helped to produce new financial institutions like Swiss Reinsurance Company in 1863 and the Swiss People's Bank in 1869. At the same time, the tourist industry expanded: Thomas Cook organized his first tour in 1863, the same year as Edward Whymper's dramatic ascent of the Matterhorn. In the following years, winter sports began to take off, encouraged in part by rail travel and Leslie Stephens's 1871 book *The Playground of Europe*.

Agriculture had long seen the slowest growth of all three sectors, and was to prove the weak link after 1873, when a flood of grain and meat from North America and Eastern Europe poured into Western Europe, thanks to railways and refrigerated ships. Small farms could not compete, even when helped by cantonal banks, and many farmers began to leave the land – whether for the cities or for places like Argentina, Australia and especially the United States – leaving mountain areas like Ticino virtually depopulated. The new wave of emigration peaked between 1880 and 1885, and particularly hit the number of speakers of Rhaeto-Romansh, which began to decline despite the growth of medical and sporting tourism to the Grisons. The agricultural labour force fell rapidly, especially in the 1870s and 1880s. By the deepest point of the depression in 1888, there were more people working in manufactures than on farms. Switzerland was one of only six European countries in which farming was not the dominant sector. Overall the agrarian labour force halved between

1850 and 1910, despite the beginnings of a modern food industry with the foundation of Maggi in 1872.

Other sectors suffered from the depression as well. In fact, the 1876 World Fair revealed how far the Swiss watch industry had lagged behind automated American production. While the industry rapidly modernized, this was not the case for textiles, which suffered badly and lost a third of its labour force. Glarus cotton and St Gallen embroideries were particularly hit. Conversely, metallurgy and chemicals (which had developed out of textile dying) did well. Brown Boveri, the largest Swiss engineering firm, dates from 1884, and Sandoz followed two years later. Increasingly, production became factory based, especially in German-speaking Switzerland: the Bally shoe factory in Solothurn is a notable example. Hydroelectric power and other forms of electricity began to spread after 1879, and two years later the first phone lines were installed. Urbanization and commercialization encouraged retail services, with the first big department stores such as Jelmoli coming in the 1880s, often opening new employment prospects for women. Banking modernized, with concentration and a move away from simple local banks to cantonal and even bigger banks with a much wider remit. Economic pressure also encouraged the emergence of Raiffeisen savings banks for small savers after 1880.

The changing structure and fortunes of Swiss industry in this period had both social and political effects. Workers were often restive, and looked for protection. This encouraged new forms of trade unionism, leading to the establishment of the Schweizerischer Gewerkschaftsbund/Union Syndicale Suisse, the umbrella organization in the early 1880s, although it at first accounted for only some 9 per cent of the workforce. Strikes also became more common, notably with Zurich locksmiths in 1886. In the next decade, works committees emerged, along with the first all-female trade unions. Workers' representatives began to call on the government for action on unemployment and other social issues. Not only was a Social Democratic Party (SPS) established in 1888, but two years later it got its first MP in the person of the veteran J. J. Treichler, who by then had become an ultra-leftist. The movement, though still small, was stronger and more united in German-speaking cantons than in the Suisse Romande, where socialist parties were more strictly cantonal.

At the same time, May Day emerged as a workers' festival, and the left began to organize its first referendum challenges. Such widely based worker participation in the new national democratic processes added a new element to Swiss politics. In contrast, a Zurich-based petition of 1886 for female suffrage led nowhere.

The way in which socialism developed in Switzerland had significant consequences both for the Swiss state and for political Catholicism. The Radical regime, still led by Welti, had to decide how to respond to the rise of a workers' movement, given that the party still saw itself as the representative of all Swiss people (and needed to keep workers' votes). It began by passing a Factory Act, enshrining an eleven-hour day, in 1877; ten years later, it set up a Workers' Secretariat as a means of balancing the combined influence of the employers' organization, the Vorort, set up in 1870, and the 1879 Gewerbeverband/USAM, the representative organization for small business and crafts.

The rise of socialism alarmed many Catholics, because, following the Syllabus of Errors, they saw it as atheistic and subversive. But combating it required new tactics. A new generation of leaders realized that they could not simply rely on *ex cathedra* condemnations, especially in light of *Kulturkampf* suspicion of the Papacy. Catholicism needed new allies and more political influence, which meant taking a more active and collaborative part in mainstream Swiss politics. The path to such engagement was eased by the accession of Leo XIII, who helped wind down the Swiss *Kulturkampf* by withdrawing Mermillod's status as Apostolic Vicar and transferring Lachat to Ticino. In response, the persecution of priests began to ease, and many were allowed to return to their posts.

On the political front, the Catholic conservatives failed to gain a seat on the Federal Council in 1875 for Josef Zemp, a leading parliamentarian from Lucerne, but they were more successful in using the new rights of challenge to block legislation of which they disapproved. Although their effort to obstruct the 1877 Factory Act failed, in 1882 they were successful in blocking the proposal to create School Inspectors, whom they nicknamed 'Bailiffs' (*Vögte*) as if they were latter-day Gesslers. Such inspectors would, of course, have undermined the Church's position in education. Proposals for military taxation, patent reform, labour conditions and constitutional revision were also rejected. Indeed, in May 1884, all four government proposals up for public vote were defeated. This made people aware of the strength of political Catholicism.

Zemp and others also sought to create a national party, as with the Conservative Union of 1881–2, but they were continually blocked by Segesser and the so-called 'Landammänner' or leaders of the old Alpine Catholic cantons. Nonetheless, in 1884 Zemp and his associates issued a manifesto calling on Catholics to take a more constructive role in national politics, coupled with proposals for quite dramatic changes in the constitution. Increasingly the interests of Catholics in non-Catholic cantons, the so-called diaspora, came to the fore. For younger Catholics working in places like Basle, restricting themselves to living in a ghetto and refusing to engage with mainstream Swiss life was not possible. They thus warmed to Zemp's programme of social and federalist change, especially as it was coupled with defence of the Church under the slogan of 'a free church in a free state'. They were also willing to cooperate with Protestant Conservatives where necessary in another move towards integrating into the national mainstream. Catholics also began to set up their own trade unions. However, the tradition of cantonal particularism and the reality of language divisions were hard to overcome. A joint Catholic agenda did not emerge until the end of the 1880s, when the first university to operate in a Catholic canton was founded in Fribourg. The Encyclical *De Rerum Novarum* of 1891 reduced tension further, though the Christian Catholic Church did not return to Roman obedience.

Both the rise of the left and the way that the Catholics used the new system to their advantage caused real problems for the Radicals, especially after they suffered an electoral check in 1878. Increasingly, they were divided both over the attitude to adopt to the left and by language, since French-speakers tended to distance themselves from many Radical projects, notably the constitutional reform of 1872. Reorganization became essential: in 1878, led by Emil Frey, a Basle journalist and former Union prisoner in the South during the American Civil War, the Radicals created their first parliamentary group to develop unity and cohesion. Building on moves in German-speaking Switzerland in the late 1870s, Frey also unsuccessfully called for the creation of a proper party. In 1881 the Radical government, where Emil Welti was still influential, moved to bring the Suisse

Romande back on board after its post-1872 coolness by finally per-
suading Louis Ruchonnet, the leading Vaudois federalist Radical of his
day, to join the Federal Council in preference to Segesser. Conversely,
the government's attempt to move to the left and bring socialists back
under the Radicals' old patriotic and progressive umbrella was resisted
by the Radical Right, the so-called Centre, which controlled government until the late 1880s, when the Zurich democrat Walter Hauser
was elected. This opened the way to the election of Frey to the Federal
Council in 1890. By then, moreover, the effects of the depression and
the socio-political stresses it had helped to produce were beginning to
wane, opening the way to new developments in state- and nation-
building.

STATE AND PARTY DEVELOPMENT

Even before this, in fact, the Radical state had begun to change as a
result of the 1874 constitutional reform. Conflict with Catholics and
the left encouraged the introduction of proportional representation
at cantonal level, which in turn forced the state to take on new tasks
and the country's main political forces to organize as parties. The
1880s thus saw a new wave of state modernization, including the
development of new direct democratic instruments and a more pluralist
party structure. At home, the Radical government promoted national
citizenship, began to spend more on primary education and the army,
and embarked on new policy areas such as forestry. It even began to
consider welfare provision. Externally, because of the depression, it
moved away from free trade to moderate protectionism in the mid-
1880s. It also became more combative in its trade policy, demanding
the opening of other markets in return for access to Switzerland's.
These trends were very apparent in a clutch of new trade treaties with
neighbouring states at the end of the 1880s. As well as being more
activist, the government sought to become more efficient and specialized. Hence Numa Droz, a Radical journalist from Neuchâtel and the
youngest Federal Councillor ever when he was elected at the age of 32
in 1875, was able to end the tradition of letting the headship of
the Political (or Foreign) Department rotate with the presidency of
the Council. He held the position for several years, becoming the first
proper Swiss foreign minister. Nonetheless, some ministers still found

the burden of the presidency of the new-style state a real challenge. Indeed, on Christmas Day 1880, Fridolin Anderwert from Thurgau killed himself because of press criticism and his fear of becoming president. Nevertheless, the Confederation was moving further down the road to being a true federal state. As a result, the cantons began to count for rather less in foreign affairs, and in 1894 the idea of giving them all customs revenues was rejected at a votation.

Diplomatically, the country was increasingly accepted as a permanent neutral whose revolutionary days were far behind it. In consequence, the International Postal Union and the International Bureau of Weights and Measures were given Swiss homes in 1874–5. Many Swiss still felt that outside conflicts were putting the country increasingly under threat, given French resentments over 1871, the way united Italy was flexing its muscles and especially the growing power of Germany. In 1889 the government had to expel Wohlgemuth, one of Bismarck's agents sent to spy on German socialists in exile. Such fears encouraged military changes, including a Defence Committee, new weapons and a lasting reorganization of the infantry into four corps. Nevertheless, the electorate remained reluctant to accept a real foreign policy, refusing to fund either an embassy in Washington in 1884 or more legations in 1895. Droz's experiment with the Political Department was also reversed after his retirement in 1892. Public pressure for tariff protection similarly forced the government to harden its stance in the 1890s, leading to a tariff war with France in 1893–5.

Despite the conservatism of the Swiss electorate, domestic politics were soon to change dramatically. In 1890 Ticinese Radicals staged the last putsch in Swiss history in response to the unfair way the first-past-the-post system rewarded Catholic conservatives with a large majority, despite their having gained only a few more votes than the Radicals. The Confederation had to intervene militarily. To avoid any further conflict, it then imposed proportional representation (PR) on the canton. PR had been talked about since the 1840s, but came to the fore after it was adopted by Neuchâtel in 1889. Following its imposition on Ticino, Geneva, Zug, Solothurn and Schwyz moved to adopt it for their own elections. By the end of the decade, an initiative demanding the adoption of the system at the national level was launched.

A national initiative was possible because the public had, in 1891, backed a government proposal to allow initiatives for partial revisions of the Constitution, as well as those proposing a complete overhaul. The change allowed 50,000 citizens to propose a votation on specific, often policy-oriented, alterations to the Constitution. The rash of referenda challenging proposed laws in the 1880s, only a third of which were won by the government, was not felt to be democratic enough, and generated the demand that the people should be able to change the Constitution themselves. What they actually got in 1891 was not formally the legislative initiative found at cantonal level, but a new partial constitutional revision facility that ended up acting in much the same way, since it allowed minorities to put their ideas on the political agenda. The issue did not arouse much public interest at the time, but it was to reshape Swiss politics over the coming decades. As a result of repeated partial revisions, the Constitution became a strange mixture of general principles and highly specific elements.

The new initiative process also forced political movements to organize, since campaigning required effective structures. The Radicals finally united under a single organization led by Emil Frey, who was now the dominant figure in the Federal Council, and established the Radical Democratic Party. He and others realized that, threatened as they were on two sides by the Catholics and the emerging socialists, the Radicals could no longer afford either indiscipline or overt objections to democratic votes. They also needed allies: when Emil Welti retired from government after the electorate refused to accept his advice and endorse the state's purchase of the Central Railway, Josef Zemp was invited to join the Federal Council, thereby breaking the Radicals' monopoly. This was only a partial step towards reconciliation with the conservatives, even though Zemp was to prove highly successful in winning support for railway nationalization.

Ironically, the divided Catholics found it more difficult to unite than the Radicals. On the one hand, there was friction between Suisse Romande circles and unions, and the German-speaking Association of Men and Workmen's Societies (VMAV), which wanted to expand westwards. On the other, the socially aware diaspora in the industrializing cities was continually at odds with the old-fashioned conservatives in the Alpine heartland of Catholicism. Even though Catholic MPs, like the leaders of the diaspora, called for an organized party, and something like a Catholic party emerged after a meeting at Olten in 1894, it was signally ineffective. The pro-Jesuit stance of some of its leaders, moreover, threatened to erect new barriers to Catholic links with Protestant conservatives. Nonetheless, the new opportunities completed the integration of Catholic conservatives into the body politic, and hence into supporting both the new state and Swiss national identity. By the turn of the century the problems of the *Sonderbund* era were largely solved: Catholic conservatives were both represented in government and still able to use democratization against the Radicals. Many Catholics, moreover, were coming to see the liberal state as a valuable protection against the growth of the extreme left. As a result, conservatism in Switzerland began to move in a different direction, more concerned with national and social integrity than with sectarian issues and opposition to the new state. In fact the latter, along with Swiss nationhood, became increasingly accepted.

At the same time as the left was seeking representation in Parliament, it was also seeking constitutional amendments providing for industrial injury insurance, the nationalization of railways – whose precariousness was shown up by a strike in 1897–8 – and its 'Right to Work' proposal. The last was roundly rejected in 1894 by 80 per cent of those voting, thanks to the activity of the peasants who had established their own lobbies, which cooperated with the Vorort and the USAM to combat the left. Although resistance to female involvement in politics remained fierce, politics did become increasingly pluralist. It also became increasingly national, with further moves towards uniformity in the late 1880s and 1890s: legal unification; civil marriage; army reform; metrification; state monopoly of bank notes; naturalization; control of inns, patents and water power. However, the state did not expand greatly in size, although a Health Office was set up in 1893 and a fund was created to bail out the railways. The Confederation was also finally allowed to subsidize primary education, continuing the development of both state and party system.

A CONSERVATIVE AND INDUSTRIAL NATION

The years leading up to the First World War saw a mixture of continuity and change. The role of the state continued to evolve in response to the heightened pace of industrialization, while the government became protectionist and defensive in reaction to the growing Great Power tensions around Switzerland. This also reflected growing national consciousness and feeling, encouraged by a growing use of historical references. The party system became increasingly pluralist, and both government and nation underwent a conservative turn, visible in the emergence of an anti-leftist *Bürgerblock* that was to prove a lasting feature of Swiss political history.

The course of the continuous changes reflected the increasingly rapid pace of Swiss economic growth, which followed on the ending of the depression in the early 1890s. A new industrial surge, sometimes seen as a second industrial revolution, emerged as the country moved into electricity, which became a major investment sector with a real domestic market and firms. Chemicals and engineering also expanded, with companies like Hoffman La Roche emerging in

6.3 A scene from the building of the St Gotthard tunnel. Taken ten years before opening the photograph shows rolling stock being prepared for further boring work. The tunnel allowed the Gotthard railway to provide a service between Lucerne and Chiasso. Linking Ticino to the main body of the Confederation, the tunnel was to be the centrepiece of the developing rail network, which was so important to the late nineteenth-century Swiss economy, society and politics.

1896, while railway mileage doubled between 1880 and 1910. Rail's value to tourism was increasingly appreciated with the development of mountain railways, such as that to the Hotel Burgenstock in 1888 and, a decade later, with electrification. By 1900, 45 per cent of the working population was employed in manufacturing (including foreign workers), leaving only 31 per cent in agriculture. Owing mostly to tourism, banking and railways, the services' share of overall employment rose from 16 per cent to 24 per cent. Exports per capita remained very high: Nestlé – which emerged in 1905 – moved into the Japanese market, and textiles and watches sold well abroad, even though the share of textiles in the overall mix fell sharply in the 1890s.

As a result, Switzerland became a significant economic power, almost equalling the UK in terms of per capita GDP. Exports and foreign investment per capita also grew, the latter outstripping that of the UK. Economic growth showed in the rapid expansion of towns, and the way they equipped themselves with new facilities like libraries, theatres and schools. The boom also helped to produce a surge in population, which rose on average by 1.2 per cent a year from 1890 to 1913, taking the total to over 3.3 million by 1900 and 3.8 million by 1914. Along with population growth, the contraction of agriculture freed up further labour for the new factories, as did the rapid decline in emigration after 1880. However, there were still jobs to be had, and an increasing number of these were filled by foreigners, notably through immigration from Italy and Germany. Switzerland moved from being a country of emigration to one marked by immigration: by 1900 there were 380,000 outsiders in Switzerland. However, conditions for workers were often difficult, since prices outstripped wages, and workers faced major problems with poor housing, alcoholism and debt. Hence the number of strikes began to increase, enabled in part by the creation of union strike pay funds.

Concerns about growth and social unrest – the 'social problem' – led to the first attempts to provide state social welfare through state accident insurance. Although such efforts were supported by workers and some industrialists (who hoped to shift their costs onto the state), the so-called Lex Forrer was successfully challenged in May 1900 by an alliance of private insurance firms, peasants and Catholics. However, the state still changed its economic policy in other ways. Its protectionism intensified, with much higher tariffs being adopted in 1903. This paved the way for a new series of trade treaties with European states. Economic intervention was also made easier by legal changes in the early 1900s.

The most significant change in the role of the state came with the nationalization of the railways. Despite sustained opposition, changing political attitudes and the rail companies' growing financial problems won the idea public favour. The door to nationalization was opened in 1897 by a popular votation, and over the next twelve years, the main companies became part of a new Swiss Federal Railways system, set up in 1902. By then the railways were already beginning to electrify their lines. This 'drift to state socialism by antisocialists' further increased the number of state employees. However, the electorate rejected the idea of creating a national bank in 1897, which showed that older more restrained attitudes also persisted. Not until 1905 was this step towards a modern, powerful and centralized state finally approved.

Acceptance of a larger role for the state, and of the taxes to support it, grew towards the end of century as a more cohesive Swiss identity emerged under the umbrella of the new federal state. Intellectuals like the novelist Gottfried Keller had called in the 1870s for national festivals to celebrate national feeling. The spread of primary schooling and literacy, the impact of railways and military service and the development of festivals all helped to develop a wider sense of national identity. In fact, the first National Exhibition, held in Zurich in 1883, attracted 1.7 million visitors. Moreover, awareness of the rising tide of nationalism in neighbouring countries led government and many others to think about how to overcome internal divisions by redefining and maintaining Swiss identity in a more difficult environment. Obviously, such an identity for Switzerland could not rest on linguistic or ethnic foundations. Instead, thinkers such as Carl Hilty emphasized the desire of the Swiss to live together as a so-called *Willensnation*. Civic nationalism of this kind emphasized that Switzerland's historical roots and long adhesion to shared constitutional rules and processes had created a nation, as well as a state, despite the lack of shared language and religion.

History thus played an increasingly central part in the mix of elements that defined the Swiss, looking beyond the divisive events of 1798 and 1848 (which were not universally celebrated) to celebrate their longer-term unity. The late nineteenth century saw ever more historical festivals and exhibitions, a boom in historical plays, and the establishment of historical museums in Zurich and Berne. The Swiss-oriented National Library and the iconic Bundeshaus in central Berne were also completed at this time.

Academics, meanwhile, were reconstructing the narrative of Swiss history using the rediscovered charter of 1291 and supplanting the traditional date of 1307 associated with William Tell, the oath against Austria and the liberation saga. However, the latter continued to be taught in Swiss schools. A new generation of historians like Dändliker, Oechsli and Dierauer, whose massive history started to appear in 1887, dismissed the mythical rebellion of 1307 in favour of a long-term voluntaristic narrative of Switzerland's formation. Oechsli relegated Tell to the realms of myth. This trend was symbolized by the national celebration in 1891, celebrating the 600th anniversary of the supposed foundation of the Confederation, and also by the way that 1 August became the key national holiday celebrated as the Confederacy's founding day, now supported by written evidence. This elite approach did not replace the older view, reliant on traditional myths, which remained strongly entrenched at the grass roots, as seen in the 1895 erection of the Tell monument in Altdorf and Hodler's 1897 heroic portrait of the hero. A further contribution to the new Swiss identity came from those, like Bluntschli, who looked to geography and landscape. For him, echoing Schiller, the Alps were a symbol of Swiss simplicity, purity, honesty, liberty and virtue. This Alpine myth encouraged calls for defence of the national patrimony, and led to the creation of the first National Park in the Engadine in 1904 and the establishment of the Swiss League for the Protection of the Homeland, the Heimatschutz, in 1905.

A negative side of such cultural nation-formation appeared in the way many Swiss also began to see their country and their identity as threatened by the presence of a superfluity of foreigners, which was called *Überfremdung* or over-foreignization. Such sentiments emerged in 1893 in the vote banning ritual slaughter of animals (which also had anti-Semitic overtones), and after 1900 became a general public concern, shared both by nationally minded Radical MPs and by Social Democrats worried about the loss of industrial jobs, notably to the growing number of Italians who were coming to work in Switzerland. These fears reflected the fact that Switzerland had seven times the European average of foreign residents: foreigners made up 14.7 per cent of the workforce nationally, a figure rising to 21 per cent in Zurich.

Many immigrants were Germans, who often took up sensitive professional posts, something that worried specialist milieus in the 1890s, despite admiration for imperial Germany in German-speaking Switzerland. Since many Germans came to Switzerland to avoid Bismarck's attacks on the Social Democrats, moreover, Swiss nationalists sought to paint foreigners as left-wing threats to the social order. Hence, whereas at the end of the 1890s there had been moves towards integrating immigrants by increasing the rate of naturalization, in the new century resistance to such policies grew. The Federal Council took no action as right-wing forces began to argue that foreigners in themselves constituted a danger. Anti-foreigner riots in Berne and Zurich, often directed against Italian workers, increased tensions, and national identity became more emotional, if not exactly ethnic, as a result.

The intensification of European nationalism based on ethnicity had a Swiss counterpart in the emergence of new linguistic divides. In German-speaking regions, moves to defend the German language emerged, exemplified by Jakob Hunziker's 1898 work *Kampf um das Deutschtum in der Schweiz* (1898) and in 1904 by the establishment of the Deutschsprachverein to promote the German language. When the terms of the 1909 Gotthard Convention with Germany and Italy became known, a vast petitioning movement spread in the Suisse Romande, demanding its abrogation not simply because it gave too much away, but because it represented a virtual German takeover of Switzerland. In the Vaud, signatures were collected for an initiative to subject future treaties to an optional referendum.

Another divide was social. The rise of the socialist movement and the growing number of strikes (over 1800 between 1900 and 1914, including general strikes in Geneva and Lausanne in 1907 and especially Zurich in 1912) caused great alarm amongst employers, middle classes and peasants. In 1907, the army was called in to deal with major strikes, and both Berne and Zurich soon passed no-strike laws. Concern was intensified when the Social Democrats, who had increased their membership greatly in 1901 by a merger with the long-established Grütli movement, developed municipal socialism and began to win more seats in parliament, gaining fifteen by 1911. The party also began to move to the left, adopting a Marxist and class-conflict-based programme in 1908.

These developments not only pushed the Radicals away from their earlier 'all nation' stance and towards the right; the years before 1914 also saw the formation of a bourgeois laager or *Bürgerblock*, a self-contained politico-social camp led by the Vorort, the USAM and the Peasants' Union, and involving both Radicals and Catholic Conservatives, all of whom believed the nation was in conflict with the left-wing camp. In 1911, this alliance was able to reduce a new law on sickness and accident insurance to a mere skeleton of the original plan. The national Social Insurance Office, established in 1913 to help with unemployment, was also slow to develop owing to middle-class and peasant reservations.

The emerging new-style conservatism was also visible in attitudes towards democratic processes. Thus, despite the adoption of proportional representation in more cantons, including Basle Country, the national electorate three times turned it down between 1905 and 1910, albeit by narrow margins. Apparently Swiss voters, despite their growing divisions, were willing to tolerate the continuance of Radical hegemony. Similarly, in 1900, direct election to the Federal Council was also rejected, while the idea of submitting treaties to popular approval, first raised in 1897, failed to progress despite the impetus given to it by the storm over the Gotthard Convention. Not surprisingly, calls for women's suffrage – pushed by an Association of Female Workers from 1893 and from 1904 by the Social Democrats – also continued to be ignored, as were demands for female representation on education and health boards. Indeed, the new Civil Code of 1907 was very unhelpful to women.

The Radical Party, although still dominant in Parliament, found itself facing new centrifugal pressures. Between 1896 and 1905, it lost its left wing, which went on to form the Democratic Party. It also lost some more conservative members to a new Liberal Party between 1904 and 1913, while agrarian and evangelical elements were also getting restive. Peasants felt that their debt problems were not being addressed sufficiently and that the party was still too close to the bitterly distrusted socialists. The unease of mainstream Protestants with the party ultimately led to a secession in 1917 by what later became the Evangelical People's Party. In fact, despite its developing organizational apparatus, the Radical Party was declining even as it moved into closer alliance with big business. The 1912 General Strike in Zurich accentuated both trends, and also drove the party closer to anti-foreigner forces, including an emerging new right led by the aristocratic right-wing controversialist Gonzague de Reynold, which, echoing the Action Française, sought a return to the Ancien Régime and traditional 'Helvetianism'.

Conservative forces could also increasingly rely on Catholic support. Although the 1894 Catholic Party had been stillborn, pressure for Catholic unity continued to grow, encouraged both by the holding of All-Swiss Catholic Days after 1903 and by outside pressures, notably from students, and by fears of atheistic socialism. Despite some resistance from old Catholic oligarchs in Fribourg and elsewhere, a new Catholic Conservative Party was finally established at Lucerne in April 1912, which brought the Swiss Catholics a step further towards full participation in the political system on the bourgeois side.

The growing social divide underlying this was, of course, a reflection of the continuing growth of the Swiss economy. After a brief period of over-heating at the turn of the century, the economy continued to expand. By the outbreak of war in 1914, although the Swiss accounted for only 1 per cent of the European population, they provided 3 per cent of its exports (four-fifths being of manufactured goods) and 5.7 per cent of its capital stock. Switzerland also had more large-scale firms than many other countries. Thriving tourism and commerce brought 22 million overnight stays in hotels, a figure not equalled until after 1945.

The intensification of industrialization brought half a million workers into 8,000 factories, often operated by electricity and sometimes found in mountain regions, thanks to hydroelectricity. Politically, economic growth meant that there was a strong, well-educated and sometimes foreign workforce. The fact that so many workers concentrated in the bigger towns meant that many in the Swiss countryside found industrialization frightening, whether despite or because of the generally decentralized nature of Swiss society. In fact, the major urban population rose from 11.6 per cent in 1900 to 16 per cent by 1914, and larger towns gained a third of all the new jobs created after 1888. Since agriculture was not expanding, rural fears are easy to understand.

For those who ran the new factories and banks, worker militancy became a major concern. Interestingly, the pre-war period brought a boom for banks, with forty-five new foundations and thirty significant mergers. The latter produced both the Basle-based Swiss Bank Corporation (SBC) in 1896 and Zurich's Union Bank (UBS) in 1912, the year the Association of Swiss Bankers was established. These were large-scale, general-purpose banks on the model already pioneered in Germany and France. Swiss banks soon began selling their services to wealthy foreigners, in part by marketing their discretion and secrecy, in response to increasing taxation in France and elsewhere. This helped them to attract business and compete with rivals in bigger states. Bankers were generally very hostile to socialism, deepening the growing political divide.

Even though Swiss respect for neutrality grew in the years before 1914, external developments added to the growing linguistic division. In 1907, a new Geneva Convention was signed on treatment of combatants at sea, the same year that the second set of Hague Conventions on neutrality and the laws of war, in the negotiation of which Switzerland had been involved, were adopted. Switzerland continued to act as a referee over the Algeciras incident in 1905–6 and later provided a home for Turkish–Balkan negotiations of 1912, leading to the Treaty of Lausanne. However, the Swiss failed to get an International Treaty Agency established in Berne, as the government wanted, while Swiss harbouring of large numbers of Albanian, Turkish and Russian dissidents was not well received abroad.

Switzerland's unease about its geopolitical situation generated increasing attention to its army, which was slowly being equipped with repeating rifles and machine guns. Reorganizations in 1907 and 1911 expanded the force to 200,000 men and revised its management, its training and its active service rules. Military costs soon accounted for two-thirds of the budget. The wide-ranging changes to the army's structures approved by the people in 1907 set off a challenge from the Socialists, but were much admired abroad.

Unfortunately, the authorities feared, wrongly, that in its quest for *revanche*, France might seek to attack Germany through Switzerland. Hence, in 1910 the army offered to share military information with

Schweizer Manöver 1912
Kaiser Wilhelm II mit dem Burengeneral Beyers

6.4 Kaiser Wilhelm II photographed with Boer General Beyers observing Swiss army manoeuvres in September 1912. Swiss officers are in the centre of the picture and other Germans to the right. The visit was politically significant, given Europe's division into armed camps. While ostensibly the aim was to meet Swiss officers and politicians as good neighbours, the Kaiser – third from left – and his staff also wanted to assure themselves that Swiss forces would be able, in the event of war, to block any French attack on southern Germany through Switzerland. The visit helped spur the feeling that the army leadership was too close to Germany, alarming French-speakers. The presence of a Boer general would have reinforced such feelings.

Germany. Two years later, the Kaiser made a very public and controversial visit to Switzerland, ostensibly to observe the annual exercises. In reality he came to ensure that, in the event of war, Switzerland would cover Germany's southern flank against France. Coming on top of the opposition to the sale of Gotthard shares to Germany and Italy, not to mention irredentist calls emanating from Minister Pedrazzini in Rome, the Kaiser's visit led French-speakers to feel that the country was getting far too close to the Triple Alliance. The sympathy the German Swiss showed for the new Germany also caused rumours of an Austro-Swiss alliance, which raised concern in the UK.

Nonetheless, by 1913, the Swiss had forged a solid, prosperous and self-aware nation, and one with both highly innovative democratic processes and a real federal state. Its politics were more organized and pluralist than before, although it had turned its back on the revolutionary impulses of the 1840s and 1850s, squeezing out extremism while bringing opposition minorities into the system and also forging a new strongly national and historical identity. Yet, as well as becoming increasingly democratic, Switzerland was also developing an increasingly conservative streak. This found it hard to cope with the demands of the new working class. Hence many Swiss were uneasy and resistant to change. Partly as a result, the country soon found itself facing new internal divisions as well as heightened external challenges.

7

The shocks of war, 1914–1950

In 1914 Switzerland was a self-confident and relatively democratic part of the European state system. However, the effects of two world wars and the intervening depression were to test Swiss cohesion and prosperity. The First World War pressed Swiss neutrality hard, especially where linguistic unity and economic security were concerned. The resulting tensions led to an explosion at the end of the war that sent the country off in new political directions, both domestically and diplomatically. The inter-war period brought further extreme economic problems, combined with violent new divisions, often stimulated from outside.

Faced with growing European tensions in the 1930s, the Swiss began to batten down the hatches and prepare to defend themselves against external threats, first through better preparation and unity than in 1914, and then through the defensive strategy known as the Reduit. Even so, they did not avoid problems, being sucked into the German war economy and, from 1944, into difficulties with the Allies. Switzerland emerged from the war proud, because the Swiss had survived by strengthening their own democratic unity and resources, but also isolated and mistrusted. In fact, overall, the country had suffered more from events in Europe and beyond than many outside realized.

NEUTRALITY AND SOCIETY UNDER PRESSURE

The First World War required a major military effort for the Swiss. This went well in terms of mobilization and guarding the frontiers. It

7.1 Mobilization for the First World War. The photograph
reveals the sheer scale of the initial Swiss call-up on the outbreak
of war. Thousands of men assembled in squares across
Switzerland, even in Zug, one of the Sonderbund cantons. The
48th Battalion of infantry is here seen taking the oath on 5
August 1914, later than some other places, but in uniform and
fully equipped. Though they were ready to be dispatched to
guard various parts of the country, few realized that this was the
beginning of a long and painful service.

was less successful in dealing with the social and economic costs of
maintaining neutrality. Equally, the country was severely tested by
the way the war divided it along dangerous linguistic lines.

However, few people foresaw these coming trials for neutrality
and society. Indeed, when the First World War broke out,
Switzerland was in cheerful mood, thanks to the successful third
National Exhibition in Berne and the creation of the New Helvetic
Society. The government responded quickly to the crisis following
the assassination of Archduke Franz Ferdinand in Sarajevo on 28
June, mobilizing 220,000 men by 3 August, who were stationed
mainly around the exposed Jura salient at Porrentruy. The same
day, Parliament voted the government full powers and elected a
General, both for the duration. The choice of a military leader fell

on Ulrich Wille, a 66-year-old professional soldier with an English poetess mother and Prussian connections. This controversial choice, pushed by President Arthur Hoffman, was aimed in part at assuaging German sensitivities, which Hoffman felt necessary in light of the army's recognized weaknesses. The following day, neutrality was formally declared.

Armed neutrality worked well enough during the war so that Switzerland's territorial integrity was never seriously threatened, even though the war went on far longer than expected. Neutrality also helped to contain the bitter division between the Germanic and Latin language communities, which had been stimulated by the election of the apparently pro-German Wille. At the same time, neutrality imposed great and unbalanced pressures on Swiss society, intensifying the emerging divisions between middle-class conservatives and the organized working class. It also proved hard to defend economically against the combatants' controls. As a result, the country ended the war in a very divided and explosive state.

Although the first deaths in the war are said to have occurred on 2 August close to the Swiss border when French and German patrols collided north of Porrentruy, the actual war never seriously threatened Swiss territory. The initial French invasion of Alsace was quickly forced back, and the two sides dug in along the crests of the Vosges mountains. The southern end of the trenches was far quieter than Flanders, though Swiss soldiers could still hear gunfire. Once the two sides had dug in, moreover, the Swiss were able to demobilize many of their men, leaving only 50,000 in place. Remobilization occurred in late April 1915, when Italy entered the war and troops were stationed in the Grisons and the south, and again in 1916–17, when there were fears that the combatants might try to cross Switzerland to attack their enemies. No major incursions took place, but about a thousand frontier incidents ensued during the war: these included misdirected artillery fire in the Grisons, but four-fifths of them were aerial, as when French planes tried to fly across Swiss territory to bomb the Zeppelin base at Friedrichshafen, or when the Germans bombed Porrentruy in 1916. Because of this, the Swiss built up an air force of some 120 planes by the end of the war, although these were not used well nor backed up by real anti-aircraft support.

Swiss neutrality rested in part on support from the combatants, both diplomatically and militarily. On the one hand, neutrality was strongly supported by Germany in an effort to offset the outrage caused in Switzerland by its destruction of Louvain. The Allies likewise undertook to respect Swiss neutrality. Emboldened by this, the government, as early as November 1914, lent its support to a peace initiative, which came to nothing. Nor did ideas of trying to create a neutral bloc come to fruition. On the other hand, the Swiss also tried to reinforce their military defences by negotiating with the combatants to forestall the possibility of Swiss territory being used for any attacks, as was the case with France in 1915–16 when a German push through Switzerland against Belfort was feared. The negotiations dragged on and ended only with a verbal understanding in 1918. A similar deal with Germany may have been contemplated when the French drew up a Plan H in 1915–16 that envisaged a push on Alsace through Switzerland. However, the French abandoned the idea once Verdun came under attack. The Italians also planned to take up defensive positions in the Ticino in case the Germans sought to attack them through Switzerland.

The government also found it hard to maintain neutrality. Its December 1916 and February 1917 attempts at mediation both failed. Then, in late May 1917, a dispatch from Foreign Minister Hoffman to the Social Democrat MP Robert Grimm, who was then in Russia, was intercepted by the French and passed to the Russian Provisional Government and the Swedish press. The dispatch showed that Hoffman, in an attempt to protect the Swiss economy, was considering a separate German–Russian peace without the knowledge of the rest of the government. This caused outrage not only in the Federal Council and among the Allies, but also in the Suisse Romande, where there were anti-Hoffman demonstrations. He rapidly resigned in an effort to placate French-speakers and those who doubted Swiss neutrality; he was replaced by the 72-year-old Gustave Ador, the President of the Red Cross and the architect of its successful work with prisoners of war.

Neutrality was also tested internally by the emergence of what was called the *Graben* or *fossé* between the language communities. Underlying pre-war tensions were rapidly exacerbated by the war. Generally speaking, German-speakers sympathized with the Central

Powers, thanks to the influence of immigration from Germany and admiration for German military prowess and culture – leading some to envisage the end of *Schwyzerdütsch*. Many also felt that France was falling apart and that the Germans were bound to win, which made it wise to be on the winning side. French and, later, Italian speakers were more sympathetic to the liberal Allies, to the extent that 7,000 Swiss actually fought under the French flag. They also feared what might happen in a German-dominated Europe, especially after the rape of Belgium. Memories of Bernese German oppression in the Jura during the *Kulturkampf* encouraged a secessionist movement there during the war.

Everything that happened after August 1914 was interpreted in terms of these underlying prejudices. Thus, the election of Wille had been seen as a deliberate affront to the Entente. Although at times the conflict took on a physical form, as when Germans were attacked in the streets of Lausanne in 1916, the *Graben* was essentially a war of words. Linguistic partisanship was encouraged by the combatants, especially by the Central Powers, who were initially the more adept at lobbying. External actors often bought up or funded the press, since the battle was fought through newspapers, books, magazines, brochures and cartoons, not to mention hearsay. Rumours, denunciations of alleged atrocities and accusations of betrayal by the other language group abounded, as did belief in foreign plots. Both sides developed organizations to defend their interests, such as the 1904 Deutschschweizer Sprachverein under Eduard Blocher and the 1916 Ligue Patriotique Romande.

Ironically, some Swiss could seem more extreme than their sponsors. Roman Rolland found some Swiss Germans more expansionist than the Kaiser, while Clemenceau sometimes claimed there were some things he could not do because the Suisse Romande papers would not stand for it. Press censorship was brought in during 1915, although the army handled it so ineptly that the government had to set up mixed committees involving journalists to take over.

So virulent did the controversy become that appeals for calm came as early as August 1914; by November, the government felt it necessary to call publicly for national cohesion. The following month, the well-known poet Carl Spittler gave a famous lecture on 'Our Swiss Standpoint', urging his compatriots not to take sides, but to remember that they were all brothers who should unite to maintain the neutral Swiss state. The Suisse Romande historian Paul Seippel made similar statements. These interventions seem to have had some effect, as things calmed down somewhat in 1915. But argument flared up again in 1916, with demonstrations and near riots after the emergence of what was called the 'Colonels' affair', in which Colonels Egli and Wattenwil of the General Staff were arrested for passing on Swiss intelligence briefings to German military attachés. The mild sentences imposed by Wille caused outrage in French-speaking regions, and the *Courrier de Vevey* accused the government of preparing to let German troops pass through Switzerland in order to attack Belfort.

The war also intensified social pressures. Soldiers had to serve an average of 608 days during the war, during which they were subject to fierce discipline and drill but long denied equipment such as steel helmets, gas masks or machine guns. The army offered few means of offsetting the boredom of frontier watch, in which tranquillity was only disturbed by the odd poacher. Most importantly, soldiers received only pocket money, and there was no compensation to families for the loss of their breadwinner. The lack of pay drove many families towards destitution at a time when prices were rising twice as fast as wages. War taxation was a further burden for many. By 1917 some 700,000 of the country's 4 million people were in distress, and the number of births and marriages fell. Food riots broke out in 1916–17 when unrestricted submarine warfare cut down food imports. At the same time, some firms and farms were making large profits. Thus, it is not surprising either that desertion occurred or that some 5,000 conscripts joined a soldiers' trade union. Unwisely, the government turned its face against helping out workers and their families. Thus, it limited rights of association and repealed factory legislation, and it was slow to introduce rationing, which did not really become widespread until 1916–17. As a result, along with resentment of the officer class, class antagonisms grew during the war.

Indeed, it was probably the economic policies of the belligerents that placed both neutrality and Swiss society under the greatest pressure. Both sides wanted to ensure that goods they sent to Switzerland were not passed on to the other side – and neither side trusted the Swiss to deliver. In August 1915, the Allies created a Swiss-based agency, the Swiss Society for Economic Surveillance, to control Swiss exports and imports, most of which were channelled through the Mediterranean port of Sète. These conditions were sufficiently constraining that Wille even thought Switzerland might have to resort to fighting on the Central Powers' side in order to maintain its independence, although the latter followed suit with the Schweizerische Treuhandstelle. Reconciling the belligerents' conflicting demands was difficult, especially as both sides knew the country would pay a high price to preserve its supplies and neutrality. Switzerland was dependent on Germany for coal and manufactured goods and on the Allies for foodstuffs and colonial goods. Coal shortages forced the government first to cancel Sunday trains and then to take direct control of the railways. Meanwhile, the subsistence crisis meant that Switzerland had to do even more trade with the Allies, which called its impartiality into question.

The war thus became a major challenge for the economy. Raw material imports fell off, making it harder to export, and after a good year in 1916, pressure increased, notably for textiles. Declining exports meant many layoffs at a time when there was no national unemployment pay. Tourism also suffered very badly, and even banks faced problems, though they managed to fight off new state controls and rules on disclosure. Some large-scale farmers benefited from rising prices, but smaller peasant farms sold less and were disproportionately hit by taxation, inflation and a shortage of labour. Financing the war was another economic burden. Borrowing pushed the national debt up from 146 million francs in 1913 to 1817 million in 1919. Conditions also weighed heavily on the Swiss franc. The state had to increase taxation through war taxes, a profits tax and a higher stamp duty, all of which exacerbated social problems, which were to explode as the war came to an end.

THE POST-WAR SOCIO-POLITICAL CRISIS

The government had not handled war conditions well, partly because of the innate conservatism it shared with much of mainstream society. This was increasingly exacerbated by the fear of 'Bolshevism' generated by the Russian Revolution. All this had both immediate political effects and even more serious medium-term implications. Worsening class divisions and economic pressures exploded in 1918, causing a dramatic social upheaval. The forces of conservatism managed to overcome the General Strike, but had to concede Proportional Representation (PR), leading to a new era in political relations. At the same time, the country moved away from absolute neutrality through membership in the League of Nations. These developments were to mark the country for years to come.

Initially, however, the government's failings – including the Hoffman affair – primarily affected the elections of October 1917, in which the Social Democrats, the Catholic Conservatives and the Democrats won seats from Liberals and Radicals. The latter party's position was further weakened when younger elements began demanding a more interventionist approach to the economy. Their agrarian allies were also getting increasingly restless and worried about socialism, seen in the growth of trade union strength and in the number of strikes. At the same time, the Swiss left was preoccupied by the emergence of a new communist movement, led by Lenin at the Zimmerwald and Kienthal conferences in 1915 and 1916, which called on the working class to wage civil war to gain power. Although the Swiss working class did not take much notice of this, the Social Democrats did begin to attack Swiss defence policy, its financing and its lack of democracy.

By 1917, Lenin famously believed that the country was ripe for revolution, as did the United States. The establishment, Wille and much of middle-class society also became increasingly alarmed by the apparent Bolshevik threat. Leftist enthusiasm and bourgeois fears both intensified suspicion of foreigners, who were increasingly seen as synonymous with political extremists. Hence, in 1917 the Federal Council took over the policing of aliens from the cantons, even though the number of foreigners went down from 600,000 (14.7 per cent of the population) in 1914 to 402,000 (10.4 per cent) in 1920.

In fact, Switzerland did experience a socio-political explosion at the end of the war – one caused not by foreign agitators, but by the social unease resulting from the catastrophic fall in living standards induced by the war, together with the government's misplaced activism. In early 1918, the government chose to impose a

7.2 Deployment of troops to put down the General Strike of mid-November 1918. The outbreak of the strike, driven by social hardship, elite intransigence and military aggression, caused Wille and the army leadership to fear that the country was facing a Bolshevik revolution. They therefore flooded Zurich with troops drawn from rural and Catholic cantons, including the threatening-looking cavalry shown here. This show of force forced the strike leaders to back down, leaving a bitter legacy of social and political resentment.

new month-long obligatory period of civilian service, centring on public works projects. This additional burden on the working classes forced the Social Democrats and the unions, grouped together in what became known as the Olten Committee, to start planning for a general strike in line with syndicalist thinking. On 30 September of that year, a strike for higher wages broke out amongst Zurich bank clerks, supported by the working class. Tensions were also increased by the October Revolution in Russia, which led to a supportive march in Zurich on 17 October. The demonstration turned into a riot in which a policeman was killed. Wille and others sought to stop the feared revolution in its tracks and, at the request of the Zurich authorities, who found themselves without military support, sent

troops under the pro-German Colonel Sonderegger into the city. On
10 November, Sonderegger's men fired on demonstrators, wounding
three; the Olten Committee responded on 12 November by calling a
strike and issuing a nine-point reform programme. Some 250,000
workers, mainly from the railway and metallurgical industries of
German-speaking Switzerland, answered the call. Although the
strike was almost entirely peaceful, Wille mobilized 100,000 men,
mainly from rural and Catholic cantons, and occupied Zurich. Faced
with this, the Olten committee ordered workers back to work, and
the strike subsided.

Nonetheless, when combined with the effects of the war and the
introduction of proportional representation, the strike dramatically
changed Swiss politics. To begin with, the new electoral system –
which soon spread to more cantons – delivered the Radicals their
worst election result since 1848. The party lost half its seats – including many moderates – and ended with sixty, only nineteen more than
those claimed by both Social Democrats and Catholic Conservatives.
This outcome was both a real political earthquake and a dividing
line in Swiss political history, moving the country from majoritari-
anism to a highly proportional and pluralist political culture.

Nonetheless, in 1919 the right still enjoyed a majority, thanks to
the vehemently anti-socialist attitudes of both the Catholics – whose
episcopate came out against socialism – and the emerging agrarian
party in Berne and Zurich, which held thirty seats and coalesced as
the Burghers, Artisans and Peasants Party (BGB/PAB) in 1921. In
fact, the election created a new bourgeois, nationalist and peasant
bloc, which used the strike as a pretext for dismissing left-wing
concerns. Opposition to the left also took an increasingly activist
form with the foundation of militant civil guard organizations like
the anti-Semitic Patriotic Federations created by a Germanophile
army doctor, Eugen Bircher. His movement reflected a growing
xenophobia in Swiss society, which continued into the mid-1920s
with a harsh new naturalization law in 1921 and complete confederal control of foreigners' affairs in 1925. That same year, Bircher's
force evolved into a new and more sinister organization, the
Heimatwehr. Nevertheless, the electorate did reject a new security
law giving the government increased police powers, the so-called Lex
Häberlin, in 1922.

The general political move to the right, reinforcing earlier trends as it did, meant that the Social Democrats, despite their new-found electoral strength, remained very much outside the charmed circle of political power. Their exclusion was intensified by their resentment of the army because of its wartime class bias and its actions against the strike. These positions, along with the intense polarization of the post-war period, meant that there could be no question of allowing the Social Democrats a seat in the government. Indeed, in 1919 Parliament chose a second, and violently anti-socialist, Catholic, Jean-Marie Musy of Fribourg, for the Federal Council. Their exclusion led the SPS to make more use of direct democratic initiatives to advance their ideas, although the continuing conservatism of the electorate meant they achieved few of their goals. For example, a 1921 social-democratic proposal for a wealth tax was heavily defeated.

International developments reinforced the growing domestic divide. In 1919, the nearly unanimous desire of the Austrian province of Voralberg to become part of Switzerland was turned down by the Swiss authorities, fearful that it would upset the religious and linguistic balance of the country, as well as raising questions about neutrality and defensibility. Much more significant were the debates on the League of Nations. Switzerland had remained largely outside the Versailles negotiations, which were not sympathetic to neutrality, but in the end it did secure special status under Article 435 that exempted it from military involvement in the League. Entry to the League enjoyed strong support from people like the independent conservative Minister Ador, who saw the League as a barrier to communism. However, the League also posed problems because it envisioned economic sanctions, which meant that Switzerland would be forced to adopt differential neutrality. Membership was therefore vehemently opposed by right-wing movements, including the Volksbund für die Unabhängigkeit der Schweiz led by Eduard Blocher. Entry was put to a popular vote, even though this was not strictly necessary, and barely passed on 16 May 1920. Had a few votes in Appenzell gone the other way, membership would not have gained a cantonal majority. Eight months later, the electorate made it a rule that long-lasting treaties had to be approved by a votation. At the same time the government annoyed the League by refusing to let peace-keeping forces pass through the country en route to Vilnius. League recognition of neutrality also ended the demilitarization of Savoy and the free zones around Geneva. When popular resistance prevented a new deal in 1923, these zones lapsed altogether. Public opinion, however, remained solidly behind Switzerland's refusal to have diplomatic relations with the USSR.

The unease underlying attitudes towards the League and towards social reform rested in part on the deteriorating economic climate. After a brief boom at the end of the war when exports soared, a new financial crisis in 1922 developed as the reparations crisis hit Europe. Swiss holdings were badly affected as old competitors – often highly protectionist – returned to the market at a time when high inflation and Swiss levies made its exports expensive. Textile and watch exports declined sharply, while unemployment rose, reaching 100,000, exacerbated by conservative resistance to any remedial measures. This was evidence that the crisis had not overturned the pre-existing political balance.

SLUMP AND IDEOLOGICAL CONFLICT

In fact fears of foreigners and the rising left not only persisted, but became stronger and more radical despite the fact that the mid-1920s were a much better period for the Swiss economy. Polarization increased when the renewed economic growth was brutally reversed by the slump that followed in 1929, which caused real hardship, especially when met by austere economic policies. Although these were eventually replaced by more interventionist stances, forced on government by the depth of the depression, the actual onset of the slump encouraged many Swiss, like others in Europe, to look for new extreme answers to their problems, at times calling post-1848 achievements into question, sometimes violently. In the end, the country largely overcame the threat from totalitarianism and kept the rising power of the left at bay.

In the 1920s, once German hyper-inflation was tamed, Switzerland began to prosper again. The economy thrived in the second half of the 1920s, seeing not just growth but also restructuring, with agriculture losing further ground to services, notably banking and tourism. Retailing also changed with the emergence of

Gottlieb Duttweiler's pioneering mobile grocery vans, bitterly resisted by conventional shopkeepers but welcomed by consumers. Manufacturing continued its shift away from textiles to metals, chemicals and food, where Nestlé became increasingly important. Both national income and wages rose. Growth may also explain why the electorate, having in May 1925 rejected a proposal to create pensions and accident insurance, accepted a government counter-project that December.

Politically, however, Catholics, farmers and the middle classes remained absorbed with fears of a communist revolution. Hence, they drifted further to the right, intellectually and practically. The influence of the French Action Française and Italian fascism was strong on writers like Gonzague de Reynold and Georges Oltremare in the Suisse Romande. A few *fascii* were set up, and Wille hosted a lecture by Adolf Hitler in 1923. By the end of the decade, such tendencies were reinforced in the Federal Council by the election of Marcel Pilet-Golaz, a Vaudois Radical, and then by Rudolf Minger of the BGB, which was then perhaps the most anti-liberal and anti-socialist party. Minger's election represented a blunt rejection of calls that the Social Democrats, who were beginning to moderate their positions, should be allowed into the government. Catholic Conservatives also made gains in the 1928 general elections, even though foreign relations were less tense at this time. The Volksbund continued to object to Swiss participation in League committees, and the government was hesitant to go beyond encouraging international arbitration and developing its good offices role. Neutrality was strengthened when service in bodies like the Foreign Legion was finally banned. Yet at the same time, Dornier was allowed to set up factories in Switzerland to circumvent Versailles bans on German rearmament, while Motta, the long-serving foreign minister, and Musy ensured a very anti-Bolshevik foreign policy. Even though by 1930 the number of foreigners had fallen to only 8.7 per cent of the population, a harsh new law on foreigners came into effect in 1931.

By then, Switzerland was experiencing the disastrous effects of the Wall Street Crash of 1929, which led the country into a wrenching depression after 1932, with consequences that had still not fully ended when war broke out again in 1939. GDP and asset values fell dramatically, the balance of payments surplus was almost wiped out by foreign protectionism, and capital began to flow out of the country. Despite its desire to reduce expenditure, the government stepped in to save some banks. Business sought to stop Duttweiler's Migros from opening new shops, leading him to start franchising his own brand of cheap, prepacked basic goods. In 1935 he branched out into HotelPlan, giving services a double boost. Industry suffered particularly badly, with watch-making losing a third of its labour force, something which helped to push unemployment up to 124,000 or 6.5 per cent of the workforce. Agriculture faced declining prices, as well.

The Great Depression brought severe social problems to Switzerland, notably poverty caused by wage cuts and limited unemployment pay. Many families were forced to look to charity. The shortage of work made female emancipation even less likely, with all cantonal propositions being rejected out of hand. Strikes also became more common, notably between 1930 and 1932, and the Social Democrats began to gain ground. By 1936, they had become the largest party, taking seats from all three right-wing parties. The latter remained cool on social measures to help the unemployed, preferring to establish higher indirect taxes and other deflationary measures. Social Democratic calls for a minimum wage, price controls and other crisis measures were all rejected. Additionally, proposals to implement pensions and accident reform were blocked, holding back Switzerland's entry into the European welfare mainstream. However, the electorate did reject structural wage cuts, directed mainly against the civil service. In November 1932, the division between the working classes and the right-wing majority came to a head in Geneva when untrained conscripts fired on a left-wing protest march, killing thirteeen and wounding sixty-three. The event became a national scandal that damaged the army's reputation.

The deteriorating economy enabled the left to gather 334,000 signatures on its anti-crisis initiative. In response, the government was forced into limited and often messy interventionism. It first sought to save the watch industry by creating a new holding company, the ASUAG, and by banning the establishment of all new watch-making firms. Next, the government was forced to take stakes in failing banks. To justify this, it sponsored a new banking law in 1934 that made the breach of banking secrecy a criminal offence, a

7.3 An election-time satire on the proliferation of right-wing Fronts in the early 1930s. It shows they shared very similar names and were led by enthusiastic publicists who fought over a very small and bemused electorate. The fact that many of these right-wing groupuscles were foreign inspired and funded is made clear by the rear of the two plinths in the foreground. The cartoonist also draws attention to the fragility of such movements. The cartoon points the way to the rapid decline of the Fronts.

step aimed at governments in France and Weimar Germany, which had sought to stop reparations money leaking to Switzerland. In 1934 a special package of measures to help farmers passed, even though these initiatives added to the state's escalating costs. Local authorities in Biel also persuaded General Motors to open a factory there. Finance Minister Musy sought to push the Federal Council into further fiscal retrenchment in 1934, and resigned when his efforts failed. This opened the way for a 30 per cent devaluation of the franc in September 1936.

The government's inability to do more encouraged far-right movements that began to push for a radical change in Swiss institutions. In the early 1930s, some forty so-called 'Fronts' on the Italian and German model emerged. Often confusingly overlapping, some were internally generated while others had international support, as did the Lega Nazionale Ticinese and the Front Fasciste Suisse of former colonel Arthur Fonjallaz, both of which gained aid from Mussolini. Germany was behind both the Eidgenössische Front and the Swiss branch of the German Nazi party under Wilhelm Gustloff. The largest movements were the Nationale Front and, in the Suisse Romande, Oltremare's Union Nationale. Usually urban, coming especially from Berne, Zurich and Schaffhausen, the Front organizations often had roots in universities and youth movements. Believing that Switzerland was degenerate and in need of renewal, they were anti-democratic, anti-liberal and anti-Semitic, and sought a Switzerland that was more corporatist than capitalist, more security conscious, and with clearer leadership. Their agendas placed them well outside the mainstream of Swiss conservatism.

The Front movements' first success came in early 1933, when they won a number of seats in Zurich and Geneva in what came to be known as the springtime of the Fronts. They attracted far fewer votes, however, than did Duttweiler's new anti-establishment and anti-extremist Landesring party. Thereafter, the Fronts concentrated on wholesale revision of the constitution, a simple target that appealed to many voters. They raised 78,000 signatures for reform, and gained some celebrity supporters like Sonderegger, but when it came to the vote in September 1935, the Fronts' initiative attracted only 196,000 votes and went down to a comprehensive defeat, along with a proposed tougher internal security law.

Electoral defeat sent the Fronts into decline. They were also undermined by a Gestapo kidnapping on Swiss territory, by internal splits between extremists and moderates, and by government action. The Federal Council, though it allowed a councillor at the German embassy to carry on organizing, demanded an end to the national structure of the Swiss NSDAP, and eventually shut it down in 1937. Economic revival also helped to reduce support for fascism in Switzerland. As the devaluation of the franc and the reopening of German markets spurred recovery in exports and tourism, new jobs were created and share values rose. The resulting increase in prosperity paved the way for a boom in new consumer goods like electric cookers, phones and radios. Nonetheless, conditions remained threatening, forcing the Swiss, who saw the swing to the extreme right as a warning signal, to decide how to confront the rising menace.

BATTENING DOWN THE HATCHES

In the late 1930s, therefore, the political mood changed. The emergence of an indigenous fascist movement, even if its dynamism had been blunted, and the increasingly vocal sabre-rattling of the neighbouring totalitarian regimes was doubly worrying. It made the Swiss increasingly self-conscious about their position in Europe, and it encouraged reassessment of their own cultural and political identity both on the governmental side and on the left. Because of the totalitarian threat, the Social Democrats moved away from their antimilitary stance and drew closer to mainstream politics. Together, these developments propelled both government and people away from international cooperation and towards greater reliance on their own resources. While the country remained suspicious of foreigners, it also began to develop a new ideology of resistance clearly demarcated from fascist thinking. Eventually, the country also began to rethink its military and political position, first rearming and preparing for war and then, after the Nazi onslaught in the West, creating a heavily defended Alpine fortress, the Reduit.

Federal Councillor Minger of the BGB, who believed that war would come by 1939, was responsible for reviving the previously neglected army. In 1936, he secured a larger budget and also established a War Loan. Next, he introduced a new strategic order, based on more, smaller and better-equipped divisions, and an extension of recruit schooling to three months. Finally, he sought to prepare society for war by creating a War Economy cell in 1937, which addressed the issue of supporting soldiers' families and encouraging both the state and households to build up stocks of basic goods: two months' reserves of food and necessities for the latter. Foreign policy remained caught in the past, at first, conservatively neutral except towards the USSR (to the extent that Switzerland sought to block the USSR's entry to the League of Nations). The government adopted an extreme position on the Abyssinian War, not even letting Haile Selassie live in his villa in Vevey. In 1939, Switzerland also recognized Franco's regime well before the Spanish Civil War had ended, even though 800 Swiss volunteered to fight on the Republican side, 300 of whom lost their lives.

In the mid-1930s, the Swiss also compromised their neutrality by their treatment of refugees from Nazi Germany. Many of these were Jews who were forced out or pressured into leaving for Switzerland. The movement of refugees led to the feeling among some Swiss that the country was being 'Jewified', even though the numbers involved actually declined during the inter-war years. Hitler's Anschluss with Austria in 1938 threatened a new flood of émigrés, moreover, which the conventionally anti-Semitic Heinrich Rothmund, head of the Federal Police Service, wanted to control by forestalling the arrival of many Jewish refugees who could not be returned to Germany. Imposing a visa requirement on all Austrians would have annoyed the Germans; instead, Rothmund accepted the Nazi regime's suggestion that Jewish citizens should have the letter J stamped on their passports. The measure solved a short-term problem for the worried Swiss, but had a permanently detrimental effect on Switzerland's reputation. During these years, rules on the registration of all foreigners were tightened, and press controls were introduced after complaints from Berlin about critical reporting on the Nazi movement.

The left was far more alarmed by the totalitarian threat than was the government, and therefore sought to move further towards the political mainstream. The Social Democrats revised their policies, abandoning both the dictatorship of the proletariat and their opposition to national defence. Their delegates voted for war credits in 1936, which turned them into an orthodox political party rather than a counter-culture. Though conservatives still felt socialism to be unpatriotic, in fact the left was increasingly falling in behind ideas of national resistance and identity. Hence, very significantly, on 19 July 1937, the unions under Ernst Dübi signed a no strike/no lockout agreement, the so-called Labour Peace, with major employers led by Konrad Ilg from Von Roll. This settlement reflected the left's realization that the division between workers and bosses had played into the Nazis' hands in Germany, something they wanted to prevent in Switzerland. Social Democratic moderation did not stop cantonal governments from banning the Communist Party, urged on by Musy's National Anti-Bolshevik Association. Nor did it persuade the other parties to elect a Social Democrat to the Federal Council, since fear of the party's revolutionary and anti-military potential remained. However, the government did promise new economic policies more acceptable to the left.

The Labour Peace turned out to be the pivotal element in a general policy switch towards greater self-reliance, producing what has been called the hedgehog syndrome. Swiss neutrality was restored to its integral form in 1938 when Foreign Minister Motta withdrew Switzerland from the League of Nations. In the same year, in a hands-off signal to Mussolini, who was making threatening noises about the *Italianità* of Ticino and the Grigioni, a referendum made Romansh a national language. Switzerland's linguistic integrity – and its difference from Nazi Germany – was also furthered by increasing public use of *Schwyzerdütsch*, which acquired a new supporting organization in 1938. The public celebration of Swiss identity continued with the opening of the Museum of Federal Charters in Schwyz in 1937 and the defence of Tell offered by historians like Karl Meyer against German doubters. Much of this was summed up in the Zurich *Landi* or national exhibition of 1939.

In addition, the government sought to give moral and intellectual cohesion to various initiatives and to the nation as a whole under the label of *Geistige Landesverteidigung*, or spiritual national defence. The term had been launched by a Radical MP in 1929 when inveighing against over-foreignization, and was taken up by the press, including some Frontist journalists. It was really brought to the fore, however, by the new Catholic Conservative Minister Philip Etter, notably in a famous government Message of December 1938 that urged a defence of Swiss culture. Promoted through stamps, children's books and official publications, the *Geistige Landesverteidigung* proved very popular by encouraging a new 'common sense' way of thinking about Switzerland, its past and identity that distinguished it from Nazi *Völkisch* thinking by stressing heroic ideals, collectivism and the Alps as a fortress. The concept thus helped the country unite, prepare for and survive the coming war.

The Second World War imposed a new set of stresses on Switzerland, because of Axis racism and totalitarianism and the perceived threat to Swiss territorial integrity. The war provoked less internal division than between 1914 and 1918, but it also raised new moral questions and practical challenges. The outbreak of war, when it finally came, saw another smooth process of initial mobilization, voting of full powers, declaration of neutrality and election of a general. Parliament's choice in 1939 was less controversial than in 1914, falling on Henri Guisan, a 61-year-old Romand farmer turned professional soldier, linguistically adept and conservative, who was to become a national hero during the war. By early September 1939, he had some 430,000 men under arms, although most of these were soon sent home after the declaration of war led not to conflict in the west, but the so-called Phoney War. The lull allowed the authorities to develop their preparations, with Guisan creating the *Heer im Haus* agency to support morale amongst bored soldiers and to encourage ideas of Swissness amongst the civilian population. Significantly, performances of Schiller's *William Tell* in the Zurich theatre were extremely popular at this time. Female volunteers were also organized into a formal Complementary Women's Service, while soldiers' pay was guaranteed in the December 1939 Compensation Fund for Mobilized Soldiers, into which firms and wage earners paid 4 per cent. By the autumn, rationing of products like flour, rice and sugar was introduced, along with controls on prices, rents and services, as the government sought to ensure that it could manage the inevitable hardships of war. The government also sought to work out its economic relationships with the belligerents, since both sides wanted to control Swiss trade – whether, in the case of Germany, to stop raw materials getting to the Allies, or in the Allies' case, to ensure continuing supplies of Swiss weapons. The latter proved harder to negotiate than a deal with Germany.

Guisan was very aware that the Swiss army was probably too weak to stop any German push into Switzerland. He therefore put out feelers to the French about providing support on the army's left flank, should the Nazis attack. Such plans went out the window in May 1940, however, when the Wehrmacht began its Blitzkrieg. The Swiss remobilized on a larger scale, but failed to avert a popular panic on 15–16 May when the Germans feinted an attack between Basle and Schaffhausen. The feint left Guisan's forces on the Limmat line in the wrong place, with Guderian's panzers on their flank and rear. Guderian's army moved on into France on 16 June, but Switzerland remained doubly exposed, because by then Italy had entered the war, meaning that the country was wholly surrounded by the Axis. The Germans found evidence of the Swiss staff talks with the French, which were discovered in a train at La Charité sur Loire. Since no corresponding talks with the Wehrmacht had taken place, the documents called Swiss neutrality very much into question. The country was in great danger, and invasion seemed to be a real possibility. Indeed, the German General staff worked on an invasion plan, known as Operation Tannenbaum, from late June until 17 October. The Swiss air force also found itself having to repel frequent Luftwaffe incursions. Swiss success annoyed Goering, who unsuccessfully sent in saboteurs to try to disrupt the Swiss interceptors.

Responding to the threat provoked a divisive domestic crisis when, on 26 June, Ministers Pilet-Golaz and Etter made broadcasts urging the Swiss to adjust to the new circumstances in which they found themselves and to accept the 'sure guidance' of the Federal Council. The addresses reflected conservatives' impatience with the slowness of the Swiss system and their desire for more authoritarian governance that they believed could ensure Swiss independence. But their ambiguous statement prompted a response diametrically different from what they intended. The army's partial demobilization and the apologies offered for the aerial clashes led many officers to fear that the government no longer intended to resist a German attack. They were also worried by the revival of the Fronts, whose actions also

7.4 Guisan at Rütli. A photograph taken on 25 July 1940,
when Henri Guisan, then head of the army, addressed virtually
the entire Swiss officer corps at the famous Rütli meadow above
Lake Lucerne, where the three founders of the Confederacy had
supposedly taken their oath to liberty centuries before. In what
was called his 'Report', Guisan – who is the single figure nearest
to the lake – sought to reassure his officers that he planned to
resist any German offensive, notwithstanding the fall of France,
and to inform them of the Reduit strategy they would therefore
be following. His initiative succeeded, and the meeting has itself
become legend. Indeed the fact that he autographed a copy of
the picture for his son Henri junior, then an army subaltern,
shows that he was aware of the historic nature of the event.

called neutrality into question, especially when some Frontist leaders were formally received by Pilet-Golaz on 10 September. One group of officers even considered a putsch, for which they were briefly imprisoned. Still, the military's concerns led to an open National Resistance Association, while at the same time De Rougemont and others founded the Gotthard League to focus civilian resistance against Nazism.

Meanwhile, Guisan was thinking of a military response to the Blitzkrieg and the country's new encirclement. The campaign of 1939 had convinced him that a mobile Swiss strategy would not work, but that, like the Finns, the Swiss might be able to hold defensive positions. A staff report was drawn up on 13 June, but Guisan remained doubtful, and it was only on 9 July that he opted for an echeloned defence, the last line of which would be in the fortified Alps. His strategy was conceived not just to dissuade invasion, but also to provide a base for counter-attacks if the invasion came. Two weeks later, he took the striking and risky step of summoning all his field officers to the historic Rütli meadow overlooking Lake Lucerne to explain his will to resist and the way in which this was to be done through the Reduit, as it became known. The meeting had an electrifying effect on the army, whose morale greatly improved, while annoying Berlin. Public opinion took longer to be impressed.

In the event, parts of the army began to fall back to the Alps to start new defensive works: series of demolition points, camouflaged gun emplacements, anti-tank barriers and hidden airfields, all backed up by barracks, stores and services. Half the army was soon dug in, and eventually 360,000 men were stationed in the Reduit, at a cost of some 900 million francs. Economic defence was strengthened by encouraging the population to join what was called the 'battle of the fields' – also known as the Wahlen Plan after one of its publicists – to increase the amount of land used to grow crops. By the use of football pitches and even the lawns in front of the Bundeshaus, the amount of land given over to crops was doubled. A merchant marine to help bring in much-needed supplies was also established. However, although the first crises of the war were thus overcome, challenges and problems were far from over.

THE ENCIRCLED HEDGEHOG

In fact, the war pressed on the country partly because of its geographical situation, surrounded on all sides as it was by the Axis, and partly because of its own economic needs. Thus the Swiss remained under uncomfortable pressure from the Axis, fearful of invasion and pressured into considerable economic cooperation, especially when the Nazi invasion of Russia made Swiss industry increasingly attractive to Germany. On the whole, the nation's hedgehog strategy and identity sustained firm resistance to Nazi ideology, as well as encouraging social and political cohesion and left-leaning reform at home. At the same time, Swiss fears also led to harsher stances over refugees and humanitarian obligations.

Early in the war, despite improvements in self-sufficiency, and even though the Swiss continued to fear a German attack, the nation found itself sucked into Germany's economic embrace. Operation Tannenbaum might have been implemented had the Luftwaffe won the Battle of Britain, or had planning for Operation Barbarossa against Russia not started in December 1940 as it did. Hitler may also have felt that encirclement and the combined effects of propaganda and internal sympathies would bring Switzerland into the Axis camp without fighting. Indeed, a number of businessmen and others, many linked with the Volksbund, presented the government with the so-called 'Petition of 200' on 15 November 1940 demanding tight control of the press, while leading officers, including Ulrich Wille Jr. and his ally Colonel Gustav Däniker, attacked Guisan's handling of the war and called for a more German-friendly stance. The government did not give way, owing in part to the arrival of the hardliner Eduard von Steiger of the BGB and Walter Stämpfli, a left-leaning Radical who won plaudits for his handling of the war economy.

Economically, Switzerland's double dependence on Germany for both raw materials and markets for its manufactures made it hard to resist German pressure. Thus, in August 1940 the government agreed to a large-scale credit for Germany. Financing this and the war weighed heavily on the population, who faced a war profits tax, a Sacrifice Tax, a National Defence tax, a levy on rich refugees and, from July 1941, a consumption tax. Rationing also tightened, as did the new controls on economic activity – running to 1,800 ordinances – which aimed, not always successfully, at keeping inflation low, creating jobs and adjusting wages to prices. The government's approach represented a major shift away from pre-war views of the state and its functions.

The launching of Operation Barbarossa on 22 June 1941 forced Germany to move to a war economy, which in turn made Swiss military production extremely attractive to the Nazi regime. Berlin's tentative invasion plans were revisited, and a *Gauleiter* was chosen to run the new client state that Hitler envisioned. Moreover, Swiss sympathy for the Nazis increased somewhat when the Wehrmacht took on the 'Bolsheviks'; Eugen Bircher even took three medical missions to the Eastern Front between October 1941 and June 1942. The German plan had again to be set aside, however, when Barbarossa ran into difficulties. And when Däniker circulated a report about a visit to Germany that urged Swiss entry into the new Nazi order, he was imprisoned on Guisan's orders. By this time, Guisan's step was in line with majority opinion. The press was almost uniformly hostile to Nazism, despite censorship and incessant German complaints. The public was more inclined to watch patriotic films like *Gilberte de Courgenay* or to celebrate the 650th Anniversary of the foundation of the Confederation – which made much use of the Tell legend – than to support totalitarianism. A wide range of forces encouraged the public's increasing hostility to the Nazi movement, including among churches and satirists. Social Democratic policies for a 'New Switzerland', which included an initiative on pensions, also had support from the Radicals, emphasizing the general move away from Nazi models. However, the establishment still remained resistant to the idea of allowing a Social Democrat into the government.

Given this lack of popular sympathy, Germany turned to economic leverage, available because Switzerland needed military markets to replace disappearing civilian orders and to provide much-needed work. Minds were concentrated by food riots in Steinen in September 1942. Neither the government nor the public was keen to ask what Swiss firms in Germany did, even when some did adopt racist language and use forced labour. The Swiss Railways also provided discounts to the Germans, including for the transit of much-needed coal to Switzerland. Concern about Nazi attitudes also affected the Swiss policy on refugees by reinforcing ingrained conservative attitudes toward foreigners. The authorities persisted in a hedgehog attitude, treating refugees as a threat partly because they were aware that taking too many would also get them in bad odour with Berlin. Even a year after news of the Holocaust had reached Switzerland, Police Chief Rothmund ordered the frontiers closed and all illegals deported; Minister Von Steiger then infamously declared that 'the boat is full' to justify the policy. The government's move was bitterly attacked in many quarters, including by the theologian Karl Barth; in response, the government somewhat relaxed its approach. However, although the policy was largely determined by *raison d'état*, because of deep-seated anti-Semitism, the policy received warm support from the Swiss Patriotic Federation and the Young Radicals. Some argued that because Jews did not share the religious affiliations of the native Swiss, excluding them did not infringe the country's safe haven tradition. Additionally, these voices noted, German Jews were not political refugees as such, and the country had no obligation towards them. For those holding such a view, refugees also posed an economic problem because they were a further burden on an already strained economy. The Police Department vehemently denied accusations of inhuman treatment of refugees, although those eventually allowed in were subject to severe conditions. A further tightening of policy occurred in December 1942 when the Nazi occupation of Vichy France increased the exodus of refugees. Public-spirited individuals like the St Gallen policeman Paul Grüninger, who helped refugees, paid a high price for doing so.

The war did bring other intense economic pressures, although not because of the refugees. National income and per capita GDP both fell to low levels while debt rose, thanks to having to spend 80 per cent of the state budget on the military, which also got preference in food supplies. As rationing became increasingly tight and prices outstripped wages, a black market developed. Women suffered particularly from difficult conditions, though births and marriages did rise during the war. The war also made the Swiss economy increasingly dependent on Germany, which by 1943–4 absorbed 50 per cent of Swiss exports, thus preventing unemployment, and provided 65 per cent of Swiss imports. However, Germany was poorly placed to pay for its purchases, forcing Berne to concede a further 500 million francs credit in July 1941. Thereafter, Germany began to sell gold to the National Bank, which was eager to buy because in June 1941, the United States had frozen 2 billion francs of Swiss assets, forcing the Bank to rebuild its reserves. The Bank also wanted to stop others buying gold that could then be used to buy francs and push inflation up.

Even though the tide of war was beginning to change, fear of a German takeover remained real. At the notorious Wansee Conference of December 1942, for example, the Nazi leadership still assumed that Swiss Jews would be included in the Final Solution. In the end the National Bank bought 1.7 billion francs from Germany, including gold the Nazi regime seized from its victims; it also bought almost 3 billion francs of gold from the Allies. Dealings with the German regime continued despite Allied pressure for a cessation of Swiss trade with Germany and for acceptance of the Safehaven programme. The latter ruled out forced transfers of property, in which Switzerland was still involved.

Despite having very good information on German army thinking through the secret Lucy espionage network, the Swiss government – as opposed to Guisan – did not fully appreciate the extent to which Germany's position had weakened. Indeed, in 1942 Pilet-Golaz was still thinking of offering mediation. His willingness to do so led his own intelligence services to accuse him in February 1943 of wanting a separate peace. But an effort to expel him failed, and he was re-elected that December. Economic need and continuing fears of German aggression still motivated government strategy. Such fears remained active from late 1942 well into 1943, and in fact real expectation of an attack developed in March 1943 after secret talks took place between Guisan and SS General Walter Schellenberg. The latter claimed that invasion plans had been active, and that he had helped to quash them. This was probably a fabrication, designed partly to help Schellenberg's own interests inside the Reich and partly to maintain economic pressure on Switzerland in the face of Allied progress in North Africa. Guisan used the meeting to ram home the Swiss determination to resist any attack, a stance made plausible by the massive increase in Swiss anti-aircraft and anti-tank guns, along with an air force that had grown from 200 to 530 planes. Guisan's

7.5 One of the twenty-six major military artillery emplacements within the Reduit. The latter was not a single construction but a network of camouflaged defensive lines round the Alps involving such things as guns hidden in old barns, anti-tank barriers, mines, blockhouses and road blocks. It also included underground hangars, stockpiles and facilities like hospitals for the 385,000 men who were stationed there in 1941–3. The Reduit was developed after the war but gradually became redundant and its remnants were sold off in 2011.

determination was also backed up by a fully functional – and now publically discussed – Reduit and the ability to mobilize 580,000 well-trained men. The Federal Council was unhappy about the talks, however, and blocked further dealings. It also went on arresting and executing Nazi agents.

Popular attitudes moved beyond the government's caution and towards the left because of reductions in rations and the resulting poverty and social unease. In the 1943 elections, which were not postponed because of the war as they were in Britain, the Social Democrats gained an unprecedented eleven seats and again became the largest party. The victory finally enabled them to secure their first Federal Council seat for Ernst Nobs, MP, a Zurich cantonal administrator and mayor of Zurich. Unions demanded higher wages and the renewal of the Labour Peace, while Stämpfli conceded the creation of the AHV/AVS pension system, setting Switzerland on the road to a modern welfare state as well as a more consensual form of governance. Even the Communists re-emerged in 1944 as the Labour party. However, the Social Democrats were not able to secure either the direct election of Federal Councillors or the expansion, from seven to nine, of the Federal Council.

The fall of Mussolini in September 1943 renewed German concern about Switzerland, whose links with the Allies it distrusted and whose mountains could provide a means of resisting an Allied push from the south. In summer 1944, rumours came through the Swiss Viking link in Budapest that an attack was imminent. The Allied attack on D-Day made this impossible, however, and the government even refused Guisan a new mobilization. The shifting balance in the war did cause Switzerland new problems, however, problems which were to outlast the war.

AT ODDS WITH THE ALLIES

Continuing German pressure made it difficult for Switzerland to respond to the new strategic situation, and made relations with the Allies harder. Indeed, Switzerland faced increasing difficulties with the latter. Disliking what they saw as the self-interestedly strict interpretation of neutrality favoured by the Swiss, they increased their demands on Switzerland as their victories accumulated. The resulting alienation foreshadowed the way that, after 1945, Swiss satisfaction at having survived the war came into conflict with critical Allied attitudes. This rendered the country unable to play a full part in the new international configurations that were emerging. For example, since the United Nations was unwilling to accommodate neutrality, the country stayed out. Growing criticism from the Allies also meant that reformism began to peter out at home.

As early as 1944, the Allies were causing more difficulties for the Swiss government than the Germans were, calling on the Swiss to break all relations with the Reich while extracting new trade and gold deals after an eight-month suspension of supplies in 1944. The Swiss did not, in fact, sign any additional agreements with Germany, which was finding it harder to provide Switzerland with the coal the country so desperately needed. As an Allied victory became more likely, the government even tried to renew contacts with the USSR, but Stalin remained hostile. His rejection of Pilet-Golaz's overtures finally forced the latter to resign in 1944. However, it was the constant overflights by Allied bombers that annoyed the Swiss the most, especially when on 1 April 1944, and apparently by mistake, the Americans bombed Schaffhausen, killing forty people and wounding many more.

By the late summer of 1944, change around Switzerland accelerated as the Allies moved closer to the Swiss borders, forcing the transfer of men from the Reduit to the north and west frontiers. Although Stalin might have liked to invade so as to use Switzerland for a further attack on Germany, there was never any question of the Allies crossing into Switzerland. Nonetheless, Allied political pressure increased: in early 1945, Roosevelt demanded that Switzerland join the Allies in their crusade against Nazism, and difficult negotiations began over art sales. Initially, the Swiss declined such demands, though they did open the frontiers a little more to refugees, and on 16 February 1945, German holdings in Switzerland were finally blocked. Yet even in March, the government, pushed by the right, refused to end trade with the Reich on the grounds that this would infringe neutrality. Indeed, Swiss banks were dealing with the Reichsbank as late as 3 May 1945, at the very time that Swiss officers were helping to end the war in Italy and refugees were again pouring into Switzerland. Swiss reluctance to change its profitable business-as-usual policy partly reflected an insistence on sovereignty, and partly an awareness that, even after its defeat, Germany would remain an important trading partner for Switzerland. Only as the war ended were relations with the Reich finally broken off. Church bells rang on 8 May, and the Federal Council broadcast to the nation to celebrate the way the army had ensured the country's survival. After a final parade in Berne, active service was ended on 20 August.

Switzerland might only have lost 84 citizens dead and 260 wounded, but the war had cost it 2.3 billion francs of assets and it had suffered 70 million francs of war damage from overflying incidents. In the long term, Swiss policy towards Germany during the war would prove far more costly politically. At the end of the war, the Swiss faced what has been called 'resentful international suspicion'. Outside opinion viewed the Confederation's economic relations with the Reich not as necessary compromises to ensure survival, but as profiteering from cooperation with evil. Despite Churchill's praise, Allied opinion generally had little sympathy for neutrality. For the Americans in particular, the matter of Holocaust assets, on which the Swiss were seen as avoiding Allied controls and demands, was another major concern. The Allies demanded that all gold held by the National Bank should be returned, because it was stolen. Although the demand caused an explosion of anger in Switzerland, the Swiss had to negotiate in order to get their own assets unfrozen. They found the Allies unsatisfied by the establishment of the Judicial Chamber for Looted Assets (Kammer zu Beurteilung von Raub), the passing of a decree on such assets in December 1945 and the Currie agreement of March 1945.

Finally, after very tough negotiations, the Swiss government accepted the Washington Agreement of 25 May 1946, in which it agreed to liquidate German assets and pay half of the 250 million francs realized to the Allies. The latter accepted this action as satisfying all their claims, and unfroze Swiss assets. The British and French were won over partly by a generous loan the Swiss government provided towards their rebuilding costs. None of this prevented further wrangling over implementation and the exchange rates used in the settlement. Switzerland also promised to identify holders of abandoned accounts in Swiss banks, but undertook no serious efforts to do so. Moreover, there was no question of Switzerland joining the United Nations, given that the Charter did not provide for

neutrality and there was little support domestically for entry.
However, it did become an Observer, and allowed the United
Nations to use the old League buildings in Geneva. Switzerland
also stayed out of UNRRA, GATT and the Bretton Woods institutions, because the latter's founding document criticized neutrals who
had traded with the Axis. Only later did it join the OEEC, the
International Court of Justice and UNESCO.

The initial post-war stand-off began to ease as Swiss anti-
communism found a new place in the widening Cold War divide.
The Cold War also provided a new opening for neutrality, so that
within a few years Switzerland was able to accept a mediating role in
the Korean War. Switzerland even received a limited amount of
Marshall Plan aid. The government's stance reflected a new policy

7.6 Churchill in Zurich, 19 September 1946. He came to
receive an honorary degree from the University and,
surprisingly, the neutral Swiss turned out in thousands to
congratulate him, both in the streets, as seen in this triumphal
parade through rainy Zurich, and in the Münsterhof. His
speech in the University Aula, 'Let Europe Arise', which urged
Franco-German reconciliation and the creation of a United
States of Europe, was a turning point in the history of Western
Europe, if not in that of Switzerland.

of 'neutrality and solidarity' adumbrated in 1947 by Max Petitpierre, Pilet-Golaz's successor as foreign minister. Since the United Nations would not provide for Swiss neutrality, he sought to give the policy a new dimension by playing up neutrality's humanitarian and universalist elements. Switzerland under his guidance joined bodies like UNICEF, despite some reservations at home, and established diplomatic relations with the USSR, Israel and China.

The Swiss reaction to the beginnings of European integration remained ambiguous. In 1946, the Swiss offered Churchill an enthusiastic welcome for his idea of Franco-German reconciliation, and issued their own Hertenstein Declaration in favour of a European federation. Swiss intellectuals like Denis de Rougemont were active in the early federalist movement, but the government was much more reserved and stayed out of the Council of Europe on its foundation in 1949, out of fear of its supranational political ambitions. Likewise, Switzerland only joined the European Payments Union after gaining assurances that it could opt out of decisions of which it disapproved. The country also ignored critical voices about its wartime role, notably from Judge Max Wolff, and became increasingly defensive. Calls for a purge of the army were ignored, and no formal response to Guisan's 'Report on Active Service' of 1947 was ever published. The Report reinforced what many Swiss felt about their experience, and began to give the war a mythical status, on which they were to build over the next forty years by stressing the *Activdienst* (active service) while underplaying the significance of relations with Germany.

Before then, the hostile atmosphere and difficult negotiations at war's end had an impact on domestic politics by undermining solidarity and reformism. However, family allowances were approved in December 1945 and AVS came into being in January 1948, defeating a popular challenge to do so. Economic Articles including consultation and government economic powers were passed, legitimating the state's new policy shift towards a welfare state. But a Right to Work Initiative was defeated, and in 1947 the Social Democrats lost seats. The restoration of the right to challenge 'urgent' legislation only narrowly scraped through. National solidarity faced an explosion of separatism in the Bernese Jura after German-speakers blocked the election of a French-speaker to the key Transport portfolio. As before, the Ticinese demanded special treatment.

Many ordinary Swiss also felt that their sacrifices during the war were not appreciated, despite having, through the army, maintained independence and neutrality against Nazism, as well as providing a haven for refugees and preserving internal cohesion. Critical outside judgements were not understood, let alone accepted. The Swiss perspective emphasized that the nation had maintained its unity, overcoming both linguistic and social divides, while the Swiss government was moving away from its earlier conservatism towards a more interventionist role. In the Swiss view, their institutions had enabled Switzerland to stay out of two wars, even though those wars and a major depression had undermined the nation's prosperity. The post-war combination of external criticism and domestic tensions thus encouraged the continuation of a hedgehog mentality and valorization of Swiss distinctiveness in a rapidly changing world, especially in conservative quarters. The hedgehog wartime experience of many Swiss, in which they had seen off slump and war, became a vital basis for developing a new self-confidence based on the conviction that Switzerland had become a special case – the so-called Swiss *Sonderfall* – even though outside opinion was far from sharing Swiss assessments.

8

The Sonderfall years, 1950–1990

If the Swiss had found themselves under a cloud immediately after 1945, they were soon able to compensate, thanks to the way history speeded up thereafter. In fact the post-war years saw probably the greatest and most rapid economic and social changes Switzerland has ever undergone. This, on top of their efforts in the war, led many Swiss, and some foreigners, to think of Switzerland as the 'Sonderfall Schweiz', as an exceptional country: more prosperous, more harmonious, more democratic, more self reliant, more able to solve its problems and more moral than most other states. Switzerland's exceptionalism was attributed to distinctive institutions like neutrality, federalism and direct democracy, and also to the way the Swiss coped with their social, religious and linguistic diversities within a nation-state, leading one foreign authority to call the country a 'paradigm of integration'. In other words, the Swiss felt themselves, along with a benign Providence, to be the main authors of their own success.

They could point to the fact that, within thirty years of the end of the war, Switzerland had become a very rich country. It had also carved out a successful new international role for itself and had been able to overcome a series of challenges from linguistic division, a renewed anti-foreigner right, environmentalism and the post-1968 new left. These challenged both the direction Switzerland was taking and the new self-image behind Swiss confidence. Such challenges, however, like the recessions of the 1970s, were at first overcome, even as the country drifted once more to the right. However, by the

late 1980s, fissures were beginning to appear in the Sonderfall, with
arguments over the UN, Green issues and state security posing
challenges that ultimately upset the complacency behind the whole
Sonderfall model.

A VERY AFFLUENT SOCIETY

The first element to be added to the wartime thinking about the
Sonderfall was pride in the country's rapid rise to enhanced prosperity,
something that was to have a considerable impact on social and
political behaviour. In fact, the dramatic economic growth that
began in the early 1950s was the dominant factor in transforming

8.1 Multinational Switzerland. Much of the post-war Swiss
economic miracle was driven by the country's surprisingly large
corps of multinational companies. First among these was the
Nestlé food enterprise. Pictured here is its headquarters at Vevey
on the northern shore of Lac Leman in the French-speaking
canton of Vaud. However, this is only the brain of the company;
its body, i.e. manufacturing and sales, is mostly based outside
Switzerland.

both Switzerland and the way it was perceived. Because Swiss industries had not suffered war damage and could call on a fresh and well-educated labour force, the country was immediately able to supply consumer and capital goods on the increasing scale required by Germany and other countries as they rebuilt after the war. Industrial productivity soared, helped by a massive shift of employment from agriculture into the increasingly efficient manufacturing and service sectors. Manufacturing was progressively concentrated and focused on new industries. Total production tripled between 1960 and 1974 alone, with GDP growth rates rising as high as 12 per cent at times. The pattern of growth was also consistent, with only minor stutters in the mid-1960s. Not until the 1970s was there really any check to the upward movement of the Swiss economy.

A vast proportion of Switzerland's growing output was exported, increasingly to the rest of Europe, which by 1974 absorbed two-thirds of Swiss exports, the value of which rose consistently. Switzerland made up part of the 'blue banana' zone, stretching southwards from London to Lombardy, which was the driving force of the European economy. Growth helped to build up large multinationals like Nestlé and Brown Boveri along with chemical firms like Hoffman and CIBA. By 1970, though the Swiss then made up only 0.15 per cent of the world's population, they were responsible for 2 per cent of global trade. The deficit in the balance of trade caused by the cost of importing fuel and raw materials was made up by growing income from thriving tourism and other invisible exports. Services thus expanded, notably with Swiss banks proving increasingly attractive to outsiders. Already in the mid-1950s, Harold Wilson felt it necessary to attack the 'gnomes of Zurich' for speculating against sterling. Books appeared on the Swiss economic and financial empire, both from the Swiss and from outsiders like T. R. Fehrenbach, who in 1966 wrote a detailed study of the *Gnomes* and their power. Economic growth, in other words, provided the first new pillar of the Sonderfall as well as generally enhancing the country's image. It was therefore true of the Swiss that 'they had never had it so good'.

Prosperity was reinforced by social change. Switzerland became a bigger, more mobile, more affluent and more cultured society. The population rose to 6.3 million by 1970, owing mainly to the influx of workers from other countries who were needed to sustain high levels of economic growth. Significantly, many Swiss did not call them guest workers (*Gastarbeiter*), as did the Germans, but less welcomingly *Fremdarbeiter* or 'foreign workers'. By 1970, non-native inhabitants numbered over a million, or 17.2 per cent of the population. Population growth accelerated urbanization and density while individuals also became more mobile. As the agricultural segment shrank, with 100,000 farms disappearing between 1940 and 1980, many people moved out of the mountain regions. Others moved from over-crowded city centres into new suburbs. Motorization made commuting much easier, but also enabled some industry to move into more rural areas. A second form of mobility resulted from the move into services and the arrival of foreign workers willing to take over low paid and routine jobs from the Swiss: a new middle class emerged, much of which was employed rather than being entrepreneurs. The expansion of higher education also allowed young people to move out of their home regions and to climb the social ladder.

Some authorities began to feel that Switzerland was ceasing to be a class society. It had certainly become a more equal society, since the wealth generated by economic growth was relatively fairly shared. Wages rose 150 per cent – often faster than GDP – in the thirty years after the war, compared to only 66 per cent in pre-war decades; in consequence, the share of income enjoyed by the top decile fell while that of lower ones grew. The increasing availability of welfare accelerated the decline of poverty, as did the virtual disappearance of unemployment. Switzerland became a high-wage, high-price economy whose growing purchasing power also made it a wealthy consumer society. Holidays, housing, medical care, cars and recreational spending all soared. Savings rose tenfold, and the Stock Exchange nearly eightfold. The rise of consumer associations in the early 1960s, along with the emergence of shopping centres and especially supermarket chains like the Coop, Denner and Migros, also corresponded to shifts in both wealth and outlook. Migros became the dominant retail force in Switzerland, spreading from groceries into education, leisure, banking and gardening, although not into alcohol. At the same time, even though the relative size of the public sector declined, the country invested heavily in high-quality public infrastructure, including airports, good motorways and even, by 1980, a road tunnel under the St Gotthard. Measured quality of life improved greatly, with life expectancy soaring thanks to enhanced public health, while crime and industrial unrest ran at remarkably low levels.

Switzerland was also becoming a more educated and aware society, as schools improved and its many newspapers doubled their print runs. The first racy tabloid, *Blick*, appeared in 1959, and entertainment became more easily available after television made its appearance in 1953. The Swiss participated in European culture, providing a number of leading film actors and directors, notably Jean-Luc Godard and Alain Tanner. Switzerland also became a more multi-lingual country, since the arrival of foreign workers, at first from Italy and then from further abroad, meant that more languages were spoken by greater numbers. Mobility and education meant that more native Swiss were likely to speak another national language too. Immigration changed the religious balance by increasing the number of Catholics, although the growing secularization of European society also affected Switzerland: increasing numbers refused to fill in the religious question on the census form, suggesting that they had no religious beliefs. Yet, despite the increase in diversity, social harmony and stability came to constitute a second new pillar of the Sonderfall.

Politically, developments at home and abroad reinforced Swiss feelings that they had found a winning recipe. Domestically, reformism continued to subside. An unemployment insurance scheme was approved in 1951 and the Social Democrats won an extra parliamentary seat, but the centre-right did better. Then, in 1953, the people rejected tax increases proposed by the Social Democratic Finance Minister Max Weber; when he resigned in pique, the party was again left outside the government, even though it won additional seats in 1955. In 1958, the electorate also rejected a law banning cartels, of which there were some 600. The government's wartime emergency powers lapsed whereas Conjunctural Articles, allowing it to act in case of depression, were held up until 1964.

In fact a certain depoliticization became visible domestically. With the collective cake growing larger, there seemed to be less need for argument or government intervention. With fewer conflicts over the distribution of resources and a decreasing desire to rock the consumerist ship, the number of problematic initiatives fell. Turnout for both

8.2 Women and politics. A highly symbolic photo of the long-standing denial of women's political rights. It shows a woman who had the temerity to try to attend the 1946 annual Landsgemeinde of Appenzell Ausserrhoden in Trogen being summarily and emphatically directed to leave by a policeman. Women's suffrage was slower coming to Switzerland than in other European countries owing to conservative masculine resistance. Some Francophone cantons gave women the vote in the late 1950s, but a national initiative failed in 1959. Protests continued, but only in 1971 did a votation succeed, after which women made rapid progress politically.

votations and elections also began to decline. Politics, in other words, seemed less necessary, and fewer voters supported innovations like female suffrage, which, despite defeats at cantonal level, was put to the vote nationally in 1959 and comprehensively defeated. Women were given the vote in Geneva, Neuchâtel and Vaud, however, ensuring that the idea did not die. Overall, politics appeared to be giving way to optimistic managerialism and to the pursuit of consumerism and entertainment.

Declining contention encouraged the parties to move towards the centre, reinforcing tendencies towards compromise and consultation. Thus, the communistic Labour Party was marginalized, while the Social Democratic party saw its traditional constituency shrinking and becoming less ideological. Trade union membership also dropped, despite the unions being fully involved in economic policy-making. The SPS had therefore to change its tune, refraining from launching provocative constitutional initiatives and dropping Marxist elements from its programme at Winterthur in 1959. The party's about-turn partly paid off: although it lost ground electorally in 1959, it still gained the two seats on the Federal Council that its support had long justified, and for which the Conservative–Christian–Social People's Party, as the Catholic Conservatives had become in 1957, had been pushing. The 1959 recasting of the Federal Council created the so-called Magic Formula of two Radicals, two Catholics, two Socialists and one member of the Peasant Party, almost precisely reflecting the parties' shares of the electorate. Remarkably, both remained relatively stable until the end of the century. In line with this trend, the Conservatives in 1970 again renamed themselves as the Christian Democratic People's party, seeking to move outside the Catholic laager and liberalize in line with Vatican II. However, the implosion of Catholic supportive organizations in the face of secularization and social change limited its growth. The next year, the BGB became the Swiss People's Party after a merger with the old Democratic Party, in an initially unsuccessful attempt to widen its appeal beyond the declining farming community.

This regression towards the centre produced increasingly harmonious politics, making it possible to agree on a permanent limitation to the size of the National Council. This was fixed at 200 from the 1963 elections onward. Concordance democracy that sought consensual policy-making also increased, furthered by the enhanced role given to organized interests in policy-making through new consultation processes. The Swiss became increasingly proud of their political cooperation, moderation and democracy, elements that came to be seen as a further pillar of the Sonderfall. Indeed, for one English politician, the Swiss had succeeded in taking the conflict out of politics. The novelist Paul Erdman suggested a slightly dimmer view in his novel *The Crash of '79*, in which everything in Switzerland was efficiently decided by a handful of top businessmen and politicians working in cahoots. Even though meant critically, Erdman's picture reinforced the commonly held view that Switzerland, by the 1960s, had become surprisingly well off and remarkably well integrated.

A NEW INTERNATIONAL ROLE

Domestic achievements were not the only new elements to be added to the Sonderfall in the post-war years. Diplomatic developments also reinforced the image as the country came in from the cold. Switzerland may have remained outside major institutions like the UN, but it still carved out a new – and well-recognized – role for itself as an active neutral and as a key member of EFTA. However, it was also surreptitiously developing new links with NATO. And its new role was not exempt from domestic criticism.

In the early 1950s, although defensiveness and resentment over criticism of its wartime record continued, accentuated by the necessity of signing a 1951 deal with the US COCOM authority that banned Switzerland from exporting arms to the East, the country increasingly came to see the real threat to its independence as coming from the USSR. Although the USSR formally recognized Swiss neutrality in 1955, and even though Switzerland stayed out of NATO and emphasized the solidaristic side of its neutrality, much of its strategic thinking and military preparation assumed that it was on the side of the West. Officially, however, Switzerland presented itself as a locking 'device' between East and West, giving both sides the assurance that Switzerland would neither attack them nor allow its territory to be used by the other side. To develop the country's commitment to solidarity as well as neutrality, Switzerland joined an increasing number of UN agencies, many of which had offices in

Geneva. On occasions, it did apply UN sanctions, as well as becoming an Observer in the Council of Europe. Switzerland also provided mediation and other good offices in conflicts such as the Korean, Algerian and Vietnam wars.

Formal neutrality between East and West did not stop the government from purging leftists from the civil service, warning the public against eastern propaganda, and secretly surveilling possible communist sympathizers, such was the strength of its anti-communism. Ten thousand Hungarian refugees were warmly welcomed after the 1956 uprising. At the same time – although this was only revealed much later – the government set up an organization known as Project 26, designed to create a shadow government and guerrilla force in liaison with NATO's Gladio network in case the Red Army rolled into Switzerland. Official military strategy moved from resistance based on the Alps to a mobile defence designed to hold off the Soviets for fifteen days until NATO could come to the rescue. This strategic posture was built into a new military concept in 1966. The Swiss also toyed with the idea of acquiring nuclear weapons, but this was soon set aside.

The development of European integration posed Switzerland new problems. The government was uneasy about the formation of the Coal and Steel Community and then the European Economic Community, since they threatened to constrain Switzerland's economic and political autonomy. Swiss foreign policy therefore supported the idea of a large Free Trade Area and, when that failed, fell in with the UK's fallback suggestion of a small free trade area. Switzerland was therefore active in the formation of EFTA in 1960. EFTA seemed to be a stepping-stone towards more involvement in Europe, since the government finally accepted that the Council of Europe did not threaten its sovereignty and became a full member in 1963. Three years later Switzerland entered GATT. However, since EFTA had been designed as a rival to the EC, the British application to join the latter cast EFTA into doubt. At first, Switzerland was disturbed by the British switch, and the government briefly considered association with the EC. Soon, however, EFTA became a very satisfactory means of managing small-state relations with the EC, and in 1972, Switzerland was one of a number of EFTA states which signed free-trade agreements with Brussels. This proved a very adequate arrangement, providing free access for Swiss goods but without incurring any of the burdens of membership. Many sectoral deals were to follow, leading the Swiss to think that they had developed a 'third way' that avoided either membership or marginalization.

This pragmatic success, along with what was seen as a successful inoculation against the Cold War, was generally popular. It reinforced the feeling that Switzerland was doing exceptionally well by adding helpful self-reliance to its other achievements, in line with *Willensnation* thinking. As a result, thinkers in the 1960s started using the term Sonderfall to describe the country's singularly fortunate condition. The term was first spelled out by anti-immigrant writers such as Adolf Guggenbühl in his 1967 essay 'Die Schweizer sind anders' ('The Swiss are different'). Such views were reinforced by the way the country rode out the oil crisis relatively unscathed, whereas neighbouring states suffered badly. Growing faith in Swiss exceptionalism reinforced the defensive, often hedgehog-like attitudes developed during the war, because awareness remained of the apparent fragility of the newly found success. Defensiveness, psychological as well as military, lay behind the 1962 establishment of the Civil Protection Office and the requirement that all new houses have nuclear shelters, even if these were usually used as wine or paint stores. The government also moved provisionally to replace *Rufst du* by the Swiss Hymn as the national anthem, a move made permanent in 1978.

Such attitudes did not go unquestioned. At first among intellectuals and then among other political forces, the country's transformation was consistently challenged. Max Frisch's 1954 novel *Stiller* sharply challenged the Sonderfall, as did writers such as Karl Schmidt and Max Imboden. Their books, *Unbehagen im Kleinstaat* and *Helvetisches Malaise* respectively, were hostile to the agenda of growth at all costs and to the commercialization of all human connections. A cottage industry of soul-searching books about a Swiss malaise developed, encouraged by a scandal over the purchase of Mirage fighters to replace British Hawker Hunters that led to a formal parliamentary inquiry in 1964, which condemned the lack of ministerial control that had let costs escalate. As a result, fewer planes were bought and Defence Minister Paul Chaudet decided not to stand for re-election in 1966. The government also agreed, in future, to submit its policy strategy to Parliament for approval, and to redefine its relationship with the cantons. The following year's elections saw the unconventional centrist Landesring make significant gains as voters protested against the failings of the system. The Labour (or Communist) Party also won two more seats, even after the Prague Spring prompted a new burst of anti-communism. There was even talk of the necessity for a complete revision of the Constitution, which had swollen considerably over the years, thanks to additions written in through popular initiatives. Some also felt the constitution to be out of line with modern liberal thinking. The breach between Sonderfall thinking and critical intellectuals came to a head in 1969 when a long-delayed government civil defence booklet, written by Albert Bachman, the founder of the P26 secret army organization and by then a fierce anti-communist and soon to be head of Swiss intelligence services, went beyond shelters by calling for social discipline and warning against flirting with left-wing and non-Swiss ideas. The booklet caused a wave of protest and a split in the Swiss Writers' Association, as the critics noisily dissociated themselves from conservative views. Although such criticisms were rarely noted outside, they were a foretaste of new challenges and splits that were developing, partly in response to the new affluence the country was enjoying. Indeed, while the country adopted William Tell's crossbow as its symbol of Swiss quality, mainstream historians were becoming increasingly critical both of the liberation saga and of prevailing Swiss conservatism.

NEW CHALLENGES

From the early 1960s the country had to face new challenges. The first of these, which was probably the most noted outside, concerned the Jura question, which was to run into the late 1970s. But there was also a significant new anti-foreigner movement that often came within an ace of rewriting the rules on population numbers. The New Left surge that derived from the events of May 1968 in France also had a lasting effect on Swiss politics, including through its encouragement of environmentalism. Although the new forces severely challenged the Sonderfall status quo, however, this proved able to absorb them.

8.3 A photograph of a big demonstration for Jurassian
independence, held in Delemont on 20 March 1965. The central
placard saying 'in French' sums up the motivation of the
movement. Other placards denounce mistreatment by Berne
and concessions made to other cantons, and also call for liberty.
The large size of the demonstration is symbolic of the militancy
of the separatist campaign, which also involved small-scale
violence. This continued for a while into the 1980s, because the
new canton did not include Moutiers and the other French-
speaking parts of the southern Jura. Their inclusion in the new
canton may soon be put to a popular vote.

The status quo was initially threatened by a resurgence of language conflict after the Bernese electorate, in 1959, roundly defeated
a call by the Rassemblement Jurassien (RJ) to allow a right of
secession for the Bernese Jura. The RJ appealed for outside help,
while its underground youth wing, the Beliers, embarked on a campaign of minor violence: dynamiting railway lines, attacking the
local arsenal and setting fire to buildings. The Federal Council stepped in, and in 1969–70 the Bernese accepted an amendment to the
cantonal constitution that recognized the existence of a Jurassian
people and allowed for a series of votes on autonomy. The resolution
of such a potentially damaging problem was hailed as another
Sonderfall achievement.

Interestingly, attempts to form a language-based Romand party came to nothing, as did moves to reunite the two Basle half-cantons in 1969, since the rural population did not wish to share the city's higher costs. However, the city became the first German-speaking canton to give women the vote, reflecting growing pressure on the issue. Indeed, the cantons remained important sites of innovation in the 1960s and 1970s, leading the way on constitutional revision as well as on women's suffrage, and accounting for a growing share of state expenditure. However, they also turned to the centre for new subsidies for the universities in 1966. Ultimately, reform of the fed-eral–cantonal relationship was a key element of the national constitu-tional revision process then getting under way.

An even more significant complicating factor in further evolution of the Sonderfall was renewed opposition to '*Überfremdung*' as opponents of immigration characterized it. The surge in worker immi-gration had proved to be nowhere near as temporary as had been assumed after the war, and the growing population of near-permanent immigrants worried many. Although clearly a by-product of the new prosperity, it also seemed to challenge the conservative view of Swiss identity on which the Sonderfall idea rested. Immigration thus proved to be a very emotive issue that cut across the political land-scape: worried trade unionists in the 1950s sought to curb numbers, while conservative single-issue parties against immigration emerged in the 1960s. Chief among these was the Nationale Aktion gegen die Überfremdung von Volk und Heimat (NA), the first anti-migrant party in Europe. Although the government took some first steps to control numbers and to examine the problems posed by migration, this did not dissuade the NA and others from tabling initiatives to reduce the number of foreigners in the population. These were then withdrawn to make room for a proposal by a leading right-wing publicist, James Schwarzenbach. He had been recruited by the NA and in 1967 became its first representative in Parliament. His initiative called for a decrease of 400,000 foreigners and a permanent quota on non-citizen residents. The hard-fought campaign over the initiative caused a real political crisis before it was defeated by 54 per cent to 46 per cent in 1970.

This was far from the end of the story: fear of foreigners con-tinued to be a hot political issue, fuelled by concessions on families which the government had to make when it renegotiated an accord with Italy. In 1971 the NA gained four seats in the lower house, while Schwarzenbach's new Republican Movement, a 1970 breakaway prompted by the NA's increasing extremism, won seven seats. However, two further anti-foreigner initiatives, directed against 'overpopulation' and easier naturalization, were easily defeated once a Europe-wide depression set in. One of the ironies of the situation was that the massive use of cheap foreign labour had probably been a disincentive to technological modernization in the 1960s.

If the *Überfremdung* movement criticized aspects of the Sonderfall from a traditional nativist position, the events of May 1968 in France helped to stimulate a wider challenge from the left. The upheaval of 1968 fostered the emergence of a range of 'new' left-wing parties, such as Trotskyists, Maoists and neo-Stalinists, some of which succeeded in entering Parliament, while others helped develop new extra-parliamentary social protest movements. Sometimes these turned to existing channels, leading to a surge in the use of direct democracy, with some years recording eight times as many initiatives as before 1968. The number of successful initiatives did not increase, however. The spirit of 1968 also manifested itself in violent demonstrations for Alternative Youth Centres, which began at the Globus building in Zurich in 1968 and spread to Geneva, Lausanne, Bienne, Basle, Berne and Lugano by 1973. Such centres encouraged a new youth culture and lifestyle that had little time for orthodox political activity, let alone for the army. The movement made conscientious objection, then still virtually a crime, fashionable, much to the alarm of the establishment. It also boosted the use of Schwyzerdütsch, producing the so-called *Mundartwelle*, a wave of dialect usage that began to dominate the media, politics and even academia.

The events of 1968 encouraged change in two main policy areas. One was the rights of women, who finally got the vote in 1971 with support from as large a majority as had been against the idea in 1959. The vote followed increased pressure from women's organizations and the embarrassment of having to consider opting out of parts of the European Convention on Human Rights, which the country had yet to accept, because of the disenfranchisement of women. The initiative also benefited from the fading stress on the comradeship of the (masculine) army that had spared Switzerland in the war – a view which left little room for female emancipation. The first women – eleven in all – entered Parliament that autumn, and progress thereafter was surprisingly rapid: by 1981, gender equality was written into the Constitution. Again, the pacific solution of this long-standing anomaly was seen by some as an element of the Sonderfall.

The other area of change came in political environmentalism. The first environmental party emerged in Neuchâtel in 1971 in opposition to a planned lakeside motorway, but environmentalism really took off with protests against nuclear power when planning permission for the Kaiseraugst power reactor came up for renewal. A site of considerable archaeological significance close to left-wing Basle, Kaiseraugst mobilized resistance to atomic energy, including a large-scale occupation in April 1975. The Federal Council was forced to negotiate with the demonstrators, and though the occupation was ended, it dealt a severe blow to nuclear power. Several initiatives demanding a moratorium on nuclear power were launched, and Whitsun anti-nuclear marches became an established part of the political scene. So did concern about nuclear waste. The damaging 1976 chemical spillage at Roche's Seveso plant in northern Italy also helped to push environmental concerns beyond mere protest and into mainstream politics. Environmental initiatives attracted up to 30 per cent of those voting, so that from the late 1970s, ecological parties began to emerge, winning municipal seats. In 1979, Daniel Brelaz of Lausanne was elected the first Green MP in Europe. A new law enshrining the principle of 'the polluter pays' entered the statute book, and the political system seemed to be innovative and flexible.

These new forms of left-wing politics sprang in large part from a new middle-class generation that had not experienced the 1930s and 1940s, and whose members were critical of the consumerism, xenophobia and repressive tolerance of their times. Despite being educated and well off, they felt themselves powerless against the legacy of the Sonderfall. This segment often sought progressive change at home and more help for the Third World, ideas that were equally vigorously resisted, notably by right-wing Radicals. Indeed, in 1971 both the Social Democrats and the Landesring lost ground, while the far right gained and the Radicals re-emerged as the largest party, suggesting that the Sonderfall was still intact, despite the pressures it had had to endure.

RIDING OUT THE RECESSION

Indeed, many came to see the way the country was able to cope with the economic depression of the 1970s as further proof of its special status. Unemployment remained very low and the overall economic situation remained comparatively rosy. By the early 1980s, after the second oil shock had been overcome, the country began to return to its centre-right leanings.

Nonetheless, by 1975, the Social Democrats regained the top spot, since the far right promptly lost half its seats. The rapid swing reflected the fact that the country was caught up in the international economic crisis unleashed by the oil-price shock of 1973. Switzerland, like most western countries, had become dependent on imported oil for three-quarters of its energy consumption, which had risen fourfold between 1950 and 1970. Increased oil prices caused rising inflation along with declining domestic demand and foreign exports. Growth ground to a virtual halt in 1973–6 and again in 1978–81 as industrial production and investment fell off. The watch industry suffered particularly, because it had not kept up with the widening use of quartz and mass production, even though it had helped to pioneer the new technology.

Economic stagnation slowed social mobility as wages began to slide and access to property ownership became more difficult. As a result, income disparities rose along with taxes. However, although 365,000 jobs, or 12 per cent of the total, were lost and as many workers went on short time, the Swiss did not suffer from unemployment as much as most of the developed world. The unemployed rose from a few hundred at the beginning of the decade to only 25,000 in 1974–6; instead, a large number of foreign workers did not have their contracts renewed and left Switzerland. Once back home, they often stayed, since they were not entitled to Swiss unemployment pay. The number of new *Fremdarbeiter* coming to Switzerland halved in the second half of the decade. All in all, about 175,000 left the country, accounting for half the jobs lost.

The economic downturn limited labour unrest, but it probably also helped to defeat new attempts to restrict the number of foreigners. The idea was wonderfully satirized in a hilarious 1978 film by Rolf Lyssy called *The Swissmakers*, which derided the way in which citizenship applications from spaghetti-eating Italians were handled.

It became the most watched film in Switzerland before *Titanic*, suggesting that many Swiss did not take the NA's ideas too seriously. Indeed, the latter made an attempt in the late 1970s to moderate its image, allowing it to continue influencing legislation on migration into the early 1980s. However, asylum policy was significantly liberalized in 1979, something which was to have a considerable impact.

Policy began to swing towards the left, along with Parliament. Welfare policy became more active, with price controls coming in after 1972, along with new Conjunctural Articles in 1978. Social security expanded, with reforms to old-age pensions in 1974, bringing in the three-pillar system of state, occupational and private provision. Three years later, unemployment insurance was made obligatory. Even if the country was moving closer towards a normal West European welfare democracy, the SPS was still unable to push through proposals for a Value Added Tax (VAT), a wealth tax and industrial co-determination (*Mitbestimmungsrecht*), let alone policies for better integration of foreigners.

Foreign policy was not greatly changed by the depression, despite being in Social Democratic hands throughout the decade. Switzerland continued to evolve hesitantly towards more openness and solidarity, but with considerable limitations. The first official visit to Moscow took place in 1973, and the country became more sympathetic to the wider world, as seen in responses to South Africa and the Chilean crisis. However, it proved far less willing to admit refugees then than it had been in 1956. The Swiss also threw a good deal of effort into the Helsinki process, proposing wide-ranging arbitration and mediation procedures in collaboration with other European neutrals and non-aligned states. Switzerland finally signed the ECHR in 1974, but did not ratify the European Social Charter. In 1976, led by the far right, the electorate resoundingly defeated a proposed loan to the International Development Agency. This corresponded to the way Switzerland stood alongside other capitalist industrial countries in the Paris Conference on North–South relations. Under Pierre Aubert, foreign minister from 1978, new efforts began to develop relations with the Third World and with the Council of Europe.

The ongoing shifts in Swiss political culture did help to reinforce ideas of domestic harmony by pushing forward the democratic processes needed to solve the Jura question. A 1974 vote accepted the idea, but not the boundaries, of a new canton: the Protestant elements of the South Jura, whose historic and geographic connections with Berne were closer than those of the Catholic north, largely voted against the idea. The actual frontier was decided by further referenda in 1975, which paved the way for the creation of the twenty-third canton in 1978–9. This, along with the way the country had escaped the worst of the European recession, served to reassure many Swiss that they were still a Sonderfall. Nevertheless, resentment amongst Jurassian nationalists, who wanted the whole region, persisted in an unsettling way.

The 'youth troubles' that flared up at the end of the decade also helped to push mainstream Swiss society back towards the right. The second oil shock seems to have made many young people realize that their educational, job and political prospects were much diminished. The perceived deception and immorality of the age of affluence came under increasing attack, as in Fritz Zorn's powerful novel *Mars* and later in Alain Tanner's film *Messidor*. Anti-establishment feelings among the young were given a powerful new focus by the decision of the Zurich City Council to spend millions refurbishing the Opera House while closing facilities for the young and their rock culture. The decision sparked major demonstrations, which were met with violence. Attempts were made to ban a film about the troubles called *Zurich Burns*. Such heavy-handed responses provoked a further wave of riots and protests in Zurich and other major cities. The Autonomous Youth Centre in Zurich then reopened in the spring of 1981 under Church supervision, but remained under pressure because of fears over drug use. The internal contradictions of the youth movement led to its decline after 1982. Nonetheless, debate on the 'youth problem' was abundant, including a government report that accepted the reality of alienation, much to the annoyance of some conservatives. To the establishment, the emergence of a counter-culture prepared to use violence seemed a real threat to the rule of law and the Swiss way of life. The establishment had earlier also been distressed by the publication of *Das Boot ist Voll*, Alfred Häsler's critique of Swiss refugee policy during the Second World War, a book that had considerable impact even though it did not directly challenge the country's role in the war.

These developments help to explain a swing to the right that began in the late 1970s. In 1979 the Social Democrats and the Landesring both lost seats, as did the Republikaner, the secessionists from the NA, while the orthodox right gained, with the FDP leading the way. This pattern was continued four years later when the Social Democrats lost a further four seats, and the far left also slumped, allowing the Radicals to re-emerge as the largest party. The FDP was then emboldened to launch its first initiative in many years, on the harmonization of the school year. When the Social Democrats put forward the first-ever female nomination for the Federal Council, that of Zurich MP Lilian Uechtenhagen, she was turned down. Her perceived extremism encouraged the conservative parties to prefer Otto Stich of Solothurn. In fact, the choice of Uechtenhagen reflected the way the SPS was being undermined by divisions between its moderate membership and aggressive intellectual left-wing leaders. The SPS's reaction to her rejection was to threaten to pull out of the Magic Formula, which would set off a crisis in Swiss politics. In the end, wiser counsels prevailed, but the unfavourable image generated by internal animosities was very damaging to the party. The fact that, later the same year, the electorate roundly rejected the party's initiative on banning bank secrecy did not help.

The shift rightwards, along with a renewed surge in the foreign population, also helped to revive the far right. The surge came about partly because economic growth created demand for yet more *Fremdarbeiter* and partly because the new asylum law encouraged applications from many Tamils fleeing the civil war in Sri Lanka. The rightist revival showed itself first in the crushing 1981 defeat of the left's Être Solidaire initiative, which proposed better treatment for foreign workers, and then in new NA extremism. The electorate rejected a new foreigners' law in 1982, and the NA launched yet another initiative against immigration. When the far-right Vigilance Party won 20 per cent of the vote in Geneva, the government moved to revise its asylum legislation in 1983, and went on in succeeding years to toughen its stance on foreigners. The far right's worry about the ability of foreigners to buy landed property in Switzerland was answered by the restrictive *Lex Friedrich* of 1985.

The right had far less success on environmental issues, which proved an even bigger problem after revelations in 1983–4 that the country's

forests were apparently dying. This led to a special session of
Parliament and new legislation, the need for which was underlined
by the Chernobyl nuclear explosion and especially the Schweizerhalle
chemical-spill disaster of November 1986. Failure to deal adequately
with a fire at the Sandoz chemicals plant, near Basle, allowed tons of
toxic chemicals to escape into the Rhine, with dire effects. The slow
public response to the disaster helped to undermine confidence, at
home and abroad, in Swiss standards of environmental protection.
The foundation in 1985 by Reaganite businessman Michel Dreher of
the Automobile Party, which campaigned for motorists and against
'ecological gauchism' and asylum-seekers, showed there was resistance
to the new trend. The AP enjoyed modest electoral success for a while,
but the number of Green parties also grew, and from 1983, they joined
in a loose federation.

Attitudes began to swing right in some other areas, as could be seen
with another rejection of a VAT proposal in 1979 and resistance to the
extension of female rights. An updated marriage law was opposed by
small businesses because it meant giving some control to proprietors'
wives, which, opponents argued, would break up firms. Nonetheless,
the law survived a challenge. The long-awaited project to make a
reality of the constitutional commitment to maternity insurance was
rejected in December 1987, however, revealing continuing doubts
about female emancipation even though the country was making
considerable progress in this respect. Traditionalists also joined the
establishment in resisting pacifist and environmentalist opposition to
the army and its needs, notably for new training grounds and expenditure. Hostility to conscientious objection remained intense. In other
words, the Sonderfall and its supporters continued to exercise a controlling influence on Swiss politics and society.

CONFLICTING CURRENTS

However, while right-wing thinking continued to lead government
policy and to block attempts to change the Sonderfall's default setting of self-exclusion from the UN, all this was subject to real challenge as the 1980s wore on. This was especially the case where the
army and the environment were concerned. The overall role of the
state also attracted massive criticism, thanks to revelations about its

past security policy. In other words, real fissures in the Sonderfall began to open up as new forces came into conflict.

Government policy also responded to the spread of more conservative economic ideas in the developed world during the 1980s. The state made limited moves towards deregulation by lifting price controls and some regulatory burdens on banks, and by encouraging local commercial radio stations. Some commentators even discerned a Swiss version of Thatcherism at this time, and worried about the future the social services faced with privatization and deregulation. Neo-liberal policies advanced once the Radicals selected the first woman Federal Councillor and Minister in October 1984 in Elizabeth Kopp, MP, a 48-year-old lawyer from Zurich. She took over the Police and Justice Ministry and became known as the country's 'Iron Lady', although she also gave further impetus to women's rights. One Social Democratic minister went as far as to accuse her party of wanting to dismantle the welfare state. Such claims were exaggerated, given that the decade saw major reform in both unemployment insurance and occupational pensions. However, the FDP did indeed campaign for 'Less of the State'. The same period saw a renewal of the SVP, whose Zurich wing, under the leadership of a wealthy entrepreneur, Christoph Blocher, was developing new sections, strategies and structures. Blocher's family originally came to Switzerland from Württemberg in the mid-nineteenth century. His grandfather had been a German-language activist and founder of an anti-League of Nations alliance, while he himself was the seventh child of a Protestant pastor from north-eastern Switzerland. Educated in law and agriculture, Blocher inherited conservative views. After a very successful business career with Ems Chemicals, where he rose to become president and chief shareholder, he entered politics at the local level with the SVP, since he distrusted the Radicals. By 1977, he was head of the Zurich branch of the party, which doubled its electoral strength under his leadership, cannily exploiting the presence of German-language television in the city. Two years later, he entered the national parliament, where he also had a considerable impact. His rise showed how the declining importance of agriculture was forcing the SVP to find a new, more confrontational, role.

The party both reinforced and benefited from the swing to the right, both in votations like that on maternity assurance and on policies which might hinder economic recovery, like extra training

8.4 The image of Christoph Blocher with which most Swiss will be familiar. The photograph shows him engaged in his powerful oratory, making much use of emphatic body language. He is flanked by Tony Brunner, a St Gallen farmer who replaced Ueli Maurer as party president a few years ago. Behind them is the party's jokey logo, involving a cheery sun appearing over the initials of the party (Swiss People's Party in German and Centre Democratic Union in French and Italian) and the ever present Swiss flag. The picture is symbolic of the party's powerful and populist image, which has developed since the conflict over the EEA in the early 1990s.

levies and taxes on energy consumption. The rise of the new SVP corresponded to a change in tone of foreign affairs, which became more open to European business and more hostile to the East. Thus the Swiss condemned the Russian invasion of Afghanistan and a rise in Eastern economic espionage, while holding back on contacts with the USSR. The 'New Freeze' of the early 1980s also revived the Swiss preference for armed neutrality. However, the Federal Council did move towards an application for UN entry, while the arrival of détente led some Swiss to question the value and virtue of the traditional armed forces, which consumed a disproportionate share of the national budget.

To some extent the new tone also reflected the way that the economy finally recovered after the second oil shock. The new recession this produced continued unabated into 1982, after which growth resumed, first sluggishly and then more vigorously. Exports recovered well, especially in manufactures like chemicals, where mergers became the order of the day. The big banks also began to expand internationally on a much greater scale. Even the watch industry began to revive after several leading companies were merged into a new holding company, SMH, in 1983. The launch that year of the Swatch fun watch allowed the Swiss to start recovering market share, first in Europe and then even in Japan. New designs, quartz technology and better promotion were enforced by Nicholas Hayek, head of the new company. Only the engineering sector experienced continuing difficulty: Sulzer and others had to reduce their labour forces, and Brown-Boverei was eventually forced to merge with the Swedish ASEA combine. Recession followed by recovery did bring down inflation by half. Unemployment also fell by 60 per cent between 1984 and 1988, even though the number of foreign workers began to creep up again. Renewed immigration helped to control wages, even though demand and profits rose. So good did things seem to be that in some years the OECD's regular economic reports forbore to offer the Swiss any advice.

Economic growth did add to social tensions by drawing in more people from Portugal, Yugoslavia and further afield who sought to better their lot by taking up new posts in construction and in hotels. The foreign population rose again from 14 per cent in the late 1970s to 18 per cent by 1990, at a time when the native birth rate was falling and the divorce rate rising. In contrast to the by now well-assimilated Italians and even the wave of Tamil refugees, traditionalists saw the new immigrants as more criminal and more alien to Swiss values. Renewed growth also heightened emerging problems of drug abuse and the linked problem of AIDS transmission among heroin users, which made itself felt after 1983. Indeed Switzerland, perhaps because of its affluence and well-developed counter-culture, became a major sufferer in the early AIDS epidemic. These trends all strengthened traditionalist unease.

However, as with the earlier shift to the left, the swing to the right was never wholehearted or unchallenged. Thus, the electorate in 1982 accepted a popular initiative to reimpose the price controls that had lapsed in 1978. Indeed, the *Economist* in 1986 accused the country of putting up a 'do not disturb' sign in face of the neo-liberal revolution. This accusation was at odds with favourable foreign assessments of the continuing Sonderfall by Peter Katzenstein and others. He admired the way the country had coped with the economic crises of the 1970s through its liberal corporatism, compensating market losses by domestic social provisions and cartelization. Swiss social welfare was also praised for avoiding welfare dependency and attacking poverty directly, rather than providing guarantees. The limited size of the Swiss government and its preference for subsidiarity, with matters handled locally when possible, also appealed to many.

Towards the end of the 1980s, it seemed as though the tide might turn once again, with the new forces liberated by 1968 again challenging the Sonderfall. Even while the Social Democrats continued to lose votes in cantonal elections, despite their move to the centre, the 'Group for a Switzerland without an Army' – a youthful and radical social movement led by the charismatic Andi Gross and others – horrified the right and many other patriotic Swiss in 1985 by launching an initiative to abolish the army. This coincided with a new surge of environmental concern, the so-called *Grüne Welle*, which called for curbs on vehicular emissions and traffic flows. A 1987 referendum provided special protection for sensitive marshy areas, while more support came to railways and public transit through the Rail 2000 programme and after. Polls suggested that environmental concerns were the greatest worry facing the Swiss; these concerns were increasingly marshalled by the new Grüne Partei der Schweiz/Parti écologiste Suisse, which was formally established in 1986 and began to win cantonal seats. Mainstream parties had to take this on board, even on the far right, where a new secession from the NA took on an environmentalist colouring and won one national and forty-four cantonal seats.

The new forces faced a rival mobilization of conservative forces, however, motivated above all by threats to national sovereignty. The right saw Foreign Minister Pierre Aubert's efforts to move the country towards international cooperation through involvement in international organizations as a challenge to the Sonderfall. They succeeded in turning the electorate against such moves, leading to the rejection not merely of the Council of Europe's Social Charter and membership in UNESCO, but more significantly a crushing vote against the government's proposal that Switzerland should at last become a full member of the UN. In March 1986, the proposal lost by 76 per cent–24 per cent on a relatively high turn-out of 50.7 per cent, showing that the hedgehog complex was still deeply rooted.

While the defeat was partly due to poor government campaigning, it owed much more to the efforts of a new populist pressure group, Action for an Independent and Neutral Switzerland (AUNS/ASIN), led by Blocher, who was viscerally opposed to Swiss entanglements that might constrain its independence and neutrality. Blocher's leadership of the AUNS/ASIN represented a move away from traditional parliamentary politics for him, and one that gave him a real boost by undermining the existing far right while showing that populist politics could deliver massive blows to the establishment. The vote also showed a real gulf opening up between inward-looking traditionalists, often rurally based, and more progressive, outward-looking and often urban groups. Although many thought the SVP might lose many seats to the Greens, including in the Federal Council, as a result of the 1987 elections, this did not happen. In fact, voters rallied to keep the SVP at 11 per cent while the Christian Democratic Party lost 4 per cent, starting what was to be a longer-term decline; the Greens made only modest gains, far removed from the expected breakthrough. However, the Green Party did win seats and began to penetrate cantonal politics, which encouraged new thinking on energy and toxic waste. The FDP and the SVP were also moved in 1988–9 to persuade Parliament to compensate the promoters of Kaiseraugst, since it was clear that building a new plant was now politically impossible.

With the initial free-trade agreements now fully in force, Switzerland faced new and growing European challenges. Along with the other EFTA states, Switzerland wanted to go further in cooperation, aware that the way the Community was enlarging and deepening would reduce EFTA's influence. The Swiss thought they might share in decision-making that affected them through the 1984 Luxembourg Agreement, but this mechanism proved to be too restricted in scope. It was soon left behind, moreover, by the renewed development of the Community under the Single European Act and the potentially dynamic effects of the '1992 Single Market Programme'. At Interlaken in 1987, the EC rejected the very idea of shared decision-making with third countries, making it clear that Switzerland was not a 'quasi-member', as some Swiss officials liked to think. A government report in August 1988 still looked to develop the 'third way', and averred that only if this did not work might membership become a possibility. Foreign policy problems outside Europe, notably over South Africa, also threatened to isolate Switzerland again.

A greater crisis began in late 1988, after which Elizabeth Kopp was forced to resign, only days after being elected vice-president. Her resignation followed her reluctant admission that she had tipped off her colourful husband Hans about an investigation by her department of his firm, Shakarchi AG, over its part in handling the largest-ever case of laundered drug money. Although she at first denied any offence, further claims that the department had hindered other inquiries forced her to offer to resign at the end of February. Inquiries set in motion by the government soon produced evidence of breaches of confidentiality, and of misleading the Federal Council, forcing her to resign immediately. Her parliamentary immunity was suspended to allow for criminal prosecution. In the end she was acquitted on a legal technicality in the spring of 1990, but this was a pyrrhic victory for her and the establishment. A parliamentary commission of inquiry had revealed that there had been serious shortcomings in the administration of both departments. More importantly, it became apparent that the departments had, along with the Defence Ministry, been keeping some 900,000 secret files on alleged subversives that were full of hearsay and unreliable information. This revelation was linked to the continuing existence of P26. The 'affair of the fiches' became a major issue in the early 1990s, raising questions about public trust in the system, something that the looming vote on the abolition of the army threatened to reinforce.

In other words, if, by the end of the 1980s, the country had been transformed economically and socially, it was not problem-free. Fissures were in fact appearing in the Sonderfall. If prosperity and social harmony remained largely untouched, the political and diplomatic pillars of the Sonderfall were being opened up by new developments inside and outside Switzerland. Evidently, not all the country's policy problems had been successfully solved either. Deepening arguments about economic policy, European relations, foreigners, forests, and the role of army and state were all to help undermine the Sonderfall in the coming years, just as Switzerland found itself in a very changed international situation.

9

Since 1989

A return to normality?

The breaching of the Berlin Wall and the ensuing collapse of the Soviet empire ushered the Swiss into a new era, even if they were not always aware of it. Alterations in the context on which the Sonderfall rested and developing resistance to change began to turn the fissures in the Sonderfall into large cracks. The country found itself forced to rethink its armed neutrality, to cope with a surge in asylum applications and to devise new relations with a changing EU, all at a time of economic depression and painful scrutiny of the country's Second World War record. These challenges stimulated a populist nationalist response, much like that found in other European countries. It was led by the Swiss People's Party (SVP), which was opposed to international entanglements, whether with the United Nations or the EU, on the grounds of their incompatibility with the Sonderfall. The rise of populist nationalism led to government crises and controversial votations and elections that posed questions about the country's future direction. Increasingly, the country faced a choice between adapting to outside demands or resisting change and maintaining the Sonderfall. Politics, in other words, became increasingly polarized and sometimes personalized.

All this put the system, and especially the government, under great pressure as it tried to navigate between the rocks of outside problems and the shoals of shifting domestic opinion. As a result, all the elements of the Sonderfall were threatened: the country's foreign policy stance, its prosperity, its cohesion, its consensus politics, its policy successes and its memories of its role in the Second World

War, along with its sense of identity. For some time, the populist response to these threats looked like fundamentally challenging the whole Swiss post-war system, but consensus reasserted itself often enough to prevent this, though it still left the country divided and uncertain. And, while such reverses as the country suffered were slight in comparison to problems elsewhere, they were still sufficient to worry the Swiss. In this, Switzerland became a more normal state, evolving in much the same way as its European neighbours.

A CHANGED INTERNATIONAL POSITION

For most Europeans, 1989 means the end of the Cold War, but this was not always the case in Switzerland, given that debates over the army, the fate of the first women Federal Councillor and secret files were all over the front pages that year. Indeed, perhaps because of concern with the Kopp scandal, the attack on the army and a controversial exhibition called 'Diamant' celebrating the anniversary of 1939, the Swiss government itself did not immediately appreciate the significance of the fall of the Berlin Wall, first telling journalists that it could not comment on every little international event and eventually admitting that it had been taken by surprise. The fact that the Swiss ambassador in Berlin was twice arrested for drunkenness at the time did not help. The country thus limped along after everyone else, even though the collapse of the Soviet satellites necessarily affected its international strategies.

In fact, the end of the Cold War immediately transformed the debate on the army. Although the Group for a Switzerland without an Army lost the votation in late November 1989, the fact that over a third of voters voted in favour of abolishing the army, despite a massive counter campaign, was a real warning shot across the establishment's bows. Public opinion was also shaken by finding that, after the 1990 agreement between Helmut Kohl and Mikhail Gorbachev on reducing the size of the Bundeswehr in return for allowing German reunification, the Swiss army – potentially 650,000 militiamen strong – was nominally the largest in Europe, an odd position for a pacific neutral country.

The government responded by initiating a programme of military reform, known as Army 95: limiting the army to 370,000, cutting the length of time served and abolishing some reserve formations. Such changes fell far short of satisfying the army's critics, who successfully pushed for a civilian alternative to military service, and unsuccessfully for rejecting the purchase of 34 F/A18 jet fighters. However, a second attempt to abolish the army was crushingly defeated in 2001, although criticisms and changes still worried traditionalist defenders of the Sonderfall, who disliked any move away from a wholly militia army.

The authorities also had to move on neutrality and foreign policy, since Switzerland could no longer claim to be a buffer state between West and East. Instead it found itself in the middle of a sea of peaceable democratic states with nobody to be neutral between. Not only was there less demand for Swiss services as an honest broker but there was also more competition to provide such services. Moreover, in order to uphold international law, the government in 1990 imposed sanctions on Iraq after the invasion of Kuwait. The contemporaneous implosion of the Neutral and Non-Aligned Group left the country even more isolated and uncertain.

Since critics believed that neutrality also prevented closer relations with the EU, which the government wanted, an expert study group was set up. Its 1992 report argued that neutrality should be seen with a clearer eye and in a new European context, no longer as a barrier to EU entry. Until a fully fledged system of European collective security emerged, and neutrality could be relinquished, Switzerland should maintain an independent defence capacity but should also show more openness and solidarity by integrating further into Europe. Like many in the foreign policy establishment, the Group believed that Swiss independence and freedom of action could only be maintained by taking part in international institutions. As with changes to the army, this belief was rejected by traditionalists, adding to their unease and turning neutrality into a source of unsettling internal debate rather than a firm pillar of a Sonderfall.

When in January 1989, Commission President Jacques Delors talked about a new deal with all the EFTA countries, involving shared decision-making, it seemed for a moment as though things were working out on relations with Europe. The Swiss leaped for joy and joined in negotiations with the other EFTA states. Unfortunately, these proved to be very difficult; Austria and Sweden ultimately applied

9.1 The new Gotthard railway tunnel. The picture shows
workers in the Gotthard base tunnel celebrating the
breakthrough in the eastern bore on 15 October 2010, waving
Swiss, Italian and Ticinese flags amongst others. They are
pictured standing in front of the cutting face of a tunnel boring
machine, which had come from the north. The project was
implemented mainly to relieve Switzerland of the pollution
caused by excessive lorry traffic through the (surprisingly
fragile) Alps. Agreed in 1992, construction started in 1996 and
full service is scheduled for 2017.

for entry because they felt the likely benefits of the proposed deal were
too limited. Switzerland's sensitive position in European transit also
proved an obstacle, since the Swiss objected – on environmental
grounds – to excessive lorry movement through the Alps. Ultimately,
the government proposed building and financing new base rail tunnels
as compensation for imposing new charges on trans-Alpine truck
transit. In the end, agreement on what was to become the European
Economic Area was reached on the night of 21–2 October 1991, but
the two French-speaking Swiss ministers negotiating coupled their
acceptance of the deal with the comment that it was incompatible
with Swiss interests and dignity, a stance that was to haunt the
government.

A major political crisis broke out in 1992 when doubts about new external initiatives came home to roost, against a background of political change and growing challenges to the establishment. The *Fichenskandal* continued to cause enormous uproar and forced a parliamentary inquiry. Three hundred thousand people demanded to see their files, and it became almost a symbol of pride to have had a file. The affair left a very nasty taste in many people's mouths, shaking their confidence in the institutions on which the Sonderfall rested. Alarm also grew over the quintupling of applications for asylum between the late 1980s and 1991, owing to instability in Turkey and Sri Lanka. The processing system was overwhelmed, and the numbers of resident foreigners rose from just under a million in 1985 to nearly a million and a half by 1995, or over 20 per cent of the population. The far right increasingly seized on these numbers, claiming that asylum seekers were flooding the country (even though only a minority of applications were actually successful). In response, the government tried to restrict migration by introducing a three-circles policy in 1991. This allowed considerable free movement to people from European states and relatively generous access for people from other white western states, but imposed severe restrictions on applications from the rest of the world. Nevertheless, as elsewhere, the issue produced a new wave of ethnic and nationalist feeling in Switzerland, which affected domestic as well as diplomatic matters. Notably, this surge increasingly overwhelmed the influence of the new social movements that had been so visible in the 1980s.

EUROPEAN AND ECONOMIC WORRIES

The new national populism showed itself most strongly in the 1992 votation on the EEA, and was strengthened by reactions to the first real recession that post-war Switzerland had known. Economic pressure in turn reinforced emerging social problems at odds with the Sonderfall image. At the same time, the very foundation of the Sonderfall, the country's Second World War record, also came under vigorous outside attack. Still, the tenacity of traditionalism had already showed itself in another rejection of VAT in 1990. In the 1991 general election, the first when votes at 18 were allowed, the small parties of the far right, including a new formation, the populist

Lega dei Ticinesi, did well, whereas Radicals and Christian Democrats both lost heavily. All told the far right won 11 per cent of the vote, nearly twice as many as the Greens, showing how radicalism and change were encouraging support for defenders of Sonderfall Schweiz. Nonetheless, the Greens did make a modest breakthrough, symbolizing different doubts about the direction in which Switzerland was heading. The Federal Tribunal in 1990 also ruled against the Landsgemeinde of Appenzell Inner Rhoden, which refused to allow female participation, finally ending electoral exclusion – if not all discrimination against women – across Switzerland. This helped to pave the way for an upsurge in women's presence and participation in society.

Left-wing and intellectual opposition lay behind the lukewarm celebration of the Confederation's 700th Anniversary in 1991. In fact, the idea of having any festivities was contested on both historical and contemporary grounds. For some intellectuals, a century of a 'snooper' state, and even 700 years of any national history, was more than enough. However, much public opinion and the leadership of the SVP disregarded such critical views, still adhering to the liberation myth, including the reality of Tell. One of the key events of the festivities was a seminar on whether Switzerland was still a Sonderfall. The term began to fall out of use after 1989, reflecting the way in which the Kopp affair and the files scandal had damaged the idea of Switzerland as an exceptional model democracy. Indeed, Foreign Minister Réné Felber was quoted as saying he never wanted to hear the term again.

The growing internal divide over armed neutrality and the lack of faith in the system came to a head over closer relations with the EC. Encouraged by the first opinion poll to show a majority in favour of joining the EC, and then by public approval in early May 1992 of Swiss entry to the World Bank and the International Monetary Fund, the government decided to apply for entry later that month. But by then, the ECJ had reduced the independence of the EEA, and Norway and Finland had also applied for entry. The Swiss application confused many voters and left the government – whose campaigning was poor and not supported by business – exposed to the charge that it was asking the electorate to vote for a step that it felt was flawed. The charge was brilliantly exploited by AUNS under Blocher, which

9.2 Populist campaigns. The poster calls on the Swiss to reject
entry to the European Economic Area in the votation of 6
December 1992. The EEA (or Espace Economique Européenne
as it was then known) is depicted as an imposition that would
prevent the country from seeing where it was going, thus
depriving it of its freedom. Published by a small magazine in
French-speaking Switzerland, the poster sums up the views of
the successful traditionalist opposition, led by AUNS and the
SVP. The votation, which rejected entry, was a key moment in
recent Swiss politics and policy.

depicted staying out as cost free, whereas entry would threaten prosperity, cohesion and independence. Such arguments mobilized many habitual non-voters, increasingly distrustful of government, so that the turnout was an unprecedented 78.3 per cent. Entry was rejected by 50.3 per cent to 49.7 per cent, but with only seven cantons, mainly French-speaking, in favour. Described by some Ministers as 'a black day', the vote was initially interpreted as revealing a linguistic problem, as there was immense unhappiness in the Suisse Romande. Many French-speakers felt, not wholly accurately, that their interests had again been trampled under foot by the German-speaking majority, even going to the extent of raising mock customs barriers along the language frontier. Such hostility led to a good deal of parliamentary soul-searching and eventually to a new constitutional article on languages in 1996.

In fact, the EEA vote was much more a symbol of a new divide between an outward-looking, mainly urban Switzerland and a more inward-looking, mainly rural Switzerland which was losing its confidence in government and doubtful about new policies on neutrality and foreigners. The government was forced to freeze the membership application and reduce its *Eurolex* legislative adaption programme, which became known as *Swisslex*. In 1994 lorry transit across the Alps became an additional complication thanks to a restrictive popular initiative. The government also found itself facing a newly energized and restructured nationalist right, of which, following the 6 December 1992 votation, Christoph Blocher had became the acknowledged symbol and leader. His Zurich wing of the SVP became increasingly influential, combative and anti-establishment, winning over the conservatively inclined. It won its first new seats for years in 1995, mainly at the expense of the Swiss Democrats, even though the Social Democrats did even better, becoming once more the largest party in the National Council. The SPS also succeeded in getting a second woman into the Cabinet in 1993 when Ruth Dreifuss, nominally from Geneva, was chosen after a male candidate was preferred over the party's original female choice. He felt it wise to refuse election, given the immense feminist pressure, leaving the way open for Dreifuss to take the seat.

The success of both SPS and SVP reflected the fact that the country was experiencing its first real depression since 1945. Starting in 1991 and continuing until 1997, the economy contracted 2 per cent as trade and demand fell, owing to downturns elsewhere in Europe, the deflationary policy of the National Bank and a continuation of the low rate of economic growth experienced in the past. The depression triggered a certain amount of deregulation and the beginnings of shareholder activism. There was also a good deal of consolidation, notably in chemicals, retailing and banks, where in 1998, SBC from Basle merged with the Union Bank from Zurich, forming the new UBS bank. Fewer of those working were independent, while more and more became employees, often for the sixty-six largest firms. Some 200,000 jobs were lost, leading to 5.5 per cent unemployment, a twenty-fold increase over the 1990s, even if less than elsewhere. Moreover, real wages fell as inflation rose above the European average. As a result, wealth became increasingly redistributed to the benefit of the rich, with the number of millionaires rising precipitously, even while as many as one in six Swiss was classified as working poor. Not surprisingly, there was a sharp rise in the number of strikes, notably in 1993–4 and again in 1997–9, along with increasing invalidity insurance claims. Equally, the depression helped to produce an unprecedented expansion in social spending on unemployment and pensions, along with the consolidation of the welfare state. As another pillar of the Sonderfall eroded, a major debate on economic policy started: neo-liberals like David de Pury and other leading industrialists called in their 1995 White Book for a radical reorganization, deregulation and privatization of the economy and, especially, of the welfare state. Its costs were already seen as responsible for declining competitiveness. The left was vociferous in its rejection, and called for more regulation. Generally liberalization was unpopular, even though Blocher, in contradistinction to many of his new supporters, was in favour of freeing the economy.

The depression also threatened social cohesion and harmony as levels of violent crime began to creep up, along with divorce and suicide rates. Many Swiss also found the escalating costs of medical insurance premiums a major burden. These developments led many, especially blue-collar workers, to respond to the appeal of the SVP, turning away from the trade unions, who were finding it increasingly difficult to deal with more aggressive and better-organized employers. To an extent, such voters accepted the SVP argument that part of the problem was caused by asylum seekers. The SVP fanned discontent with a failed popular attempt to curb clandestine immigration in December 1996.

The party was also helped by a head-on challenge to the foundation of the Sonderfall, Switzerland's role in the Second World War. In 1995, encouraged by Edgar Bronfman, head of the revived World Jewish Congress, survivors and their lawyers used the US courts to launch a class action against Swiss banks for refusing to release dormant accounts originating with victims of the Holocaust. The case was taken up by Senator Alfonse d'Amato and US Undersecretary of State Stuart Eizenstat, who issued a report drawn from the archives. The accusations against Switzerland soon broadened out to embrace claims that it had collaborated in the Holocaust by accepting gold from concentration camps (or looted from occupied states) and refused Jewish refugees entry, not to mention prolonging the war by its economic assistance to the Nazis. The temperature was raised by accusatory books, which proposed boycotts of Swiss goods.

Aware that they could be heavily penalized if they did not cooperate, the banks agreed in August 1998 to pay $1.3 billion in compensation, a sum boosted by contributions from insurance firms and manufacturers whose German subsidiaries had used forced labour during the war. The Swiss government had felt it necessary in 1995 both to apologize for its wartime treatment of refugees and to sponsor an assessment of the dormant accounts issue and an international historical commission – led by economic historian Jean-Francois Bergier – to investigate Switzerland's behaviour in the war. It also offered to create a $5 billion general Solidarity Fund for victims of distress. The Bergier Commission produced a host of studies and two reports, one in December 1999 and a final one in March 2002. It found that Switzerland had been restrictive in its treatment of refugees and in its response to the needs of the time. It also accepted that anti-Semitism had affected Swiss behaviour, and that neutrality had been biased towards Germany. However, many of the more extreme criticisms were shown to have been exaggerated. In any case, the American Volcker Committee found that, contrary to earlier claims, Swiss banks held 54,000 accounts that may have belonged to victims of the Holocaust, along with 25,000 other relevant accounts.

Repayments soon began, but this still left many questions pending, such as the economy and Europe.

The criticisms of the country's behaviour between 1939 and 1945, whether from inside Switzerland or abroad, were bitterly resented by many Swiss who had endured the difficult wartime years and who refused to be transformed from heroes into villains. Their memory, which was the ultimate source of the Sonderfall, was offended, and their fears for national institutions and identity carried over into resistance to European integration. On both topics Blocher and the SVP spoke for them, denigrating Bergier and his methods and providing a 'clarification' that played up Swiss successes and the country's need for access to neighbouring states during the war so as to ensure its survival. Blocher even called for a 'war' against the United States, believing that Switzerland was being unfairly 'lynched' and that the government had given in to blackmail. Not surprisingly, the electorate in 2002 rejected the financing suggested for the proposed Solidarity Fund, showing that the Swiss were still having difficulty in facing up to their wartime past. As a result, the affair deepened the emerging rift between inward-looking Swiss and the non-SVP parts of the establishment. The former were particularly alarmed that the latter did not stand up for traditional Swiss rights and identity. This reflected the way in which, while European elites continued with attempts at international cooperation, in Switzerland as elsewhere, a significant part of society and politics reverted to more old-fashioned national thinking.

This rift revealed itself in a new initiative to limit the foreign population to 18 per cent of the total population. Although this was decisively rejected, two years later the SVP enjoyed what it called a 'triumphant' defeat when its initiative against abuse of the asylum system failed by only 1.2 per cent. The outcome reflected a renewed surge of asylum seekers produced by the bitter wars in the former Yugoslavia, which often overwhelmed facilities and produced a number of attacks, often violent, on foreigners. The votation also reinforced the SVP's belief in direct democracy as its ultimate political and populist weapon. The initiative process became more a right-wing bludgeon than a left-wing goad. In fact, six of the eighteen initiatives that have been successful since 1891 were accepted between 2000 and 2010. The SVP's new approach transformed Swiss politics, making these more aggressive, more personalized, more polarized and more media-dominated. Rather than involving discreet pragmatic cooperation and consultation, Swiss politics increasingly involved almost permanent campaigning and electioneering.

Traditionalist national populism also showed up in hostile attitudes towards European integration, which was seen as threatening sovereignty and self-reliance. The authorities consistently underestimated such sentiments as they pressed ahead with bilateral negotiations to fill the gap left by Switzerland's absence from the EEA. Negotiations proved immensely difficult, especially after the electorate voted in 1994 for the Alpine initiative, which required a dramatic transfer of trans-Alpine traffic from road to rail. In the event, an agreement was finalized only in June 1999, after the public backed related financial proposals. The agreement consisted of a phased package deal, tied together by what was called a guillotine clause, which meant that if the Swiss rejected any element, then all would fall. This approach testified to Brussels's awareness of the power of Swiss direct democracy. For the Swiss, the significant elements of the package included transport and especially the free movement of labour. The Swiss gave up their ban on lorries over 28 tonnes and lowered transit taxes in return for acceptance of the principle of charging EU vehicles to use the roads. The deal also allowed Swiss airlines free access to EU air space with rights of cabotage, the lack of which had been undermining Swissair. Free movement was even more controversial. It was to be phased in with a review in 2009. Switzerland was also allowed flanking measures to protect against what was called 'social dumping' (paying EU workers in Switzerland at lower EU rates). Such worries led the Swiss Democrats and the Lega Ticinese to challenge the deal, forcing a referendum. With the SVP nominally neutral, the unions won over by flanking measures and the business community actively in favour, the whole deal was approved in May 2000 by a two-to-one majority.

The challenge was nevertheless a sign that the citizenry was getting worried about Swiss identity as well as the economy. This had already been visible in controversies over the celebration of Swiss

9.3 The annual Landsgemeinde of canton Glarus, one of only two remaining in Switzerland. The assembly meets on a Sunday in early May in the Glarus town's Zaunplatz beneath the Glärnisch mountain and attracts up to 7,000 people. Of late the authorities have erected a temporary wooden ring of raised terraces on which citizens can stand to get a view of the authorities on the central dais. The meeting, which can last eight hours, discusses all kinds of political issues, with voting carried out by raising a yellow card.

confederalism in 1998. The establishment planned to celebrate 1848, but the Latin cantons believed this overlooked 1798, the more significant (for them) bicentenary of their freedom from 'colonial oppression'. Language questions also underlay arguments about the growing use of English in academia, business and, from 2000, schools, where some German-speaking cantons sought to make it the first foreign language, ahead of French and Italian, causing alarm in Latin Switzerland. The SVP took the opportunity to appeal more vigorously to more traditional nationalist narratives of Swiss history, and to rebut the critical views found in the modern historiography favoured by the establishment, whether on the longer-term past or, especially, where the Second World War was concerned. Such historical traditionalism reinforced inward-looking attitudes and resistance to change. Hence, despite the way the cantons were rewriting their own constitutions, there was little enthusiasm, and some opposition, to the modernization of the national constitution. A draft was put out to consultation in 1995, and a revised version was submitted to Parliament in 1998. This produced a final text later that year, which was approved in April 1999. Significantly however, only 36 per cent of the electorate bothered to turn out, while some conservative voices remained vehemently opposed.

The new draft was shorter, better organized and more rights-oriented than its predecessor. It also encouraged further revision of cantonal constitutions. Thus, the people of Obwalden abolished their Landsgemeinde in 1998, leaving only Glarus and Appenzell Inner Rhoden with public mass decision-making. Federalism also encouraged increasing consolidation of small communes, so that by 2011 there were only 2,500 compared to the 3,000-plus of the 1980s. In Glarus, two dozen communes were reduced to only three. New legislation also rearranged the distribution of tasks and funding between the cantons and the Confederation, and also amongst the cantons. The latter began to play a larger role as a corporate body, notably through the conferences of cantonal ministers, especially the Conference of Governments set up in 1993 and the House of Cantons in Berne. The cantons used their new rights to challenge legislation for the first time in 2004, as well as appointing permanent representatives in the capital to lobby and protect their interests. Talk of reuniting the Basles and creating a new super-canton in the Jura hills seem likely to remain unfulfilled, to judge by the failure of an attempt to merge Vaud and Geneva. However, it is possible that the existing canton of Jura may succeed in expanding southwards.

The federal element of the Sonderfall was also affected by the way that politics was becoming increasingly national. In the 1999 parliamentary elections, the SVP made an unprecedented breakthrough by winning an additional fifteen seats, taking its strength to forty-four and making it the second largest formation in the Lower House. Moreover, it polled the same percentage of the electorate as the Social Democrats and won two seats in the Upper House. Its gains came mainly at the expense of the small far-right groups, notably the

Autopartei (now rebranded as the Freedom Party), and some of its victories were in those German-speaking cantons where a few years before it had had no representation. The SVP won despite a recovering economy and a fall in the numbers of unemployed.

Although it was not able to win extra seats in cantonal executives or the Federal Council, the party was clearly on the move. It continued to build on its gains, alarming the mainstream parties and liberal public opinion and dividing the country as it did so. Increasingly it followed the line of other Western European populist movements, painting the native majority as the new minority, 'victimized' by foreigners, by an untrustworthy political elite and by the left. The party blamed the post-1968 left for most of Switzerland's problems. However, despite using the Sonderfall as a political weapon and despite its claim that the Bergier Report had been interested only in cataloguing Swiss offences, the party was unable to change all the policies it disliked, such as further reform of the army. Nor could it prevent either the Federal Council issuing a critical report on Swiss relations with South Africa during the apartheid years or, in 2002, the electorate's very narrow approval of UN entry.

The party was more successful on the European front. The government was again embarrassed in 2001 when it failed to get the New Swiss European Movement (NEBS/NOMES), the pro-European lobby, to withdraw an initiative calling for immediate entry negotiations. Because it knew that the time was not ripe, the establishment urged people to vote the initiative down, which they did massively. This was wrongly seen as a formal rejection of the whole principle of entry. In any case the government pressed on with a second round of bilateral negotiations. Progress on technical issues was rapid, but the process was bedevilled by Swiss refusal of automatic exchanges of information on foreigners' bank accounts, on grounds of banking secrecy. Access to the Schengen system of free movement also became an issue; Switzerland sought access to the system because this would remove the danger that tourists might be put off if they had to obtain a special visa for Switzerland when visiting EU countries, or that the country would be targeted by would-be asylum seekers. In the end, in 2003, the EU agreed to allow Switzerland and other states to retain bank confidentiality in return for a withholding tax, three-quarters of which would be passed to relevant EU states. The Swiss negotiating position was constrained by SVP opposition, which carried increasing weight because of the party's electoral progress. At the cantonal level it gained 150 seats between 1995 and 2003, when it also made a further eleven national gains, many of them in the Suisse Romande, reinforcing the nationalization of politics. While the SVP increased its share of the vote to 26 per cent and the Social Democrats held their own, the Radicals and Christian Democrats both lost heavily. In other words, the Sonderfall was not giving up the fight.

POLARIZATION

The increasing challenge from the SVP and its supporters was powerful but not uniformly popular. Although other parties and forces lacked its solid support and resources, they did their best to resist and on occasions scored some surprising victories. All this meant that politics became increasingly polarized between the hard-line Zurich wing of the SVP on the one hand, and, on the other, a progressive alliance of Social Democrats and many Greens. This was not just a left–right divide, it was also a divide between outward-looking winners from globalization and inward-looking losers who opposed it. Hence, many workers switched between the Social Democrats and the SVP, with the result that policy-making became more difficult.

Changing voting patterns, in other words, reflected a new and more divisive politics: people increasingly voted on their values and not their socio-economic interest, making compromise more difficult. Unsettled by globalization with its encouragement of multinational enterprises and with growing economic pressure on Swiss farms – whose numbers fell by a third between 1990 and 2010 – and with the increasing inequality it promoted, many saw themselves as losing out in terms of crime, welfare and language. They were also aware that although income inequalities were growing, as was happening throughout the western world, they were not benefiting. A series of accidents that called into question the country's reputation for quiet efficiency and policy success involved with the Sonderfall may also have made voters look for new reassurance. The closure of the Gotthard auto tunnel after a fire, the grounding, merger and forced sale of Swissair in 2001–2, the massacre in the Zug cantonal parliament in September 2001, the Uberlingen air crash of July 2002 and troubles over the 2002 Expo in the western lakes (from which Swiss flags were supposed to be banned), helped to increase doubts at home and abroad whether Switzerland was as reliable a model as it had been. The *amour propre* of the Sonderfall seemed to be in danger.

Many worried voters were attracted by the SVP's clearly focused message on identitarian themes, whereas the SPS drew less on workers and more on middle-class voters who gained from the gathering Europeanization, which continued despite popular opposition to political links with the EU. The confluence of cultural issues with rapid change made the open/shut divide, and general polarization, almost more acute than in other European countries. This was reflected in increasing politicization, which saw higher turnouts (especially amongst the elderly, whose views were marked by the war years), more petitions and even rising party membership. The SVP both encouraged and profited from all these trends, creating a mass populist party just as similar parties in other countries were running into difficulties. The party was unique in Swiss terms as well. It was media-savvy, well-funded, well-organized and led not just by Blocher, but also by a new generation of highly committed and charismatic MPs, often more inflammatory (and French-speaking) than Blocher himself, and equally capable of dominating television arenas and the columns of the popular press. The other parties found it virtually impossible to compete with the SVP, allowing the party to set the political weather.

With all this going for it, immediately after the 2003 elections the SVP demanded the second seat in government it felt had been denied it in 1999, refusing to accept any other candidate than Blocher. He was eventually elected in place of Ruth Metzler, the first time an unblemished sitting minister had been set aside since 1874. Since Hans-Rudolf Merz, a conservative Radical, was also elected, the balance of government was changed. Old consensual conventions about gender and cantonal representation, let alone the right of ministers to decide on the time of their own departure, were swept aside. Many MPs in other parties were distinctly unhappy with all this, but they learned the lesson and were to apply it four years later.

The election of Blocher did not, as some had hoped, domesticate him; instead, the tone of government began to change. The Federal Council became increasingly politicized, since Blocher remained openly critical of the government and its policies, wading into things outside his remit and never missing a chance to promote his own and his party's ideas. His supporters saw this as cleaning out the Augean stables of a corrupt elite, whereas critics saw it as undermining the system of collegial responsibility and ministerial solidarity that had been in effect for a century. The atmosphere got so bad that the majority censored Blocher in 2006 for some of his outbursts, and one minister stepped down early because of the uncomfortable atmosphere.

Nonetheless, the remaining checks and balances of the system meant that domestic policy did not change all that much, even though in 2004 Parliament, for the first time ever, turned down the government's policy programme. The government was further embarrassed when the electorate agreed to an SVP-inspired initiative condemning those guilty of sexual crimes to perpetual imprisonment, since this was impossible to square with European human rights law. Blocher did succeed in toughening asylum policy, as well, while the electorate in 2006 rejected government ideas on making naturalization easier for long-established young foreigners. The same year, however, the electorate heavily rejected an SVP challenge to new proposals on educational harmonization, and after nearly half a century, a maternity insurance plan was finally approved in 2004. This more or less completed the welfarization of the Swiss state. Nonetheless, the costs and complexities of the welfare state, as in other countries, were a constant source of argument and unease. As in other countries, the government also launched a programme of measures to help revitalize the still sluggish economy. Partial liberalization of the electricity market was achieved, while two new regulatory agencies, COMCO (for competition) and FINMA (for financial markets), were established.

The SVP also failed to prevent foreign policy from taking on a more international dimension; under the new Social Democratic foreign minister, Micheline Calmy-Rey, Switzerland played an active role in the United Nations and beyond, prompting the SVP to call for her resignation for breaching neutrality. The party's opposition to closer links with Europe met with only limited success. In 2004 it failed to prevent either the negotiation of a second set of bilaterals (including entry to Schengen and a deal on savings) or the extension of the solidarity payments and rights of free movement to the ten states who then joined the EU. Nor could it force the government to take the symbolic step of withdrawing, rather then freezing, the 1992 application, something which led the party to promise a twenty-year war to prevent entry. However, the government did downgrade entry into the EU from its key aim to a mere option.

Despite some setbacks, the SVP also continued to prosper electorally, although growing at a slower rate than before. By 2007, it finished up for the first time as the largest party in cantonal parliaments. The Social Democrats steadily lost cantonal seats, and saw their cherished project for a single national health insurance scheme heavily defeated in 2006. They were also threatened by the advance of the Greens. In the centre, the Radicals found it hard not to be sucked into the SVP's wake, although the Christian Democrats seemed to have started to reverse their long-term decline. The apparent slackening off in the SVP's rate of expansion and the economic recovery – which saw growth rates of 3 per cent, increasing domestic demand and no rise in unemployment – suggested that the SVP would not make much progress in 2007. In fact, the party launched itself into the campaign with vigour, jointly focusing on Blocher and on its 'Contract with the Swiss'. This committed the party to cutting taxes, deporting foreign criminals and staying out of the EU. This won it seven more seats, and a record 29 per cent of the popular vote, mostly at the expense of the SPS, which fell below 20 per cent, and to a lesser extent the Radicals, thereby enhancing polarization and leaving open the possibility of an SVP-led system change.

A CONSENSUS UNDER CONTINUING PRESSURE

It was at this point that the consensus whirligig brought in its revenges, leading to Blocher's eviction from the cabinet and a failed attempt by the SVP to go into 'opposition'. Nonetheless, the party remained the agenda-setter, along with outside events. In fact, at the same time the Sonderfall was further undermined by the credit crunch and the related assaults on banking secrecy, while in the

9.4 An official portrait of Mrs Eveline Widmer-Schlumpf, Minister of Finance and President in 2012. However, in 2007 she became a hate object for the SVP after agreeing to accept nomination to government after the defeat of Christoph Blocher. She did this in order to ensure the party kept its second ministerial portfolio, but because she was both a moderate and the person who kept the party leader out of office, she was regarded as a traitor and forced out into a new party. Nonetheless, she successfully took over Blocher's Justice and Police portfolio before moving to Finance.

2011 elections, the SVP's onward advance was partly halted and its governmental ambitions reined in. The country thus remains uneasily poised politically between possible futures even though, comparatively speaking, its situation is an enviable one.

In late 2007, just as it seemed as though the SVP was on the cusp of a real breakthrough, things rapidly changed. Voters moved to defend consensus, dealing the party several blows in the second round of the elections for the Council of States. Then, in the National Council, the Christian Democrats, Social Democrats and Greens copied the SVP's 2003 tactics and worked together to eject Blocher from government, replacing him by Eveline Widmer-Schlumpf, the respected SVP Finance Director in Grisons. Although Blocher's ejection was carried out completely within the existing rules, the SVP was outraged and went into opposition. This proved to be ineffective, and remained limited to a mean-spirited attempt to expel Mrs Widmer-Schlumpf and her fellow moderate SVP minister, Samuel Schmid, from the party. This was done, but only at the cost of driving them and many other moderates out into a new Conservative Democratic party, the BDP/PBD. The SVP also found itself stymied in Parliament, being able to block policies only when it could find allies. Even when the party turned to direct democracy, it lost on initiatives about allowing secret local decisions on naturalizations, and on banning government campaigning during votations, while the act it supported on cutting business taxes only just scraped through. The party's internal divisions and its U-turns on extending free movement to Bulgaria and Romania, which it completely failed to prevent, did not help it. Hence, the SVP eventually gave up insisting on Blocher's return to the Federal Council and abandoned formal opposition. In consequence, it was just able to secure the election of Ueli Maurer to the Federal Council in December 2008, although once again a rogue SVP candidate pushed by the centre and left nearly claimed the seat. With five parties represented in government for the first time, many thought that consensus governance was at an end.

In the event, however, party strife was overshadowed when the country got caught up in the credit crunch and the ensuing depression, which called the economic pillars of the Sonderfall further into question. While the economy did relatively well in 2007–8, the summer of 2007 revealed major difficulties at UBS, the country's biggest bank. This had expanded aggressively in the United States, abandoning traditional conservative Swiss approaches for rampant Anglo-American risk-taking and a heavy exposure to the emerging sub-prime mortgage crisis. UBS had to write down large sums and admit to large losses. Investors began to withdraw their funds, and its shares lost much of their value, leaving Credit Suisse as the largest Swiss bank. Chairman Marcel Ospel admitted defeat and stepped down in the spring of 2008, but the problems endured, especially as the Swiss were badly hit by Lehmann Brothers' collapse. In October 2008 the government had to step in and follow Ireland in propping its banks up by taking a 9 per cent share in UBS and arranging for the National Bank to buy UBS's toxic assets and put them in a new offshore 'bad' bank. After the bank had racked up the country's greatest-ever corporate loss of 20 billion francs in 2008, a fresh management team was installed at UBS in spring 2009, and set about making large staff and service cuts.

The recession put the economy as a whole into negative growth, with bankruptcies and unemployment both rising, which forced the government to produce three stimulus packages. The effects of the downturn elsewhere also put Switzerland under new pressure because of its tax and banking policies. The EU took issue with low cantonal tax rates, pioneered by Zug, which it felt unfairly – and against the terms of the 1972 agreement – incited firms to leave their homelands for Swiss tax havens. The French also objected in particular to the special tax deals devised for people like the racing driver Michael Schumacher, especially when rock hero Johnny Hallyday decamped to Switzerland ahead of the French presidential election of 2007. Moreover, the EU did not feel it was getting sufficient returns from the withholding tax on income from holdings at Swiss banks.

The OECD and the United States also assaulted banking secrecy and the role of Swiss banks in encouraging Americans to evade US tax obligations. The Americans were helped in this by the revelations of a UBS whistle-blower, Bradley Birkenfeld. Faced with the threat of being placed on an OECD blacklist, the government first allowed UBS to release 250 names of American clients to the US authorities, and then, in March 2009, agreed to relax the banking laws in line with OECD norms, accepting that tax evasion as well as tax fraud provided a legitimate reason for lifting bank secrecy. This change was written into the new dual-tax treaties needed to get Switzerland's name removed from an existing OECD grey list. Such measures did not stop the United States from launching a suit against UBS, seeking access to 52,000 names of allegedly illicit American clients who had been attracted by UBS to take out confidential accounts in Switzerland. The government was forced to step in, and in August 2009 agreed to allow the American Internal Revenue Service full access to 4,450 accounts. In theory, this agreement preserved banking secrecy, but in practice it opened a further breach and left the Swiss open to further incursions. These steps, taken under intense foreign pressure, undermined what many traditionalists saw as a major element of the Sonderfall and intensified concerns about a national identity defined by traditional institutions and practices. The Lega even launched an initiative to write banking secrecy into the Constitution. Nonetheless, the right was also very critical of excessively high business salaries, reflecting the way that Switzerland, like much of western society, was experiencing a growing disparity between elite and mainstream salaries and wealth.

Swiss international standing also came under attack from Libya after the brief arrest of one of Colonel Gaddafi's sons in Geneva for abusing his servants. Oil supplies and flights were cut off, billions withdrawn from Swiss banks and Swiss businessmen taken hostage, leading the president in office, Radical Hans Rudolf Merz, to make an unauthorized and unsuccessful visit to Tripoli. Only painful negotiations and further humiliations, including having EU envoys defend the Swiss embassy, allowed the hostages to be released. This humiliation revealed Switzerland's lack of real allies and weight, and may explain why the government tipped off US authorities that the filmmaker Roman Polanski was due to visit Zurich to receive a lifetime achievement award, enabling them to seek extradition. Although this was not in the end conceded, the affair won Switzerland widespread loathing among the international cultural elite.

The government, and the country as a whole, came under even greater pressure because of the SVP's successful initiative of 29 November 2009 banning the construction of minarets in Switzerland, even though there were only a handful of them existing or planned. Designed by the SVP as a warning shot against possible Islamization, the initiative caused uproar abroad, especially in Arab countries. At home, it gave the party a new boost, because it had been able to win over non-core voters and push its own agenda forward. The SVP argued that Switzerland should resign from the European Convention on Human Rights if the ECHR declared its initiative illegal. It also went on to demand that the divided and incapable government resign, and to bring further pressure, it launched an initiative to secure the direct election of the Federal Council.

Banking secrecy again added to the country's difficulties after a former employee of HSBC in Geneva handed over an illicit list containing the names of some 3,000 French citizens with undeclared accounts in Switzerland. This caused a good deal of tension with

9.5 SVP Poster. A typically aggressive, not to say inflammatory, example of the campaigning style, which had brought the SVP so many successes in recent years. Used in its successful campaign for the 29 November 2009 votation on banning the construction of minarets, it combines an attack on Islamic treatment of women with the suggestions that burka-wearers, no matter how pretty, are terrorists and that minarets are akin to long-range missiles. The implication is that Islam is threatening the destruction of Switzerland and its Christian heritage.

France, as did a German purchase of a similar list. The government tried to de-dramatize the issue, but many voices inside Switzerland argued that Switzerland could not go on refusing to recognize tax evasion as a crime and claiming that everybody else was in the wrong. The Federal Administrative Court's decision that FINMA had exceeded its powers in transferring names of American clients of UBS to the US also left the government with a major problem. It seemed that banking secrecy might be lost and the country forced to accept automatic exchange of information about accounts with Swiss banks. However, the initiative to write banking secrecy into the constitution failed to garner enough signatures for a votation.

Although the Libyan hostage crisis was finally resolved in June 2010, the government was further battered by revelations that it had toyed with the idea of attempting an armed rescue, and then by a damning parliamentary report on the way it had managed the affair. This forced Merz to step down, but despite a spirited challenge from the SVP, the Radicals and Social Democrats both held on to their seats. The election of Simonetta Sommaruga for the latter meant that, for the first time, the Federal Council had a female majority. A controversial switch of portfolios also took place, with Doris Leuthard moving to Environment, Transport, Energy and Communications and Eveline Widmer-Schlumpf to Finance, relegating the new Social Democrat Minister to the Police and Justice Department.

In November 2010, 52.9 per cent of those voting rejected the government's counter-project and backed an SVP initiative on expelling foreigners guilty of crimes. The SVP then increased its pressure on the establishment by launching a new programme and seeking to reverse prevailing schools policies. The party was also able to burnish its martyrdom image by holding its winter assembly in a snowy field, after having been banned from using a public hall. This helped it to maintain its support, whereas the SPS's new anti-capitalist programme was badly received and its fair tax initiative failed badly on 28 November. The rejection in February 2011 of a pacifist initiative to ban the keeping of army weapons at home, because they were too often used in domestic murders, also showed the continuing strength of conservative feelings. The SVP was also able to snatch the Bernese seat in the Council of States left vacant by

Ms Sommaruga, and to exploit the collapse of an apparent agreement to open negotiations with Brussels on a new framework deal with the EU, involving acceptance of the acquis. This helped effectively to block all progress on the EU dossier, notably on an agricultural free trade deal.

The attention of both the electorate and the SVP was then caught by two unexpected issues that came to dominate the early stages of the 2011 election campaign. One was the panic caused by the Fukushima nuclear crisis in Japan, which turned opinion around and led the authorities to pledge an end to nuclear power by the 2030s, although no adequate replacement was agreed. The second, which soon overcame such environmental concerns, was alarm at the ever-increasing value of the Swiss franc, which became an increasing problem for exporters and many others, prompting fears of a depression. Attempts by the National Bank to check the franc's rise proved of some effect, however, and may be developed further. The discovery of major fraud in the London branch of UBS also helped to focus attention on the growing European financial crisis.

The SVP sought to offset these new concerns by reviving fears about foreigners and asylum seekers; the party launched an initiative to establish draconian controls on the foreign population, attacked Sommaruga's handling of asylum policy and made control of immigration one of the three planks of its revised 'Contract with Switzerland', in place of tax cuts. The SVP initiative ignored an actual fall in the number of asylum seekers and criticisms that Swiss policy was already in breach of human rights provisions. The party also brushed aside suggestions that its stance on Islam was close to that of Norwegian mass murderer Anders Behring Breivik. The initiative was part of a huge surge of proposals made to attract public attention prior to the election. However, the party did not, at first, benefit hugely in the polls.

From early September a new element entered the equation with the announcement of the forthcoming resignation of Madame Calmy-Rey from the government, which focused attention on government formation. Yet the 2011 election campaign did not take off in the way that that of 2007 had done. This was despite the fact that, on the one hand, the election raised fundamental questions about the direction the country would take: would it remain consensual and outward looking, or would it continue to veer inward, changing both the political system and Swiss foreign policy? On the other hand, the election failed to rouse much excitement despite the presence of an increased number of candidates and heavy spending on poster and press advertising, not to mention more use of new technology and social media. Habit, the proliferation of parties and a recovering economic situation seem to have led voters to overlook the strategic dimension. The desire of the mainstream parties to avoid excitement, in case this might aid the SVP, also contributed to a lacklustre campaign and an only slightly increased turnout.

In the event, the election did not produce a further destabilizing shift away from consensus politics. In fact, the SVP suffered its first losses in some twenty years, in both houses. It failed either to achieve a last-minute mobilization in elections to the National Council or to find sufficient allies in the non-proportional elections to the Council of States and the government. However, all the major parties initially lost ground, because the electorate seems to have been dissatisfied with party strife and the lack of clear answers to its economic needs. Conversely, the Green Liberals and the BPD both did well, together harvesting a tenth of all votes cast. The Ständerat run-off elections partly reinforced the resistance to polarization by inflicting several humiliating defeats on the SVP, often at the hands of the Social Democrats.

This partial rejection of polarized politics meant that, although the SVP remained by far the largest party and retained considerable potential for disturbing the system, it had to negotiate on its claim to a second minister when the time came to elect the Federal Council. In the event, its selections and strategy backfired, and it failed to win back the second seat that, on its psephological reading of consensus, it believes it deserves. Rather, its bête noire, Ms Widmer-Schlumpf, was both re-elected and nominated as President for 2012. More conventional understandings of consensus and the new-style Magic Formula, which stressed parliamentary balance and policy agreement, were thus reinforced at its expense. Indeed, the party briefly considered whether to withdraw again from government in protest against the denial of its governmental claims. It decided not to so so. It also maintained its direct democratic pressures on the system, even if these did not always succeed.

Yet the SVP remains a powerful and popular force. Consequently, a major shift in the political balance and the governance of Switzerland remains a possibility, although 2011 at least delayed it. For while religion, language and, to an extent, class have faded as sources of internal division, the identitarian divide remains. This still draws on history, as well as on institutions like direct democracy, with realities still being challenged by myths both old and new. In other words, if the Sonderfall's appeal is weakening, it has not yet gone away.

Moreover, the country still has to decide on its attitude to an outside world that is presenting the Swiss with increasingly pressing challenges. Finding consensus on responses to new pressures from global population movements, new security problems, overdevelopment, the EU, the US, and the OECD, not to mention from currency markets disturbed by the Eurozone crisis, will not be easy. For even if the country's economic, financial and social position remains stronger than that of many other European states, its political divisions are increasing and the system is no longer as stable as it was. Being a *Willensnation* thus poses problems of its own. In fact the country has to decide whether it will stick to a cooperative line or build on Switzerland's own xenophobic and ultra-right-wing tradition – which had emerged as its nineteenth-century revolutionary tendencies evaporated – and follow the present Europe-wide trend back towards a more competitive international order. Both at home and abroad, the SVP offers the country a very different future from that championed by majority opinion – and one which, despite the party's stress on tradition, could lead to drastic change in the Swiss system.

Switzerland therefore remains under tension from within and without. In other words, it is going through yet another phase in its long evolution, showing again that it is not the pacific, politics-free place so many imagine. It remains, as it has long been, a real polity with real – and often conflictual – politics. And these are, more than ever, a matter of the interaction between a sense of distinctiveness, intellectually and especially because of its political system, and the country's intimate connection with Europe. Out of this interaction will come the decisions which will continue the making of the Swiss.

Although it may not yet be clear either how Swiss politics will evolve in future or where Swiss history may lead, we can be sure that Swiss history is far from coming to an end. Switzerland will continue to have a far more complex and striking history than most outsiders realize, and one most unlikely to follow a single simple trajectory. Indeed, because of its very particularity, Swiss history cannot serve as a model for others – anymore than can Swiss politics – but it remains fascinating and worth studying both for itself and because it offers a better understanding of the full range of possibilities that European polities have produced. It deserves to be rescued from the way it has been overlooked and misconstrued in recent years, and presented in its full richness and significance.

CHRONOLOGY

58–15 BC	The Romans establish control over most of Switzerland.
AD 370	Burgundians and Allemanni begin to invade and settle.
c. 400	Earliest bishoprics established in region.
610–12	Missions of Columban and Gallus in eastern Switzerland, leading to the founding of the St Gallen cloister. Christianity spreads among the Alemanni and becomes primary religion in the region by end of century.
730–887	Swiss lands under Frankish control.
950–82	Ottonian Emperors influential in the Duchy of Swabia and Kingdom of Burgundy.
1025	Building of Habichtsburg ['Happisburg'] castle as feudal structures become predominant.
1030	Waning of the Kingdom of Burgundy and the Duchy of Swabia.
1190	St Gotthard pass route opened up by Teufelsbrücke/ Devil's Bridge. Trade route from Milan through Val Leventina, Uri and Lake Lucerne creates new political alignments.
1191	Berne (and then Fribourg) founded by Dukes of Zähringen.
1200	Extinction of local dynasties (including Zähringens in 1218) accelerates and urbanization increases
1231	Uri granted charter establishing Reichsfreiheit.
1240	Schwyz given charter suggesting Reichsfreiheit, which remained disputed.

1243	Bernese alliance with Fribourg, followed by others with Valais and Solothurn (1295), begins the formation of a western network of alliances.
1250–73	Imperial interregnum, ended when Rudolf of Habsburg becomes Emperor.
1291	Death of Rudolf and accession of Adolf of Nassau. A document describing a pact among Uri, Schwyz and Unterwalden is dated 'early August'. Peace alliance among Zurich, Uri and Schwyz extends eastern network of alliances from Lake Constance to Alpine foothills.
1298–1308	Albrecht of Habsburg Emperor, until his murder by his nephew disrupts Habsburg network. No further undisputed Habsburg Emperor until 1438.
1300–15	Territorial disputes between Schwyz and Abbey of Einsiedeln flare into violence, culminating in Habsburg campaign and Battle of Morgarten. Inner Swiss victory over Habsburgs and regional forces in 1315.
1309	Unterwalden made Reichsfrei by Emperor Henry VII of Luxembourg.
1315	Assembly of Inner Swiss after Morgarten; alliances updated in Pact of Brunnen. Emperor Louis the Bavarian confirms Reichsfreiheit of Uri, Schwyz and Unterwalden.
1320	Zehnden/Dizains of Valais given legal recognition by Bishop of Sion.
1332	Lucerne allies with Uri, Schwyz and Unterwalden during campaign against Habsburg bailiffs.
1336	Rudolf Brun leads an artisans' revolt against Zurich oligarchy and creates guild regime with dictatorial powers for Brun.
1347	Black Death comes to Switzerland.
1350s	Social conflicts in Uri. Extinction or expulsion of local noble families.
1351–3	Zurich and Inner Swiss occupy Glarus and Zug after alliance; Berne allies with Inner Swiss, linking the eastern and western networks of alliances.

1367	Formation of League of House of God in Graubünden by subjects of the Bishop of Chur. Beginning of a period of federal networking that continues to 1526.
1370	Priests' Charter (*Pfaffenbrief*) regulates judicial organization and arrangements for Gotthard traffic among most of the Confederates.
1377	Appenzell joins Swabian League in resistance to Abbott of St Gallen.
1386–7	Sempach War. Confederates defeat Duke Leopold of Austria at Sempach and seize Rapperswil. Consolidation of the Old Confederacy (*Alte Eidgenossenschaft*). After Landsgemeinde in Glarus declares autonomy, Archduke Albert III of Habsburg's forces defeated by Glarners at Näfels.
1389	Zurich briefly allies with Austria, but Confederates force it to end the alliance and remain part of Confederacy.
1393	Sempach Charter adds military codes to the network of alliances forming the VIII Orte League. Beginning of regular oath-taking among Confederates.
1395	Grey League established in Grisons.
1401–10	Appenzell allies with St Gallen and Schwyz. Defeat of Abbots' and south German forces, expansion of Bund ob dem See around Lake of Constance in opposition to regional nobility and Habsburg officers. First peace in 1410, final settlement in 1429.
1410	Alliance of Uri, Urseren and Val Levantina extends Uri's reach south of Gotthard pass into Ticino valley.
1411	Schaffhausen becomes an imperial free city.
1414–18	Council of Constance at edge of Confederacy, ending of papal schism. Conquest of Aargau after Habsburgs are banned by Emperor Sigismund for supporting rival papal claimant.
1415–26	Organization of western Aargau as Bernese subject territory; eastern Aargau as condominium of VIII cantons, who begin meeting yearly in Baden.
1422	Milanese defeat Swiss at Arbedo and reverse early Swiss expansion south in Italy.

1436	Jews expelled from Berne. Death of Frederick VII of Toggenburg. Schwyz and others seize Toggenburg lands, Zurich's claims unsuccessful.
1438	Habsburgs regain Holy Roman Empire under Frederick III. Habsburg family provides Emperors provides continuously until 1742.
1439	League of Ten Jurisdictions forms in eastern holdings of Frederick VII of Toggenburg, joining Grisons network of alliances. Zurich, having been excluded from Toggenburg alliance, denies markets to Schwyz and turns to Habsburgs: hostilities of Old Zurich War begin.
1443–4	Zurich defeated at St Jacob an der Sihl. Armagnac mercenaries win pyrrhic victory over Confederacy's forces near Basle at St Jacob an der Birs; France signs peace treaty with Basle.
1449	Zurich accepts defeat, ceding most Toggenburg claims and returning to its old place in the Confederacy.
c. 1450	The Tell myth starts to circulate.
1451–4	The abbey and city of St Gallen become parallel allies of Confederacy. First Appenzell treaties with Confederates.
1458	Plappart War in Constance triggered by insults against Swiss.
1460	Thurgau annexed as condominium (common bailliage) after raid by free-lance companies triggers invasion by Lucerne and others.
1463	First printed book in Basle, three years after University founded there.
1467	Count Sigismund of Habsburg-Tirol sells Winterthur to Zurich.
1469	Social conflict in Berne (*Twingherrenstreit*) between regional/urban nobility and guilds.
1474–7	Charles the Bold, Duke of Burgundy, turns on Berne and the Confederacy but is defeated at Grandson (1474), Murten/Morat (1476) and Nancy (1477). White Book of Sarnen records the full Tell myth.
1477	*Combourgeoisie* of Berne and Fribourg with Geneva, as Fribourg escapes from Habsburg rule. *Saubannerzug* of disaffected troops against Geneva.

1478	Battle of Giornico sees the Swiss begin to reassert their position in Ticino. Obwalden leads resistance to Lucerne over Entlebuch.
1481	*Stanser Verkommnis* brings Fribourg and Solothurn into Confederacy, but not as equals to VIII original cantons.
1489	Death of Mayor Hans Waldmann in Zurich (dominant *c.* 1485) at the hands of rural rebels and disaffected Zurich burghers, angry at his taxes on countryside.
1497–8	Two Grison leagues form alliance with Confederacy.
1499	So-called Swabian War triggered by territorial conflicts in Graubünden. Maximilian I seeks to reassert Habsburg and imperial authority, with support of Swabian nobles and south German towns. But multiple Swiss victories lead to Peace of Basle and recognition of Swiss exemption from most imperial jurisdiction. Basle and Schaffhausen then enter Confederacy (1501), but not on equal basis with VIII original cantons.
1500	Betrayal of Novara outside Milan: clash between Swiss mercenary armies avoided, but claimant to Milan betrayed to French.
1503	*Pensionenbrief*: unsuccessful statute that attempts to restrict mercenary recruitment to cantonal magistrates.
1507	Etterlin's *Chronicle of Swiss History* published.
1510	Conquest of Milanese by Swiss troops allied with Papacy.
1511	*Erbeinung* treaty ends hereditary conflict with Habsburgs.
1512	Three Grisons leagues seize the Valtellina.
1513	Battle of Novara. Last major Swiss infantry victory over French. Entry of Appenzell to Confederacy, which is thereafter stable in membership until 1798.
1515	Divided Swiss troops defeated by French at Marignano, outside Milan.
1516	Perpetual peace with France, reinforced in 1521, giving France privileged rights to recruit mercenaries.
1517	Martin Luther protests about indulgences and theology in Wittenberg.
1519	Zwingli opens his preaching campaign in Zurich.

1522   Reformation in Zurich. Battle of Bicocca reveals Swiss military weaknesses.

1523   Diet counsels against 'innovation' but Zwingli's teachings spread. Earliest Anabaptist thinkers appear.

1524–6   Union of the Three Leagues in Grisons establishes permanent alliance, limits Bishop of Chur, allows communes to decide on religion. Peasant attack on Ittingen cloister in Thurgau.

1525   German Peasants' War rages in southern and central Germany. Appenzell lets communes decide on religion. Battle of Pavia ends Swiss military predominance.

1526–7   Geneva–Berne *combourgeoisie*. Bishop of Geneva expelled from city.

1528–9   Reformation adopted in Berne, Basle, St Gall, Schaffhausen, and Bienne. First Kappel War halted before battle. Supposed milk soup of Kappel and First Landfrieden.

1530   Berne and Fribourg relieve Geneva from Savoyard siege. Reformation in Neuchâtel.

1531   Second Kappel War; death of Zwingli and peace (Second Landfrieden) with balance in favour of Catholics.

1532   Farel comes to Geneva and spreads Reformation. Bullinger leads Zurich church.

1535–6   Berne and Fribourg again come to aid of Geneva against Savoy and occupy Vaud and part of Valais.

1536   Calvin's Institutes published in first Latin edition.

1540   Calvin permanently appointed head of Church in Geneva. Bishopric of Basle allies with Catholic cantons. Consensus Tigurninus between Bullinger and Calvin unites the Zwinglian and Calvinist movements into a single Swiss Reformed church.

1543–62   Council of Trent crystallizes Catholic Reformation.

1559   Treaty of Cateau-Cambresis ends Habsburg–Valois wars in Italy.

1560   Civil strife in Glarus over religious adherence.

1561–93   Religious Wars in France, in which Swiss mercenaries are involved on both sides. Huguenot exiles flow to

	Geneva, greatly increasing population and bringing new industries.
1564–9	In face of Savoyard revival, Berne, Geneva and Valais yield Gex, the Genevois and Chablais. Geneva refused admission to Confederacy by Catholic cantons.
1566	Second Helvetic Confession of Faith of Heinrich Bullinger is published.
1570	Archbishop Carlo Borromeo of Milan on pilgrimage to Disentis and Einsiedeln.
1580	Establishment of Jesuit college in Fribourg. Peter Canisius active in Fribourg until his death in 1597.
1576	Simmler's *De Respublica Helvetiorum* published.
1586	Golden League amongst Catholic cantons allies them with Savoy and Spain, and places religion above previous alliances.
1597	Division of Appenzell into two Rhoden, one Catholic and one Protestant.
1602	Escalade of Geneva. Attempt at a pro-Savoyard coup fails.
1618–48	Thirty Years War rages around Switzerland. Zurich proposes a confederal defence agreement in 1629. After Swedes briefly invade Thurgau to attack Constance, Schwyz prosecutes the confederal commander, Killian Kesselring, for alleged collusion.
1620	Political disturbances in Valtellina and massacre of some 400 Protestants (*Sacro Macello*). Expulsion of Grisons (until 1639), and Austrian invasion of the III Leagues.
1623	Divisions in Glarus lead to creation of two Landsgemeinden.
1627	Fribourg closes patriciate to newcomers.
1647	*Defensional of Wil* establishes joint militia to defend the borders. Berne ends new admissions to full citizen status.
1648	Johann Rudolf Wettstein of Basle attends Westphalian peace congress and secures explicit Swiss exemption from imperial authority for Confederacy.
1650	Start of economic downturn and agrarian crisis.

1653	Swiss Peasants' War spreads from Entlebuch across central Swiss regions. Suppressed through cooperation of Catholic and Reformed cantons.
1656	Purge of Anabaptists in Schwyz sparks off First Villmergen War, in which the Protestant cantons are defeated, leading to Third Landfrieden.
1663	Treaty with Louis XIV renewing mercenary contracts and alliance with France.
1669–83	Zurich, Uri, Fribourg and Solothurn end enrollment of new full citizens.
1675	*Formula Consensus* drawn up for Swiss Reformed Churches.
1685	Revocation of Edict of Nantes sends many Protestant Huguenot exiles to Switzerland.
1680–1700	Watch-making begins in Jura hills. Expansion of printed calico to Zurich, Neuchatel, Schaffhausen and elsewhere as proto-industrialization thrives.
1712	Troubles in Toggenburg lead to Second Villmergen War and Peace of Aarau (Fourth Landfrieden), in which religious parity replaces previous Catholic advantage. Confessional tensions hinder further consolidation.
1707	Social mobility further restricted with closure of Lucerne, Schwyz and Basle's citizenship rolls to new families; Bernese ban on oligarchs' participation in industrial occupations.
1723	Davel affair in the Pays de Vaud opens wave of troubles in western Switzerland, notably in Geneva.
1740s	Cotton spinning and dyeing spreads in Glarus and eastern Switzerland.
1760s	Creation of learned associations, notably the Helvetic Society.
1762–8	Further troubles over banning of Rousseau's works in Geneva, and over tax changes in Neuchâtel.
1768	Restriction of government of Berne to seventy-eight families opens further aristocratic reaction.
1777	Last mercenary alliance with France.
1781	Social troubles in Fribourg and elsewhere.

1789	Outbreak of French Revolution spurs abolition of serfdom in Bishopric of Basle and troubles in Hallau, Valais, Vaud and Zurich.
1796	Conservative cantons welcome French émigrés and forcibly repress popular dissidence.
1798	Diet breaks up on 28 January after renewal of oaths, while French invasion prompts revolts and military defeat. Switzerland overrun and the Helvetic Republic declared. Nidwalden insurrection in September violently repressed.
1799	War of Second Coalition badly affects Switzerland.
1803	The Helvetic Republic collapses because of internal rivalries and conservative opposition. Napoleon imposes a compromise 'Mediation' regime, while Neuchâtel, Ticino and Valais are detached from Switzerland.
1813	Battle of Leipzig undermines Napoleonic Empire and leads to invasion by Allies and restoration of some Ancien Régime constitutions.
1814–15	Long Diet leads to a new Charter for Confederation and constitutions for the cantons; the Vienna Congress grants the Bishopric of Basle to Berne and recognizes Swiss neutrality as being in the general interest of Europe. Geneva, Neuchatel, Ticino and Valais join Confederation permanently.
1820	Revolutions in Europe encourage domestic Philhellenism and liberalism in press and politics, with the emergence of bodies like the Shooting Society (*Schützengesellschaft*).
1823	Conclusum against press and émigrés passed at behest of Holy Alliance.
1830	Ticino initiates the Regeneration ahead of July Days in Paris. Liberal constitutional reforms in many cantons, accepted by the Diet.
1832	Siebner Concordat prompts the *Sarnerbund* of conservative cantons, while near-civil war breaks out in Schwyz and Basle.
1834	Articles of Baden open religious conflict with recall of Jesuits and Nunciature to Schwyz; revolutions in Ticino and Zurich.

1841	Trouble in Aargau over new constitution and Liberals' forced closure of seven convents. Catholics start thinking about resistance while radical *Freikorps* twice fail in attacks on Lucerne.
1845–6	Radical revolutions in Vaud and Geneva.
1846	Creation of the Sonderbund among Catholic cantons.
1847	First internal railway between Baden and Zurich (*Spanischbrötli Bahn*). St Gallen election gives Radicals majority in Diet, allowing prohibition of Sonderbund. Dufour defeats Catholics in Fribourg, Zug and at Ghislikon.
1848	First Federal Constitution drafted and approved by votation. First factory legislation, in Glarus.
1856–7	Neuchâtel crisis results in Prussia abandoning its claims.
1859–60	Swiss refuse to buy North Savoy, but get customs-free zones round Geneva.
1864–70	Democratic movement in cantons brings direct-democratic reforms.
1866	Referendum gives Jews full rights but rejects other constitutional reforms.
1870–1	Franco-Prussian War leads to mobilization and internment of Bourbaki's French army.
1871–84	*Kulturkampf* in Switzerland after First Vatican Council.
1872	Revision of Federal constitution fails because of opposition from French speakers and Catholics.
1873	Start of economic depression.
1874	Federal constitutional revision succeeds.
1878	Completion of St Gotthard railway line.
1888	Creation of Social Democratic party triggers modernization of parties and party system. Rise of *Überfremdung* feelings against immigrants.
1891	Right of constitutional initiative at federal level reformed and extended. Election of first Catholic conservative to Federal Council.
1912	Health Assurance starts. Kaiser's visit to Swiss army manoeuvres.

1914	Mobilization and fortification on frontiers because of First World War. Ulrich Wille elected General; the Federal Council assumes special wartime powers.
1914–17	War imposes political, economic and linguistic (the *Graben/fossé*) stresses.
1918	Olten Committee and General Strike spurs adoption of proportional representation. Peasants, Artisans and Bourgeois Party (BGB) founded.
1919	Introduction of PR elections; Radicals then lose absolute majority. Formation of the Patriotic Federation (*Volksbund*).
1920	Second Catholic Conservative enters Federal Council. Entry into League of Nations approved by votation.
1929	Rudolf Minger the first BGB representative elected to Federal Council.
1931	Harsh law on foreigners agreed by votation
1932	Army fires on anti-fascist demonstration in Geneva.
1933–4	Growth of quasi-Fascist Fronts. Right-wing programme from Bernese BGB.
1935	Defeat of initiative for total revision of constitution.
1936	Devaluation of franc.
1937	Labour Peace signed between unions and business representatives.
1938	Rhaeto-Romansh declared national language. *Geistige Landesverteidigung* and return to integral neutrality. J Stamp affair for Austrian Jews seeking refuge.
1939	Outbreak of war. Guisan elected general and mobilization begun. Federal Council assumes wartime full powers and reasserts neutrality.
1940	Panic as German blitzkrieg moves west. Pilet-Golaz speech, Guisan's Rütli speech. Reduit policy and Wahlen Plans adopted amid fears of German invasion.
1940–2	Reduit constructed and occupied.
1943	Further German plan to invade Switzerland. First Social Democrat elected to Federal Council. Frontiers closed, and Steiger says 'Boat is Full'.

1944	Bombing of Schaffhausen by US air force. Tensions with the Allies grow.
1945	Nazi assets finally blocked. Switzerland refuses to join UN.
1946	Washington Currie Agreement on Nazi gold. Churchill's Zurich speech.
1947	Economic articles agreed in constitutional revision. Old age and health insurance finally introduced. Language and political tensions rise in the Jura.
1950	Beginnings of post-war economic surge.
1959	Social Democrats become a reformist party at Winterthur. Magic Formula arrangement for Federal Council membership established. Defeat of proposals for female suffrage at national level and for Jura separation.
1963	Talk of a Swiss malaise begins.
1970	Schwarzenbach initiative. BGB merges with the Democratic Party to form the Swiss People's Party (SVP/UDC).
1971	Female suffrage approved at federal level.
1972	Free Trade agreement with European Community.
1973	Oil crisis and start of economic downturn. Report on Constitutional revision tabled.
1974–6	Foreign workers contracts not renewed; their departure curbs unemployment.
1978	Acceptance of new canton of Jura through referenda in Berne and nationally.
1980	Youth troubles over Opera House costs spread from Zurich to other cities. St Gotthard Road Tunnel opens.
1984	Elizabeth Kopp elected as first female Federal Councillor, but resigns in early 1989 after leaking privileged information to her husband.
1986	Schweizerhalle environmental disaster. Entry to UN defeated by 75.7 per cent
1989	'No Army' vote gains 35.6 per cent, on 69 per cent turnout.
1990	Fiches scandal reveals government spying on citizens.

1992	Switzerland joins IMF and World Bank, and applies to join EU. EEA entry rejected in votation on 6 December. Economic downturn begins.
1995	First significant SVP gains in elections.
1996	World Jewish Council and others begin campaign against Switzerland for banks' failure to return Jewish assets after the Second World War.
1998	First bilateral agreements with EU negotiated; Nazi gold agreements signed by banks and Federal government.
1999	New constitution accepted in votation. SVP makes second large gains in cantonal and national elections but fails to get second seat on Federal Council.
2001	'Yes to Europe' initiative on immediate entry to EU rejected. Publication of Bergier final report on Swiss economic policy and policy on Jewish assets during Second World War.
2002	Entry to UN narrowly approved by electorate.
2003	Third SVP electoral breakthrough leads to election of Christoph Blocher to Federal Council.
2005	Entry to Schengen and Dublin treaties get popular approval; approval of extension of free movement rights to ten new EU member states.
2007	Tax disputes with EU start. Fourth SVP electoral gains. Blocher voted off Federal Council and replaced by Eveline Widmer-Schlumpf, who is expelled from SVP; SVP declares itself in 'opposition'. Formation of PBD.
2008	Swiss National Bank and government carry out 60 billion francs bailout of UBS. Samuel Schmid resigns, Ueli Maurer elected to Federal Council as SVP opposition ends.
2009	SVP-sponsored initiative banning minarets passes.
2010	Conflict with Gaddafi family in Libya, failed diplomatic responses, Libya Report criticizes foreign policy establishment.
2011	Fukoshima crisis and announcment of planned withdrawal from nuclear energy. Stagnation in talks with

EU. SVP fails to make further electoral gains, loses seats in the Ständerat. In elections for the Federal Council the SVP fails to eject Mrs Widmer-Schlumpf or otherwise regain a second seat.

2012   SVP decides not to leave government but loses ground politically. Proposals emerge that would allow Canton Jura to expand.

2012–13   Continuing difficulties over banks, taxes and EU relations.

GLOSSARY

Ancien Régime – Concept derived from pre-revolutionary France to describe the static and status-bound socio-political order of the European eighteenth century, including in Switzerland, as opposed to the more dynamic post-1798 situation.

Canton – Name given in French from the late fifteenth century to describe the '*Orte*', that is, the thirteen (XIII) sovereign political units in pre-modern Switzerland. German began to use the term from the late seventeenth century, along with *Stände*, and it was formally adopted for the whole country after 1798.

Challenge – One of the two main procedures that characterize Swiss direct democracy: the right of 50,000 citizens to call for a national vote on most new legislation passed by Parliament to which they are opposed. If the legislation fails to get a popular majority it lapses. It is known as a referendum in Switzerland.

Concordance/consensus – Swiss style of decision-making, which looks for the widest possible agreement and cooperation, as with the composition of the Federal Council, in contrast to the more antagonistic Anglo-American political style.

Condominium, condominiums – Territories annexed by the Swiss and ruled jointly by groups of cantons. Examples are Aargau, Thurgau and Ticino. They are also referred to as 'common bailliages' since they were ruled by bailiffs representing, on a rotating basis, the controlling cantons. They also sometimes appear as 'Mandated Territories'.

Confederacy/Confederation – Terms used to describe the overall Swiss polity as distinct from component cantons. In this book we use 'Confederacy' to denote the looser organization found prior to 1798 in which the cantons were formally autonomous actors; and 'Confederation' to describe the polity defined by mixed national and cantonal sovereignty that prevailed from 1803 to 1848, and, surprisingly, by the mixed federal structure which succeeded it. Confusingly, in French (and hence often in English as well) the term Confederation is also used, rather than Federation, to describe the post-1848 situation. However, although after 1848 Switzerland was technically a Federation, normal usage has remained 'Confederation'.

Democratic Movement – Series of cantonal processes of constitutional change in the 1860s away from domination by upper-middle-class liberalism and towards direct popular control of decision-making, elections, finance, justice and legislation. The movement was often led by smaller towns and the countryside.

Direct Democracy – Political system in which citizens themselves vote directly on major decisions, as well as electing parliamentary representatives to decide issues for them. Citizens can vote on federal constitutions, legislation and treaties. Swiss direct democracy is more extensive at the cantonal than at the federal level, extending to finance, government formation and policy matters, and includes the ability either to propose or to abrogate measures.

Eidgenossenschaft – The traditional German word for the Swiss polity, meaning a fellowship or companionship based on a bond oath or treaty. It still remains the official description of Switzerland in German.

Federalism – Both the underlying principle of Swiss governance – which means conciliating local autonomy with central co-ordination – and a political programme. Contrary to British misuse of the term, in Switzerland federalists are supporters of cantonal rights, not of the centre.

Freisinnig/Radical – Political movement and party that helped to steer Switzerland from loose confederation to federal unity in the 1840s, and then developed into a conservative force linked to big business. The Radicals held absolute majorities for Parliament for much of the late nineteenth century but have seen their strength decline since.

Geistige Landesverteidigung – Concept of defence strategy embracing social and cultural matters as well as military ones; emerged in the late 1930s and guided Swiss thinking into the 1970s.

Graben/Fossé – The split between the German- and Romance-speaking communities over attitudes to the belligerents in the First

World War. A symbol of underlying linguistic division, it spawned the more modern Swiss-German term 'Röstigraben' for the barrier, defined in terms of culinary preferences, *Rösti* being a favourite potato dish in German-speaking regions.

Guilds – Urban confraternities of artisans in specific trades that controlled careers, business organization, marketing, and that sometimes played a formal role in city politics. In the eighteenth century, guilds came to be seen less as a form of quality assurance and more as a restraint on the economy.

Helvetianism – Intellectual current emerging in the eighteenth century, which stressed the underlying unity of the Swiss and sought to reflect this in political organization.

Initiative – The second major element of direct democracy, in which a modest number of citizens' signatures (currently 100,000 at the federal level) triggers a votation on adding a new article to the Federal constitution; or, at the cantonal level, on adding a new article to legislation or to the constitution.

Laager – Dutch-derived term used to describe the defensive and introverted world of Swiss catholic society from the mid-nineteenth to the mid twentieth century. Also used of bourgeois politics.

Landfrieden – Name for four peace treaties between Catholic and Protestant cantons, often focusing on rights of worship and control of the condominiums (1529, 1531, 1656 and 1715).

Landsgemeinde (pl. *Landsgemeinden*) – Traditional form of male popular assembly embodying local sovereignty used in most pre-modern rural communes, including the Inner Swiss cantons. Now only found in the Inner Rhodes of Appenzell and in Glarus.

Magic Formula – Proportional allocation of seats in the Federal Council in relation to the share of the votes cast for each party in elections to the National Council. A major symbol of concordance democracy, especially as the precise allocation formula remained unchanged between 1959 and 2003. Since then many people believe it no longer really operates.

Mittelland/Midlands – The central geographical heartland of Switzerland, sometimes called the Plain, although it is rarely flat. Situated between the Jura hills in the North West and the Alps to the South, and running from Geneva to Thurgau.

Neutrality – The third of the main pillars of modern Swiss identity, along with direct democracy and federalism. Seen as an essential means of preserving national independence, Swiss neutrality was declared permanent, universal and in the interest of Europe in the Treaty of Vienna (1815). It commits the country to staying out of all armed conflicts (unless invaded) and maintaining universal relations. It is essentially a governmental affair and does not affect popular behaviour or economic relations, provided these are balanced and in line with preceding norms.

Populism – Term now given by outsiders to the assertive and rhetorically aggressive style of politics adopted by the Swiss People's Party (SVP/UDC), which has encouraged polarization in Swiss politics. Populism rests on the assumption that the party is the mouthpiece of the virtuous little people in their just struggle with a corrupt and unrepresentative elite. The party is also marked by charismatic leadership, its stress on direct democracy and its traditionalist nationalism, but it is more focused and organized than similar parties in other European countries.

Pre-Alps – Lower reaches of the Alpine Massif, which often provide access points into and through the mountains.

Regeneration – Period of constitutional change between 1829 and 1832, which brought in liberal institutions and authorities while also ending the territorial imbalances on which the Ancien Régime had been based.

***Reichsfreiheit* (Imperial Liberty)** – Medieval legal status of a community free of intermediate feudal control, being answerable only to the Holy Roman Emperor – and thus a form of independence, since the Emperor was often far away.

Schengen and Dublin Accords – Schengen is a EU system for allowing visa-free movement within the participating countries, within policed borders, while the Dublin Convention makes the country that initially receives them responsible for asylum seekers.

Schützenverein – Shooting Club or Carabiniers' Society – a popular association that played a part in developing national feelings in the nineteenth century.

Schwyzerdütsch – Generic term for the variety of (largely mutually comprehensible) Alemannic dialects of German, spoken in the eastern two-thirds of Switzerland.

Sonderbund – League of Catholic cantons opposed to religious and political change, the existence of which was held to be contrary to the 1815 Charter, thus triggering the civil war of 1847.

Sonderfall – The belief, popular from the 1940s onward, that Switzerland is an especially blessed 'special case' – thanks to first surviving the Second World War and then achieving remarkable stability, prosperity, political consensus, social harmony, industrial peace, international independence and general calm.

Stillstehen – Early modern strategy of avoiding commitment in international conflicts by 'staying still', out of which neutrality grew.

Überfremdung – Belief, starting in the 1890s, that the country was overwhelmed by foreigners, to the detriment of Swiss wealth and identity. Became a major political theme from the early 1960s onward as Germanophone right-wing politicians increasingly insisted that there were too many foreigners in the country.

Urschweiz – Sometimes known as Inner, or Primitive Switzerland: the group of Catholic, German-speaking cantons clustered round the northern access to the Gotthard, including Uri, Schwyz, Unterwalden, Lucerne and Zug.

Vorort – Term meaning 'pre-eminent place' used first to describe the presiding cantons in the Confederacy and then the employers' peak organization, founded in the late nineteenth century. The latter's official title is now 'Économie Suisse'.

Votation – Latinate version of the German term *Abstimmung*, meaning any kind of popular vote other than for electing parliaments or governments. Following the suggestion of Christopher Hughes it is used to avoid the misleading impression given by the use of the English term 'referendum'.

Willensnation – The idea that Switzerland is not an ethnic community but a deliberate political creation deriving from a continuing decision of different language and religious groups to live together within a political structure based on grass-roots democracy.

FURTHER READING

Switzerland poses special problems for the English-speaking reader. To begin with, three languages are regularly necessary, which discourages easy access in many cases. Moreover, much of the literature is focused on the cantons rather than on the nation as a whole, which makes things even more difficult. This has meant that the country has received relatively little attention from foreign writers. Hence, whereas a hundred years ago there was a goodly – and well informed – literature in English on the country, of late relatively little has been produced on Switzerland by English-speaking writers. Much of what is available is also dated or simply inaccurate. It also often misses the fact that Swiss history is a more sensitive subject than many outsiders realize. History is much more salient to the Swiss than their history is to the English – if not to Americans – and relies on myths which are not always known, much less shared, outside Switzerland. History is also controversial at home. An account of what has been written in English can be found at <www.kent.ac. uk/politics/cfs/csp/pdf/MaxiAndrey%20Festschrift.pdf>.

In light of these conditions, we thought it wise to list the most important general resources not in English, before turning to the Anglophone literature. These include, amongst older works, the *Handbuch der Schweizer Geschichte* (Zurich: Berichthaus, 1972), and the *History of Switzerland and the Swiss* (1982; available in all three main national languages). Of more recent works Francois Walter's *Histoire de la Suisse*, George Andrey's *L'Histoire Suisse pour les Nuls* (also available in an updated German version), Tobias Kaestli's two volumes and, in Italian, Emilo Papa's *Storia della Svizzera* have been useful. Most recently, Thomas Maissen produced a fresh survey in German, *Geschichte der Schweiz* (Baden: Hier+Jetzt, 2010). A few crucial works covering major themes or particular periods synthesize the most important research or present provocative new views: these include Roger Sablonier, *Gründungszeit ohne Eidgenossen* (Baden: Hier+Jetzt, 2008), Bernehard Stettler, *Die Eidgenossenschaft im 15. Jahrhundert: Die Suche nach einem gemeinsamen Nenner* (Zurich: Verlag Markus Widmer-Dean, 2004), and Thomas Maissen, *Die Geburt der Republik: Staatsverständnis und Repräsentation in der frühneuzeitliche Eidgenossenschaft* (Göttingen: Vandenhoek & Ruprecht, 2006). William Rappard's *La Révolution Industrielle et les origines de la Protection Légale du Travail en Suisse* (Berne: Staempfli 1914) has also informed some of our thinking, as has

Rudolf Braun, *Das ausgehende Ancien Régime in der Schweiz* (Göttingen: Vandenhoek & Ruprecht, 1984). Finally, we should mention that for many cantons, excellent new official histories have appeared in the last decades; these present up-to-date interpretations of the detailed and frequently complex material.

For more recent periods, there are good bibliographies in M. Furrer et al., *Die Schweiz im kurzen 20. Jahrhundert* (Zurich: Verlag Pestalozzianum, 2008). We have also found the electronic version of the Swiss Historical Dictionary (www.dhs.ch), which is available in the three national languages, an indispensable work of reference. It is also currently appearing in print. To date twelve of the projected thirteen volumes have appeared, again in three languages.

In listing books in English, whether by British or American writers, or, increasingly, by Swiss authors, we have largely restricted ourselves to books published in the last twenty years or so. This is because there has been a revolution in historical research and thinking in Switzerland since the 1970s, and most works published before then are now rather out of date, as well as being less accessible to readers. We have also deliberately excluded studies of individual cantons. However, we have included a number of scholarly articles, as these are often more recent and more frequent than are single volumes. The bibliography is divided into sections roughly corresponding to our chapters, although books cited in one section can often throw light on other periods as well. The imbalances among the sections reflect the dominance of religious history and Second World War studies. Nonetheless, we hope that the result will be of help to readers who want to go further into the fascinating intricacies of Swiss history.

BACKGROUND AND GENERAL

Butler, Michael, 'The Politics of Myth: The Case of William Tell', in W. C. Donahue and S. Denham, eds, *History and Literature* (Tubingen: Stauffenberg, 2000), pp. 73–90.

Charnley, Joy, *The Swiss and War* (Berne: Lang, 1999).

Farhni, Dieter, *An Outline History of Switzerland: From the Origins to the Present Day*, 8th edn (Zurich: Pro Helvetia, 2003).

Fossedal, Gregory A., *Direct Democracy in Switzerland* (New Brunswick NJ and London: Transaction Publishers, 2002).

Kuntz, Joelle, *Switzerland: How an Alpine Pass became a Country* (Geneva: Historiator, 2008).

Luck, James Murray, *History of Switzerland: The First 100,000 Years. From the Beginnings to the Days of the Present* (Palo Alto, Cal.: SPOS, 1985).

Marchal, Guy P., 'National Historiography and National Identity: Switzerland in Comparative Perspective,' in S. Berger and C Lorenz, eds,

The Contested Nation: Ethnicity, Class, Religion and Gender in National Histories (Basingstoke: Palgrave, 2008), pp. 311–38.

Meier, Heinz K., *Switzerland* (Santa Barbara, Calif.: Clio Press, 1990).

Nappey, Gregoire, *Swiss History in a Nutshell* (Basle: Bergli, 2010).

Schelbert, Leo, *Historical Dictionary of Switzerland* (Plymouth and Lanham, MD: Scarecrow Press, 2007).

Steinberg, Jonathan, *Why Switzerland?* 2nd edn (Cambridge University Press, 1996).

PRE-MODERN SWITZERLAND

Baker, Wayne, 'Church, State, and Dissent: The Crisis of the Swiss Reformation, 1531–1536', *Church History* 57/2 (1988), 135–152.

Burnett, Amy N., *Teaching the Reformation: Ministers and Their Message in Basle, 1529–1629* (Oxford University Press, 2006).

Campi, Emidio and Gordon, Bruce, eds, *Architect of Reformation: An Introduction to Heinrich Bullinger, 1504–1575* (Grand Rapids: Baker Academic, 2004).

Davis, James C., 'Coping with the Underclasses: Venice, Lille, and Zurich in the Sixteenth and Seventeenth Centuries', *Journal of Urban History* 19/4 (1993), pp. 116–122.

Ehrstine, Glenn, *Theater, Culture, and Community in Reformation Berne, 1523–1555* (Leiden: Brill, 2002).

Gordon, Bruce, *The Swiss Reformation* (Manchester University Press, 2002).

Groebner, Valentin, *Liquid Assets, Dangerous Gifts: Presents and Politics at the End of the Middle Ages* (Philadelphia: University of Pennsylvania Press, 2002).

Hacke, Daniela, 'Church, Space and Conflict: Religious Co-Existence and Political Communication in Seventeenth-Century Switzerland', *German History* 25/3 (2007), pp. 285–312.

Harder, Lelan, *The Sources of Swiss Anabaptism: The Grebel Letters and Related Documents* (Eugene, OR: Wipf & Stock, 2001).

Head, Randolph C., 'Fragmented Dominion, Fragmented Churches: The Institutionalization of the *Landfrieden* in the Thurgau, 1531–1630', *Archive for Reformation History* 96 (2005), pp. 117–44.

  'Shared Lordship, Authority and Administration: The Exercise of Dominion in the *Gemeine Herrschaften* of the Swiss Confederation, 1417–1600', *Central European History* 30/4 (2001), pp. 489–512.

  'William Tell and his Comrades: Association and Fraternity in the Propaganda of Fifteenth- And Sixteenth-Century Switzerland', *Journal of Modern History* 67/3 (1995), pp. 527–557.

Kingdon, Robert, *Adultery and Divorce in Calvin's Geneva* (Cambridge, MA: Harvard University Press, 1995).

Kümin, Beat, 'Public Houses and Civic Tensions in Early Modern Berne', *Urban History* 34/1 (2007), pp. 89–101.

Lister, Frederick K., *The Early Security Confederations: From the Ancient Greeks to the United Colonies of New England* (Westport, CT: Greenwood Press, 1999).

Locher, Gottfried, *Zwingli's Thought: New Perspectives* (Leiden: Brill, 1981).

Mathieu, Jon, *History of the Alps*, trans. Matthew Vester (Morgantown: West Virginia University Press, 2009).

McCormick, John, *One Million Mercenaries* (London: Leo Cooper, 1993).

Miller, David and Embleton, Gerry, *The Swiss at War 1300–1500* (Oxford: Osprey/Men at Arms, 1979).

Sablonier, Roger, 'The Swiss Confederation 1415–1500', in Christopher Allmand, ed., *New Cambridge Modern History*, vol. 7 (Cambridge University Press, 1998), pp. 645–70.

Wandel, Lee Palmer, *Voracious Idols and Violent Hands: Iconoclasm in Reformation Zurich, Strasbourg and Basle* (Cambridge University Press, 1994).

Watt, Jeffrey R., *Choosing Death: Suicide and Calvinism in Early Modern Geneva* (Kirksville, Mo.: Truman State University Press, 2001).

THE EIGHTEENTH CENTURY

Biucchi, Basilio, 'Switzerland, 1700–1914', in Carlo Cipolla, ed., *Fontana Economic History of Europe: Industrialization* , vol. 2 (London: Fontana, 1979), pp. 627–55.

Braun, Rudolf, *Industrialisation and Everyday Life*, trans. Sarah Hanbury-Tenison (Cambridge University Press, 1990).

Holenstein, Andre et al., eds, *The Republican Alternative: The Netherlands and Switzerland Compared* (Amsterdam University Press, 2008).

Kirk, Linda, 'Genevan Republicanism', in David Wootton, ed., *Republicanism, Liberty, and Commercial Society, 1649–1776* (Stanford University Press, 1994), pp. 270–309.

Körner, Martin, 'The Swiss Confederation,' in Richard Bonney, ed., *The Rise of the Fiscal State in Europe 1200–1815* (Oxford University Press, 1999), pp. 327–57.

Larminie, Vivienne, 'Life in Ancien Regime Vaud', *History Today* **48/4** (April 1998), pp. 44–50.

Lerner, Mark, *A Laboratory of Liberty: The Transformation of Political Culture in Republican Switzerland, 1750–1848* (Leiden: Brill, 2011).

Mason, Stanley, *Albrecht Von Haller:'The Alps.' An English Translation* (Dubendorf: Amstutz/De Clivo Press, 1987).

Zimmer, Oliver, *Contested Nation: History, Memory and Nationalism in Switzerland, 1761–1891* (Oxford University Press, 2003).

Zurbuchen, Simon, 'Switzerland in the Eighteenth Century: Myth and Reality', *Eighteenth-Century Studies* **37/4** (2004), pp. 692–694.

THE REVOLUTIONARY ERA

Birmingham, David, *Switzerland: A Village History* (London and New York: Palgrave/St Martin's Press, 2000).

Bullen, Roger, 'Guizot and the "Sonderbund" Crisis, 1846–48', *English Historical Review* 86/340 (1971), pp. 497–526.

Church, Clive H., *Europe in 1830: Revolution and Political Change* (London: Allen & Unwin, 1982).

Frei, Daniel, 'The Politics of the Artificial Past etc.' in James C. Eades, ed., *Romantic Nationalism in Europe* (Canberra: Humanities Research Centre, Australian National University, 1983), pp. 116–133.

Lerner, Mark, 'The Helvetic Republic: An Ambivalent Reception of French Revolutionary Liberty', *French History* 18/1 (2004), pp. 50–75.

Lister, Frederick K., *The Later Security Confederations* (Westport, CN: Greenwood, 2001), pp. 99–120.

Orr, Clarissa C., 'The Swiss Romantic Movement', in Roy Porter and Michael Teich, eds, *Romantic Nationalism in Historic Context* (Cambridge University Press, 1988), pp. 134–69.

Müller, Thomas C., 'Switzerland 1847/49', in Dieter Dowe, ed., *Europe in 1848: Revolution and Reform* (New York and Oxford: Berghahn Books, 2001), pp. 210–41.

Remak, Joachim, *A Very Civil War: The Swiss Sonderbund War of 1847* (Boulder: Westview, 1993).

Speich, Daniel, 'Switzerland', in Guntram H. Herb and David H. Kaplan, eds, *Nations and Nationalism: A Global Historical Overview* (Santa Barbara, Cal: ABC CLIO, 2008), pp. 244–55.

Tilly, Charles, 'Switzerland as a Special Case', in C. Tilly, *Contention and Democracy* (Cambridge University Press, 2004), pp. 168–205.

LATER NINETEENTH CENTURY

Altermatt, Urs, 'A Century of Conservatism', *Journal of Contemporary History* 14/4 (1979), pp. 581–610.

Argast, Regula, 'An Unholy Alliance: Swiss Citizenship between Local Legal Tradition, Federal Laissez-Faire, and Ethno-national Rejection of Foreigners 1848–1933', *European Review of History* 16/4 (2009), pp. 503–21.

Craig, Gordon A., *The Triumph of Liberalism: Zurich in the golden age, 1830–1869* (New York: Scribner's, 1990).

Gossman, Lionel, *Basle in the Age of Burckhardt: A Study in Unseasonable Ideas* (University of Chicago Press, 2000).

Moorehead, Caroline, *Dunant's Dream* (London: Harper Collins, 1998).

Studer, Roman, 'When did the Swiss get so rich? Comparing Living Standards in Switzerland and Europe, 1800–1913', *Journal of European Economic History* 37/2 (2008), pp. 405–52.

Zimmer, Oliver, 'Competing Memories of the Nation: Liberal Historians and the Reconstruction of the Swiss Past 1870–1900', *Past & Present* 168 (2000), pp. 194–226.

THE EARLY TWENTIETH CENTURY

Guex, S., 'The Origins of the Swiss Banking Secrecy Law and its Repercussions for Swiss Federal Policy', *Business History Review* 74/2 (2000), pp. 237–66.

Leimgruber, Mathieu, *Solidarity without the State? Business and the Shaping of the Swiss Welfare State, 1890–2000* (Cambridge University Press, 2008).

Segesser, Daniel M., '"Common Doctrine Rather than Secret Staff Conversations": Military Co-operation between France and Switzerland in the 1920s and 1930s', *War in History* 10/1 (2003), pp. 60–91.

Vogler, Robert U., 'The Genesis of Swiss Banking Secrecy: Political and Economic Environment', *Financial History Review* 8/1 (2001), pp. 73–84.

Volmert, Andrew, 'The Reinterpretation of Political Tradition: The Catholic Roots of Jurassian Nationalism', *Nationalism and Ethnic Politics* 14/3 (2008), pp. 395–427.

THE SECOND WORLD WAR

Bergier, Jean-François, 'Enterprises in Switzerland during the Second World War', in Harold James and Jakob Tanner, eds, *Enterprise in the Period of Fascism in Europe* (Aldershot: Ashgate, 2002), pp. 105–14.

Bergier, Jean-François et al., *Switzerland, National Socialism and the Second World War: Final Report* (Zurich: Pendo, 2002).

Bower, T., *Nazi Gold: The Full Story of the Fifty-Year Swiss-Nazi Conspiracy to Steal Billions from Europe's Jews and Holocaust Survivors* (London and New York: HarperCollins, 1997).

Halbrook, S. P., *Target Switzerland: Swiss Armed Neutrality in World War II* (New York: Sarpedon/Da Capo Press Inc., 2003).

Kreis, Georg, *Switzerland and the Second World War: Responding to the Challenges of the Times* (Zurich: Pro Helvetia, 1999).

Kreis, Georg and Cesarani, David, eds, *Switzerland and the Second World War* (London: Frank Cass, 2000).

LeBor, Adam, *Hitler's Secret Bankers: How Swiss Banks Profited from Nazi Genocide* (London: Birch Lane Press, 1997).

Levin, Ira C., *The Last Deposit: The Swiss Banks and Holocaust Victims' Accounts* (Westport, CN: Greenwood Press, 1999).

Ludi, Regula, *'Why Switzerland?' Remarks on a Neutral's Role in the Nazi Program of Robbery and Allied Postwar Restitution Policy* (New York: Berghahn Books, 2007).

Rickman, Gregg J., *Swiss Banks and Jewish Souls* (Piscataway, NJ: Transaction Books 1999.

Urner, Klaus, *Let's Swallow Switzerland* (Lanham, MD: Lexington Books, 2002).

Vincent, Isabel, *Hitler's Silent Partners: Swiss Banks, Nazi Gold, and the Pursuit of Justice* (New York: W. Morrow, 1997).

Wylie, Neville, *Britain, Switzerland and World War II* (Oxford University Press, 2003).

POST-1945

Butler, M. et al., eds, *The Making of Modern Switzerland, 1848–1998* (Basingstoke: Macmillan, 2000).

Church, Clive H., 'The Political and Economic Development of Switzerland, 1945–1991', in M. Butler and M. Pender, eds, *Rejection and Emancipation* (New York and Oxford: Berg, 1991), pp. 7–21.

Erdman, Paul, *The Crash of '79* (New York: Sphere Books, 1978).

Fehrenbach, Thomas, *The Gnomes of Zurich* (London: Frewin, 1966).

Ganser, Daniele, *NATO's Secret Armies: Operation Gladio and Terrorism* (London: Cass, 2005).

Hilovitz, Janet E., ed., *Switzerland in Perspective* (Westport, CN: Greenwood Press, 1990).

Hughes, Christopher J., 'Cantonalism: Federation and Confederacy in the Golden Epoch of Switzerland', in Michael Burgess and Alain G. Gagnon, eds, *Comparative Federalism and Federation* (London: Harvester-Wheatsheaf, 1993), pp. 154–67.

'Switzerland (1875): Constitutionalism and Democracy', in Vernon Bogdanor, ed., *Constitutions in Democratic Politics* (Aldershot: Gower/PSI, 1988), pp. 227–40.

Katzenstein, Peter J., *Corporatism and Change* (Ithaca, NY: Cornell University Press, 1983).

Gabriel, Jürg M. and Fischer, Thomas, eds, *Swiss Foreign Policy, 1945–2002* (Basingstoke: Palgave, 2003).

Lembruch, Gerhard, 'Consociational Democracy and Corporatism in Switzerland', *Publius* 23/2 (1993), pp. 43–60.

Milivojevic, Marko and Maurer, Pierre, eds, *Swiss Neutrality and Security* (Oxford: Berg, 1990).

Skenderovic, Damir, *The Radical Right in Switzerland* (London: Berg, 2009).

CONTEMPORARY SWITZERLAND

Bewes, Diccon, *Swiss Watching* (London: Nicholas Brealey, 2010).

Braillard, Pierre, *Switzerland and the Crisis of Dormant Assets and Nazi Gold* (London: Kegan Paul International, 2000).

Church, Clive H., 'Switzerland: An Introduction', in Christian Kalin, ed., *Switzerland Business & Investment Handbook*, 3rd edn (Zurich: Orell Füssli, 2011), pp. 3–18.

Church, Clive H., ed., *Switzerland and the European Union* (London: Routledge, 2007).

Dardanelli, Paolo, 'Federal Democracy in Switzerland', in Michael Burgess and Alain Gagnon, eds, *Federal Democracies* (London: Routledge, 2010), pp. 142–59.

Goetschel, Laurent et al., *Swiss Foreign Policy: Foundations and Possibilities* (London: Routledge, 2006).

Haller, Walter, *The Swiss Constitution in a Comparative Context* (Zurich: Dike, 2009).

Handschin, Lukas, *Swiss Company Law* (Zurich: Dike, 2008).

Kloti, Ulrich et al., eds, *Handbook of Swiss Politics*, 2nd edn (Zurich: NZZ Libro, 2007).

Kriesi, Hanspeter and Trechsel, Alex, *The Politics of Switzerland: Continuity and Change in a Consensus Democracy* (Cambridge University Press, 2008).

Ladner, Andreas and Brändle, Michael, 'Switzerland: The Green Party, Alternative and Liberal Greens', in E. Gene Frankland, ed., *Green Parties in Transition* (Abingdon: Ashgate, 2008), pp. 109–28.

Linder, Wolf, *Swiss Democracy*, 3rd edn (Basingstoke: Palgrave, 2010).

Lutz, Georg, 'The 2011 Swiss Federal Elections etc', *West European Politics* 35 (2012) 682–93.

New, Mitya, *Switzerland Unwrapped: Exposing the Myths* (London: I. B. Tauris, 1997).

Oesch, Daniel, *Redrawing the Class Map: Stratification and Institutions in Britain, Germany, Sweden and Switzerland* (Basingstoke: Palgrave, 2006).

Schwok, René, *Switzerland–European Union: An Impossible Membership?* (Brussels: Peter Lang, 2009).

Turk, Eleanor L., *Issues in Germany, Austria and Switzerland* (Westport, CN: Greenwood 2003).

Vatter, Adrian and Church, Clive H., 'Opposition in Consensual Switzerland: A Short but Significant Experiment', *Government and Opposition* 44/4 (2009), pp. 412–37.

INDEX

Items which also figure in the Glossary are marked in bold

310